Logotype
Michael Evamy

LAURENCE KING

Published in 2012 by
Laurence King Publishing Ltd
361–373 City Road
London EC1V 1LR
United Kingdom
Tel: +44 20 7841 6900
Fax: +44 20 7841 6910
e-mail: enquiries@laurenceking.com
www.laurenceking.com

A catalogue record for this book is
available from the British Library.

ISBN 978 1 85669 894 8

Book design by Company
Cover design by Pentagram
Picture research: Samantha Evamy

Printed in China

logo type

Michael Evamy

Laurence King Publishing

14 It's all in the font

16	Sans serif
16	Title case
22	All upper case
30	All lower case
32	Serif
32	Title case
36	All upper case
40	Mixed case
42	Small/large
44	Mixed font
48	Modular and grid-based
60	Superbold
64	Stencil
70	Cursive
80	Handwritten
86	Outline
88	Inline and multilinear
92	Blurred/repeated
94	3-D
98	Retro

100 More or less

102	Flourishes
108	Rules and dividers
110	Cropped
114	Negative space
118	Missing parts
124	Minimal

130 Alternative arrangements

132	Rotated
138	Slanted
140	Circular
142	Multilayered
156	Reflection and inversion
160	Word/monogram lock-ups

Contents

164 Colourful characters

166 Single-letter marks A–Z
194 Linked letters
210 In a word
230 Typographic marks
230   Dots and full stops
234   Slashes
236   Ampersands
238   Underlined
240   Other punctuation
246   Numerical and mathematical

250 Carriers & corners

252 Letter carriers
254 Carriers
254   Circles
262   Squares
264   Rectangles
270   Other shapes
276 Frames

282 East

284 Chinese
286 Arabic
292 Hebrew
294 Bilingual

300 Symbolic

302 Windows and patterns
306 Illustrative characters
310 Combination marks

Introduction

The words we see in books and magazines, on signs and online are designed to be read. This book is about words and letters that are designed to be recognized.

Logotypes – wordmarks, monograms and single-letter marks – are where the verbal becomes visual; where elements that are usually designed to speed the eye across the page invite it to linger; where the choice of font is never less than meaningful; where spaces and spacing are significant; where the composition of words and characters carry weight; where letterforms and even fragments of letterforms can evoke attributes, atmospheres, emotions, events, places, personalities and periods in history.

Once it has become familiar, a logotype is registered by the brain in much the same way as a symbol: as a single, visual entity rather than a set of related verbal ones. Is there anyone who actually reads the words 'Facebook' and 'YouTube' in the way they read text, when they see them in their familiar fonts and settings?

However, the symbol logo and the logotype are different creatures. Language is no barrier to a symbol, generally; to a logotype, it can be. On the other hand, a logotype needs no accompaniment to do its job of identifying its owner. While it is establishing itself, a symbol needs its hand held by a written name, in the form of a wordmark or other logotype. Only once an association with a brand has taken root in the minds of the audience can a symbol shed its words. There are a handful of symbols – such as those of Shell, Apple and Mercedes-Benz – that require no introduction anywhere; others take a risk if they go it alone.

For Sagi Haviv (1974–), a partner at Chermayeff & Geismar, the logotype is the default option. He told identity blog Logo Design Love: 'I start off with the premise that there has to be a good reason for a symbol. Examples of good reasons for a symbol include: a very long name; a need to bring together different entities, sub-brands or divisions; or a need for a visual icon as a shorthand. Without a good reason such as these, the focus should be on the name of the entity represented.'

Verbal and visual unite in logotypes. So do art and craft. This book celebrates all four. The art is in the concept of a logotype; in the crystallization of a visual idea. This can emerge from extended, educated experimentation with type and letterforms until something – a solution – appears. It can arrive as the result of a chance observation – a misspelt word, a slip of the tongue or a fortuitous reflection. Occasionally, the idea drops into the mind when least expected. There is a eureka

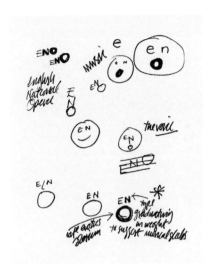

moment. For Archimedes, it came as he stepped into the bath. For Alan Fletcher (1931–2006), searching for the perfect way to marry an ampersand with an 'A' in the V&A monogram, it came during his morning shower.

Let no one think, though, that such moments, and such visionary, deceptively simple ideas, arrive completely out of the blue. They are usually the outcome of weeks, even months, of immersion in a client's brand issues, positioning and business challenges. Inspiration is hard won. As Paula Scher (1948–), the designer behind the current identities for Tiffany & Co., Howcast and New York's Museum of Modern Art (MoMA), memorably said of her 'umbrella' logotype for the financial group Citi: 'It took me a few seconds to draw it. But it took me 34 years to learn how to draw it in a few seconds.'

And, once a potential solution is identified, the work doesn't stop. Other routes have to be explored to exhaust the possibilities; there may be an even better idea around the corner. 'We only know it's the right idea if we have more than one idea,' says John Dowling of Dowling Duncan. 'We had two logos that "came" on day one,' says Michael Johnson of Johnson Banks. 'In both cases, the other 19 days of the design stage were spent looking for something better, but we never bettered that first idea. Having said that, we have many more

examples that came after arduous and exhaustive design stages.' According to Atelier Works' Quentin Newark, 'The months of background work are crucial. Only by understanding the organization, its past, its competitors, the industry situation, its ambitions and its audiences – which are all facets of the "problem" – can you begin to think of solutions. You could argue that it's because of the spadework – leading to a concise and exact definition of the problem – that a clever, elegant solution becomes possible.'

The idea is only part of the solution, though. After the art comes the craft. Specialist type designers are regularly asked to help to achieve the idea in the designer's mind: a particular union of letters, for example, or a harmonious, balanced composition of words. On occasion, the demand is for a completely new, bespoke font in several weights as part of a corporate identity system, on which the logotype will be based. (See pp. 12–13: Logotypes: The type specialist's view.)

Type designers are the modern descendants of pioneering craftsmen like Nicolas Jenson (1420–80) and Claude Garamond (1480–1561) who carved letterforms with astonishing precision from small wooden blocks in the earliest days of printing. But logotypes have a much longer lineage. They arrived with the Greeks and the Romans, when new coins bore designs

Clockwise from above:
Sketches made by Mike Dempsey on the number 38 bus that led to the identity for the English National Opera (ENO), proving that inspiration can strike at any time; the final ENO logo, by CDT Design; Victoria & Albert Museum identity, conceived in the shower by Pentagram's Alan Fletcher; YouTube logo, designed by co-founder Chad Hurley; Facebook logo, designed by Cuban Council and Test Pilot Collective.

of interwoven letters to represent contemporary rulers. This was the birth of the monogram (meaning 'single line'), the kind of logotype usually seen today on the doors, uniforms and menus of smart hotels, restaurants and department stores.

Craftspeople painted or inscribed their own monograms on to tiles, vases, bricks and other ceramic products. This form of artistic signature was probably also the first form of the commercial logotype, and it grew in sophistication until monograms came to be designed not to be read, but simply to be recognized. This tradition never died; craftspeople through the ages have done the same.

The Romans also gave us the Latin alphabet – the basis for much of the modern world's written communication – and their stone carvers laid the foundation for the 'roman' typefaces developed soon after the invention of printing. Etruscan and Roman lapidaries painted their capitals on to the marble surface before inscribing them with such fidelity and sensitivity that the carved letters bore many of the subtle, human qualities of the painted ones: thick and thin strokes, graceful 'tails' and thicker areas at the start of strokes, where the brush made contact with the stone. These qualities can be seen in the strokes, tails and serifs of early, non-calligraphic typefaces such as Bembo

(c.1495) and Garamond (sixteenth century), and in their modern, digital-friendly counterparts.

Probably the first logos in the modern sense (of being widely distributed, for the means of identifying commercial entities) were the marks used by the earliest printers in the fifteenth century on the title or end pages of their publications. These displayed enormous invention and visual economy, ranging from decorated monograms, such as William Caxton's, to orb-and-cross designs with initials, and from pictorial puns on the printer's name to allegorical engravings. Later, it was the printing trade that gave us the word 'logotype': in the days of hot-metal typesetting, 'logotype' was the term for a single piece of type bearing two or more distinct elements.

Today, there are logotypes wherever you look. The most traditional forms – monograms, signatures, plain type – still offer possibilities to designers of corporate identities. But the accelerating advances in printing, media and design technologies have opened the door to infinite variety. Designers can manipulate, integrate and decorate letterforms and words with almost total freedom, and realize visual ideas that, a generation ago, would have had to remain in the imagination.

They also have an enormous palette of typefaces with which to work.

LOGOTYPE

Logotype

logotype

Logotype

Logotype

Logotype

Logotype

Logotype

Logotype

Logotype

Giving character to
characters: Typefaces
have a Jekyll and Hyde
effect on words, and today
the range of personalities
available is greater than at
any time in the past.

Beginning with the boom in display faces in the ninet eenth century – big, bold, attention-grabbing alphabets for bellowing the headlines of theatrical bills and 'wanted' posters – the development of typefaces for advertising and branding (as distinct from text) has been unrelenting. Font fashions have come, gone and come back again. And, in their search for the new, designers have revived the old. Even fonts that had been cast into type wilderness are finding new audiences. Bookman, Cooper Black, Avant Garde: nothing is off-limits. There is even a logotype in this book that makes use of Souvenir (see Tomorrow by KentLyons, p.33), a font first designed in 1914 but not a hit until released by the International Typeface Corporation (ITC) in 1970, and whose instant over-use by designers and ad agencies consigned it to eternal association with soft-focus advertising, soft rock and soft porn.

Of course, the digital revolution hasn't just helped to give old faces a makeover; it has democratized type design and unlocked a flood of new typefaces. FontShop, the world's first digital font reseller, stocks thousands of high-quality, hand-picked fonts from major foundries and independent type designers. With the right software package, anyone can experiment with type design, and turn out a font to his or her own taste, whether that's a stern slab serif, a faux cyrillic, an extra-light script or something bold and brutalist.

It is not a development that impresses everyone. Italian-American designer Massimo Vignelli (1931–), the man most responsible for instigating corporate America's love affair with Swiss-made Helvetica (1957) in the mid 1960s, maintains that any designer worth his or her salt can get by on half a dozen cultured, tried-and-tested typefaces. For many years 'ideas-led' design consultancies such as Pentagram promoted the same philosophy. But, in logotype design at least, character and distinctiveness in type design have trumped 'good' taste and breeding. More, not less, is more in this particular field of design.

It is also a field where change has become the norm. Commercial pressures, changes of senior personnel in companies and developments in technology and media all test the resolve of organizations to stick with the identity they already have. But every rebrand is a risk; there are almost always those who will defend an existing identity, no matter what its formal qualities. Brands are very much more than logos, but logos are what people grow attached to; they offer a focal point for all the feelings, good and bad, about a brand. No other element of a brand ever draws a more impassioned defence than a logo under threat of replacement. Just ask clothes retailer The Gap, whose switch to Helvetica caused uproar among sections of its customer base, or United Airlines, whose Saul Bass-designed double-U mark was lost, to the publicly voiced disgust of thousands of travellers, in the merger with Continental. There are countless other examples.

This state of restlessness applies to identities themselves. Some clients have experimented with alternative ways of commissioning identities, such as crowdsourcing and public competitions – department store JC Penney recently replaced its Massimo Vignelli-designed wordmark with one submitted by a third-year graphic-design student at the University of Cincinnati. The development of the 'flexible' or 'dynamic' identity – the kind that has multiple, interchangeable variations

– and the widening number of media and experiences through which brand identity is being expressed have led some designers and commentators to question the value of a fixed, never-changing logo in a brand world of constant flux.

Is the logo dead? The rich diversity of ideas in this book would suggest that the logotype, at least, is more alive than ever. And, in a future in which logos will have to work ever harder, with ever less media time and space in which to operate, the kind that communicates both visually and verbally in a single, self-contained mark could easily come to dominate the creation of brand identity.

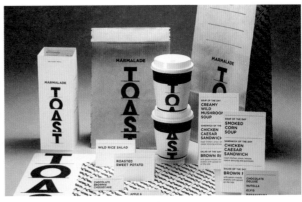

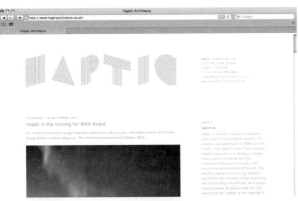

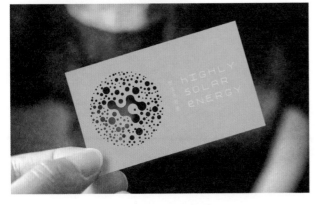

Logotypes: The type specialist's view

On high-profile branding programmes, where the fine detail of a logotype needs to be faultless, design companies often seek the expert input of a specialist type design studio. Fontsmith, based near London Bridge, is known for its development of commercially available fonts such as FS Albert and FS Lola, as well as fonts for clients such as Channel 4 and BBC One. But the studio also provides a logo design service, with projects ranging from refining the draft logotypes of other agencies to developing a typographic 'route' as part of a brand pitch or presentation, to taking the brand brief and crafting a fully formed, ready-to-use logotype from first principles.

The studio was founded by Jason Smith in 1999. Here, he talks about its work, and how an in-depth knowledge of letterforms can lead to better logotypes.

'When I learned to draw type at Monotype, the first thing I was asked to do was draw a 12-inch-diameter circle without a compass: turning the paper, sketching it out, looking at it, shaving bits off and so on. It was a brilliant exercise: when I thought I had a perfect circle I marked it out, and it wasn't.

'Everyone can see when a painting or a building or a logotype is aesthetically pleasing, but it's the job of painters, architects and type designers to figure out why it is. I look at a lot of logotypes and I see missed opportunities. I'll look at one and see a loop or a different ending, or a ligature that would have made it distinctive.

'The arrow in the FedEx logo – people love having that pointed out to them. That kind of feature makes every client and every customer happy. And that's what you're always reaching for: that special element where the penny drops. 'Something every designer should do is learn how to achieve expression through type. How do you make a word like "fizzy" look fizzy? It's not about typing out the name in Helvetica and applying a "fizzy" filter to it. It's about thinking of an idea and drawing it.

'Here, we always start with a blank piece of paper. We start sketching, and we develop an idea. Everyone here can draw really well; they've all got an eye for shapes, curves and balance. We search the words in a name for any interesting relationships between the letterforms that can become the hook. Then we apply an essence or vibe to it to capture the personality of the brand.

'An identity in its most basic form is a name. The next layer is the way you present it. That's the clever bit: conveying a message through a name. If you can build an identity in black and white, with just the name and something going on inside it, that's the holy grail.'

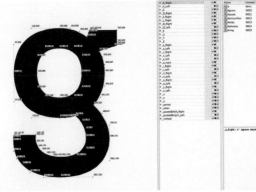

We begin with a survey of logotypes at their simplest: a word or an abbreviation set in a typeface chosen to convey something of the nature, stature or character of the organization. It is where the focus falls squarely on the letterforms themselves and on the communication of basic, essential values through type. It is where logotypes most closely follow typeface fashion, and where simplicity can lead to longevity.

AmericanAirlines

Cubus

fhrid™

THE
HEPWORTH
WAKEFIELD

VITSŒ

the Chelsea

INDITEX

Kemistry Gallery

Heller

amazee

Vanity

Campbell's

⊏+⊏

MIDI

Fenwick

cupcake

stadium

It's all
in the **font**

sirca

SONY

Jeep

rtve

BRAUN

ferrovial

Moulinex

Syfy

Canon

GREENPEACE

acca

loft

HOUSE OF
PROPELLERS

great.

Dafi/Academy

BREE

BETTYS

Blokk

AmericanAirlines

1. American Airlines
International airline, USA
Designed by Unimark International (Massimo Vignelli), 1967
In a book dedicated to expressive wordmarks, we start at the more taciturn end of the scale. Helvetica, the typeface that forms the basis for the logotypes of American Airlines, Jeep, Crate&Barrel, Microsoft, Panasonic, 3M and dozens of other global brands (as well as many more fashionable names that would shun associations with traditional big business), was considered the height of efficient, unruffled modernity when it was first applied in logotypes in the mid-1960s.

A new generation of American design firms, led by Unimark International in Chicago, adopted Helvetica as their house typeface. It responded to a need for a compact, effective, highly readable text font, and it became the modernist cornerstone of a look that signalled a new, expansive technological era in American commerce.

One of the first projects for Milan-born Massimo Vignelli (1931) after he started Unimark's New York office was to develop an identity to replace American Airlines' signature eagle symbol. His solution – the name in bold Helvetica in red and blue – outraged employees, who demanded an eagle on their aircraft tails. Vignelli, equally outraged at the demands for what he saw as superfluous and sentimental decoration, eventually relented and grudgingly crafted a highly stylized eagle to take a back seat within an 'AA' version of the identity.

Vignelli, who claims that no graphic designer needs more than six typefaces in his/her armoury, went on to apply Helvetica in numerous logotypes – including the New York City Subway's iconic signage – that survive to this day.

2. Streetlab
Skateboard retailer, Sweden
Designed by We Recommend (Martin Fredricson, Nikolaj Knop), 2010
The neutrality of Neue Helvetica (a revision of Helvetica developed in 1983) helps this skate retailer steer clear of visual clashes with the brands it stocks.

3. Sadie Coles HQ
Contemporary art gallery, UK
Designed by Farrow, 1997
Like the gallery space, the logotype plays an almost silent role, in subservience to the art it encompasses.

4. Cristina Guerra Contemporary Art
Contemporary art gallery, Portugal
Designed by Atelier Pedro Falcão, 2001
Art gallery names, like fashion brands, frequently echo the identity of their founders. Pedro Falcão's aim with this gallery identity was legibility and timelessness, 'similar to a perfume brand'.

5. ST Holdings
Record distribution and label management, UK
Designed by Give Up Art (Stuart Hammersley), 2010
An unassuming wordmark for a self-proclaimed 'boring box-packer' of the music industry.

Street ™**lab**

2

Sadie Coles   HQ

3

CristinaGuerra
Contemporary Art

4

ST Holdings Ltd.

5

6. Asprey
Luxury goods brand, UK
*Designed by Pentagram
(Angus Hyland), 2002*
For the company that has
enjoyed royal patronage
since 1862, a logotype
with stately letterspacing
and a final flourish
to mark its split from
Garrard in 2002.

7. BurdaStyle
Online sewing community
and resource, USA
*Designed by Area 17
(Audrey Templier), 2008*
A digital offshoot of
Burda Style, Germany's
leading DIY sewing
publication, with a
reinterpretation of the
magazine's logotype that
centres the brand on
fashion and style.

8. Cubus
Family fashion retailer,
Norway
*Designed by Stockholm
Design Lab, 2007*
A clean, modern identity
that repositioned this
major retail brand and
helped to consolidate
its presence in the rest
of Scandinavia and
northern Europe.

9. LazyLazy.com
Online family fashion
retailer, Denmark
*Designed by We
Recommend (Martin
Fredricson, Nikolaj
Knop), 2010*

10. Nailxpress
Nail polish strip brand,
Spain
*Designed by Talking
(Gonzalo Sanchez, Fabián
Vázquez), 2009*
Simple, straightforward
typography on
monochrome packaging,
displays and collateral
helps put the focus on
the brand's main asset:
the spectrum of colours
in its product range.

**11. Douglas
Entertainment**
TV and film producer,
Denmark
*Designed by We
Recommend (Martin
Fredricson, Nikolaj
Knop), 2010*
A simple, versatile
wordmark based on
a modified version of
the Akzidenz-Grotesk
typeface (the 1898
precursor of Helvetica
and Univers), designed
to sit comfortably with
the look of any of the
company's productions.

12. Heller
Furniture and
housewares
manufacturer, USA
*Designed by Vignelli
Associates (Massimo
Vignelli), 1972*
Not only did Massimo
Vignelli create Heller's
Helvetica wordmark,
he also designed
the company's first
ever product: a line
of melamine stacking
dinnerware. As well as
developing corporate
identities, Vignelli and his
wife Leila have applied
their modernist, objective
design language to
numerous products
and interiors.

13. Hertz
International car rental
company, USA
*Designed by Landor
Associates (Charles
Routhier, Bina Kijmedee
and Juliane Freitas),
2009*
Landor's identity loses
the dated drop shadow of
the old Hertz wordmark
but keeps the italics and
yellow (as a background),
retaining a connection
with the past while
seeking to catch the eye
of modern customers:
cash-strapped but
demanding personalized
service.

14. Spiritualized
Rock band, UK
Designed by Farrow, 1997
Created to coincide with
the release of the third
Spiritualized album,
*Ladies and Gentlemen
We Are Floating in Space*,
Farrow's utilitarian
Helvetica identity
perfectly complemented
its packaging for the
CD, which parodied
packaging for
prescription medicine.

15. Jeep
Off-road vehicle brand,
USA
*Designer unknown,
1960s*
Pure, no-nonsense
Helvetica Bold for
the original off-road
vehicle. The origin of
the name itself is still
disputed among Jeep®
enthusiasts, with some
claiming it emerged
from the designation
'GP' (short for 'General
Purpose Vehicle') and
others maintaining
that GIs named it after
Popeye's magical,
otherworldly pet,

Eugene the Jeep. The
wordmark first appeared
on vehicles in the 1960s.
(Courtesy of Chrysler-
Jeep LLC)

Asprey

6

BurdaStyle

7

Cubus

8

LazyLazy.com

9

Nailxpress®

Douglas
Entertainment

10

11

Heller

12

Hertz®

Spiritualized®

13

14

Jeep®

15

Crate&Barrel

16. Crate & Barrel
Housewares retailer, USA
Designed by Tom Shortlidge, 1968
When a young American couple, Gordon and Carole Segal, opened the first Crate & Barrel store in December 1962, their aim was to put before a discerning American audience the kind of well-designed, modern, durable products they had seen on sale in European cities while on honeymoon. The name was inspired by the bulk packaging in which their stock arrived from Europe, which they overturned to create product displays.

When the company started to branch out in the late 1960s, the Segals turned to Tom Shortlidge, a young art director at Young & Rubicam who had worked weekends in the original Chicago Old Town store to earn a little extra cash. His opinion was sought by Segal on a proposed new logo to replace the existing all-caps stencil wordmark.

'I thought it was a nice logo – but for someone else,' recalls Shortlidge, who has rarely spoken about his involvement with the iconic US brand. 'It was a stylized C+B, and would have been very appropriate for a glass manufacturer. The warmth of the name "Crate and Barrel" and what that implied was missing.'

Segal invited Shortlidge to have a go. 'To reflect the store's European-ness, I started looking at Helvetica, then a relatively new typeface in the US and one that I had introduced to the in-store signage during my brief tenure as a part-time employee. But I needed to alter Helvetica a bit to make the logo more distinctive. The "C" was made rounder and closed into more of a circle. The tail on the ampersand was extended, and other characters were tinkered with subtly.'

It was the application of the black, bold logo around the corners of boxes, bags and displays from late 1968 that really impressed the Crate & Barrel brand on the American shopper's consciousness. Every carrier bag became a commercial for the store on the streets of American cities, conferring on its bearer a chic European sophistication. With more than 100 storefronts in the USA, the brand plans to go global, bringing its American take on Euro-chic to, it says, 'every corner of the world' – including Europe.

17. Syfy
Cable TV channel, USA
Designed by Proud Creative, 2009
Launched in 1992, the SciFi Channel changed its spelling in 2009 and thereby turned a genre into an ownable, marketable trademark, freeing it to move into other genres such as reality TV, fantasy, paranormal and horror. Likewise, Proud's identity aimed for timeless, non-genre-specific simplicity.

18. Teach First
Educational charity, UK
Designed by Spencer du Bois (John Spencer), 2010
Calm, solidity and understated confidence for a highly regarded independent charity.

19. Knoll
Furniture manufacturer, USA
Designed by Unimark International (Massimo Vignelli), 1966
Massimo Vignelli and his co-founders at Unimark International in the mid-1960s were passionate about objectivity, systems and functionality in design and typography (see American Airlines, pp16–17). Knoll, a US-based company with roots in European modernism and pledged to the values of the Bauhaus, was the perfect client for the Unimark treatment. Helvetica's unusually large x-height (i.e. the height of standard lower-case letters like x, n, o, a and e) gave individual words and names – like 'Knoll' – an internal stability and visual strength that traditional typefaces with long ascenders and descenders couldn't generate. A company like Knoll needed nothing more, nothing less.

20. Openfield
Grain supplier, UK
Designed by Purpose (Rob Howsam, Stuart Youngs, Justin Davies), 2008
A wordmark to reflect the positive, inclusive spirit of a grain distribution company that shares its profits with farm owners.

17

TeachFirst

18

Knoll

19

Openfield.™

20

ERCO

1. Erco
Architectural lighting manufacturer, Germany
Designed by Otl Aicher, 1974
A font whose letters are composed of thick strokes is said to be 'bold'; one whose letters have fine strokes is termed 'light'. Erco, a company that illuminates architectural environments, has for almost 40 years been graced by a logotype that gets lighter with every letter.

The designer responsible for these strokes of brilliance was Otl Aicher (1922–91), a pioneering graphic designer and educator whose career is closely tied to Germany's post-war recovery. Having actively opposed the Nazi regime, then helped the recovery of his hometown Ulm by co-founding the highly influential Hochschule für Gestaltung in 1953, he immersed himself in creating a unified look for an event that symbolized his country's restoration to international respectability: the 1972 Olympic Games in Munich.

Aicher and his studio created graphic systems that covered every element of the Games, from his much-celebrated pictograms and posters to mascots and memorabilia. Aicher extended his pictogram system for use at Munich Airport, and it was this set of symbols that Erco wished to license – for a series of directional sign luminaires – when they approached Aicher in 1974.

With a new marketing motto of 'Light not luminaires', and a new target audience of architects and interior designers in mind, Erco commissioned an entire identity system from Aicher, from logo to exhibition stands to catalogues and brochures. The typeface Aicher chose was Univers, designed by Swiss typographer Adrian Frutiger (b.1928). What made it perfect for Aicher's purposes was its multiplicity of weight and width combinations, each connoted by a different two-digit number.

The 'E' of 'ERCO' is set in Univers 65 Bold; the 'R' in Univers 55 Roman; and the 'C' in Univers 45 Light. The 'O' was lighter than the lightest weight of Univers, and was individually cut to complete the progression.

It is usually logos, not their designers, whose lives are cut short. In this case, though, it was the reverse; the Erco logo lives on, but Aicher was tragically killed in a traffic accident in 1991, aged 69.

2. Ruth Tomlinson
Bespoke jeweller, UK
Designed by Felt Branding (Scott Manning, Tom Rogers), 2009
Jeweller to the A-list, Ruth Tomlinson raised her profile with an elegant, restrained identity that complements the intricate, handcrafted nature of her creations.

3. Indie
Advertising agency, The Netherlands
Designed by The Stone Twins (Declan and Garech Stone), 2009
A name and a launch event apparently influenced by the new frugality (in its most relative sense) in the advertising industry. The name suggests creativity on a low budget, while the launch simply involved spreading a giant branded beach towel on a public beach in Cannes during the annual Cannes Lions Festival. Indie personnel placed a few bottles of wine in an ice bucket next to the towel, and walked off.

4. Lichthaus Arnsberg
Contemporary art and performance space, Germany
Designed by Hesign International, 2010
A simple wordmark with an enigmatic appendage, apparently referring to the angular architecture of the glasshouse space and its ambient conditions, which fluctuate between light and dark.

5. Good
Print and online magazine, USA
Designed by Area 17 (Arnaud Mercier), 2006
Good calls itself the 'integrated media platform for people who want to live well and do good'. Its two main outlets are a quarterly magazine and a website (www.good.is), with each edition devoted to a topic or theme, such as water, food, transport or work.

2

3

4

5

6. Foodily.com
Online recipe finder, USA
Designed by Six (John Kariolis), 2010
Started by a group of food lovers in San Mateo, California, Foodily claims to be 'the world's largest recipe network'. Its wordmark reflects the spirit of well-fed joie de vivre.

7. International Center for Journalists
Non-profit professional organization, USA
Designed by Siegel & Gale, 2009
Established in the mid 1980s, the ICFJ promotes journalistic quality and integrity worldwide, in the belief that it can help bring about positive change. Its no-nonsense, interlocking letterforms suggest strength and plain speaking with considerably more success than its old symbol of a globe encircled by a bendy pen.

8. Inditex
Fashion distributor, Spain
Designed by Summa (Wladimir Marnich), 1999
Founded in 1975 by the reclusive Amancio Ortega – Spain's richest man in 2011 – Inditex owns around 100 businesses, including Zara, Massimo Dutti and Bershka. The group's 2001 flotation was preceded by the launch of this new identity and an extremely rare, headline-making public appearance by Ortega.

9. JW Trading
Consumer goods trading company, Hong Kong
Designed by Loovvool (Hannes Unt), 2008
An identity designed to convey a sophisticated, European, fashion-oriented positioning to the premium retailers and spas with which it trades in China and Hong Kong.

10. Hearst Corporation
Media conglomerate, USA
Designed by Chermayeff & Geismar, 2005
To coincide with the opening of the showpiece Hearst Tower headquarters at 300 West 57th St, Manhattan, Hearst also invested in a new brand architecture and logotype that

would identify its many divisions and products in a consistent, distinctive way.

11. Heal's
Department store chain, UK
Designed by Pentagram (Domenic Lippa), 2005
After almost 200 years in business with only tentative expansion beyond its Tottenham Court Road headquarters in London, Heal's felt safe and predictable. Domenic Lippa's monochrome identity and packaging, echoing that of Crate & Barrel in the USA, made the Heal's brand relevant and contemporary, and looks set to last. Not 200 years, perhaps, but for a while yet.

12. Okinaha
Health and anti-aging treatment store, Belgium
Designed by Coast (Frederic Vanhorenbeke), 2009
Named after the Japanese archipelago with the world's highest percentage of centenarians, Okinaha is based on principles of health, longevity, purity and oriental simplicity.

13. Guggenheim Partners
Investment management services, USA
Designed by Chermayeff & Geismar, 2002
The name is legendary in American business and this logotype, for a group of financial services brought together by the Guggenheim family and a small group of partners, makes visual capital of it.

14. Braun
Consumer products brand, Germany
Designed by Wolfgang Schmittel, 1952
The world knows Braun best for its electric shavers; the design world loves the company for the serenely simple products designed by Dieter Rams from the 1950s onwards, and for the logotype that graced them.

The blueprint for the famous wordmark was created in 1934 by Will Münch. It featured white characters (curiously, all upper case until the 'n') with a black drop

shadow, and an extra-tall 'A', whose shape echoed that of the 'n' as well as the profile of the radios Braun was best-known for. Black letters, without shadows, were adopted in 1939.

Wolfgang Schmittel, a freelancer in the company's design department at the time, redrew the logotype on a square grid, so that the four smaller letters all followed a consistent 2:1 height-to-width ratio. The 'A' remained taller with a ratio of 8:3, and the white space within the letterforms was of equal thickness to the black strokes. This systematic revision gave the wordmark balance, symmetry and instant recognition.

15. Gravitas
Game manufacturer, Canada
Designed by Hambly & Woolley (Bob Hambly, Frances Chen), 2008
A logotype with weight and authority to represent a game that encourages bold personal responses to deep questions.

16. Hahmo Design
Cross-disciplinary design company, Finland
Designed by Hahmo (Pekka Piippo, Antti Raudaskoski), 2003

6

7

8

9

HEARST

HEAL'S

10

11

GUGGENHEIM

12

13

BRAUN

14

GRAVITAS

HAHMO

15

16

17. Mass LBP
Public engagement consultancy, Canada
Designed by Concrete (Diti Katona, John Pylypczak, Jordan Poirier), 2008
Mass LBP's identity makes the organization feel more populist and accessible, and creates impact in applications with very limited budgets.

18. Jerwood Gallery
Contemporary art gallery, UK
Designed by Rose, 2010
For a gallery that sits on the seafront in Hastings among the famous, tall black fishing huts, a logotype inspired by the hand-painted registration numbers of local boats.

19. Samuel H Kress Foundation
Art history education fund, USA
Designed by C&G Partners, 2008
Samuel H Kress was father of a national empire of dime stores selling affordable, durable housewares. With his wealth, he established a foundation to advance the conservation of pre-20th-century European art. C&G Partners' custom typography includes a 'K' inspired by decorative details on one of SH Kress & Co.'s art-deco stores.

20. Terry Moore Design
Interior design company, UK
Designed by Kimpton (David Kimpton, Katie Alger), 2010
A monogram that repeats the founder's initials to emphasize his ownership of his firm's design output.

21. MediaCom
International media agency, UK
Designed by Rose, 2009
A high-visibility logotype for a business built on making its clients more visible.

22. Ricoh
Office equipment and camera manufacturer, Japan
Designed by Landor Associates, 2010
Established in 1936 as Rikagaku Kogyo, the business machine maker westernized its name, step-by-step, over nearly 30 years, ending up with Ricoh in 1963. Landor's revisions to its logotype are intended to enhance its 'readability on a global scale'.

23. Lisson Gallery
Contemporary art gallery, UK
Designed by A2/SW/ HK, 2007
Sometimes, a little typographic refinement can make all the difference. The finely judged tweaks made by A2/SW/HK to the Lisson Gallery's letterspaced Gill Sans wordmark – such as reducing the space between the two words, widening and opening out the 'G' to complement the 'S', shortening the mid-stroke of the 'E' and deepening the 'v' of the 'Y' – made for a more unified, balanced and optically pleasing logotype.

24. Vitsœ
Furniture manufacturer, UK
Designed by Wolfgang Schmidt, 1969
In the late 1950s, Danish furniture entrepreneur Niels Wiese Vitsœ was introduced to Braun's chief designer, Dieter Rams, by designer-maker Otto Zapf. Vitsœ and Zapf set up their own business to manufacture the Rams-designed 606 Universal Shelving System – a precision-engineered design classic. When Zapf left in 1969, Vitsœ & Zapf became Vitsœ, with a wordmark in Univers 75 Black, whose 'Œ' ligature was hand drawn by Wolfgang Schmidt to include the full counter (internal space) of the 'O' element – the standard Univers ligature resembled a reversed 'D' fused to an 'E'. In so doing, Schmidt created a unique typographic glyph, and a highly distinctive logotype.

25. The Savoy
Luxury hotel, UK
Designed by Pentagram (John Rushworth), 2008
To coincide with its roof-to-basement refurbishment, The Savoy gained a logo that is a contemporary evocation of its theatrical heyday, based on its most distinctive and flamboyant visual feature: the 12 m (40 ft) neon sign that greets guests as they arrive.

MASSLBP

17

JERWOOD GALLERY

18

KRESS

19

TM™

20

MEDIACOM

RICOH

21

22

LISSON GALLERY

23

VITSŒ

24

SAVOY

25

SM

26. Stedelijk Museum
Modern art museum,
The Netherlands
*Designed by Total Design
(Wim Crouwel), 1963*
It is a sign of how timeless
the simplest logotypes
can be that this section
of the book includes
many wordmarks still
in use 40 years or more
after they were designed.
Their longevity, though,
also has much to do with
their owners' enduring
attachment to the
values and ideas that
brought their identities
into being, such as
modernist principles of
simplicity, accessibility,
functionality and clarity.

When Edy de Wilde
was appointed head of
Amsterdam's Stedelijk
Museum in 1962, he
brought with him a young
designer, Wim Crouwel,
who had designed
a series of daring
posters and catalogues
for De Wilde at the
Van Abbemuseum in
Eindhoven.

One of the first tasks for
Crouwel was to establish
a modern identity for
the museum. He aimed
for a typographic style
that would be easily
recognizable and
individual to the Stedelijk,
but that wouldn't detract
from the artistic subject
matter.

An admirer of rationalist
Swiss design, Crouwel
found what he needed
in Univers, a typeface
designed in a wide
range of weights almost
a decade earlier by
Swiss typographer
Adrian Frutiger. Crouwel
employed Univers for the
museum's monogram
and the text on its
communications. Univers
had been designed as
a neutral, functionalist
typeface, but in Crouwel's
hands, on a long series
of Stedelijk posters, it
became the core element
of what became known in
The Netherlands as the
'SM style'.

It was Crouwel's
relationship with the
Stedelijk that helped
to get Total Design,
the pioneering
multidisciplinary
consultancy that he co-
founded, off the ground.
He remained responsible

for the museum's identity
and graphics until 1985,
when De Wilde stepped
down. Through his design
of radical typefaces,
such as the pixellated
New Alphabet in 1967,
and a series of identities
for TD's corporate clients
in the 1960s and 1970s,
Crouwel influenced
generations of graphic
designers. Not many of
his wordmarks remain
in use, but one of his
very first does. For the
Stedelijk, the visual
identity Crouwel created
to complement the
museum's displays is as
relevant and powerful
as ever.

27. Republic
Fashion retailer, UK
*Designed by B&W Studio
(Lee Bradley, Andrew
Droog), 2009*

28. Restaurant Tschine
Restaurant, Switzerland
*Designed by Hotz & Hotz
(Roman Imhof), 2007*
Tschine is the casual
dining restaurant at the
five-star Carlton Hotel
in St Moritz. Its identity
needed to reflect its more
contemporary tone, while
still conveying prestige
and sophistication.

29. Quintessentially
Private members' club, UK
*Designed by Rose (Garry
Blackburn), 2002*
A case of letterspacing
spelling luxury
and exclusivity.

**30. The Hepworth
Wakefield**
Contemporary art
gallery, UK
*Designed by A Practice
For Everyday Life
(APFEL), 2009*
The Hepworth Wakefield
opened in 2011 and
houses a collection of
20th-century art that
includes many works
by Barbara Hepworth
(1903–75), Wakefield's
most celebrated artistic
offspring. The gallery's
logotype echoes the
British modernist
typefaces of Hepworth's
era, and the oblique
tips of the letters
reference the pitched
roofs of the building
forms, designed by David
Chipperfield Architects.

REPUBLIC™

27

TSCHINE

CASUAL DINING

28

QUINTESSENTIALLY

29

THE
HEPWORTH
WAKEFIELD

30

1. aarrkk
Property developer and
invester, UK
*Designed by Brownjohn
(James Beveridge), 2009*

2. Evo
Fitness centre chain,
Norway
*Designed by Mission
Design (Gary Swindell),
2009*
Hints of wheels and legs
in this wordmark for a
fitness centre chain
attempting to evolve
(hence the name) this
established market.

3. Sirca
Financial data provider,
Australia
*Designed by Naughtyfish
(Paul Garbett), 2009*

4. Loft Investments
Financial services
provider, Sweden
*Designed by
Lundgren+Lindqvist, 2010*
In a highly conservative
market, Loft's identity
suggests a fresh
approach without ringing
alarm bells, employing
strong typography to
establish trust.

5. Ferrovial
Infrastructure and
construction company,
Spain
*Designed by Summa
(Andreu Balius, Daniel
Bembibre, Tilman Solé),
2008*
Summa developed a
typeface to identify
Ferrovial and its
many subsidiaries.
Following rapid growth
and evolution from a
construction company
into an international
designer, sponsor
and builder of major
infrastructure projects,
the group is given a
human, contemporary
face through the
logotype.

**6. Nederlandse
Staatsloterij**
National lottery,
The Netherlands
*Designed by Teldesign
(Jaco Emmen, René de
Jong), 2007*
A simple, durable
wordmark to sit easily
with the many brands
under the lottery's wings.

7. Urban Splash
Property developer and
regenerator, UK
Designed by North, 2008
For Urban Splash,
one of the UK's most
enterprising residential
property developers,
North created a
typographically led
identity system based
on an 'organic', custom
font designed with type
design house Dalton
Maag. The alphabet
includes alternative
designs for many letters,
such as 'g', 'e', 'a' and 'y'.
This offers designers
numerous options when
branding individual
developments while
ensuring their designs
remain recognizably on-
brand. It also allows the
type family to be added
to over time. Like an
Urban Splash property,
it's a work in progress.

8. Golla
Personal electronics
carriers, Finland
*Designed by Hahmo
(Pekka Piippo), 2000*

9. seymourpowell
Product design
consultancy, UK
Designed by GBH, 2002
On the face of it, a simple
lower-case wordmark.
But, by highlighting the
'we' and adding words like
'think' and 'transform',
the identity doubles as a
strapline. And, by doing
something similar with
the 'our' and appending
nouns such as 'foresight'
and 'proposal', it marks
the firm's ownership of its
skills and creations.

aarrkk

1

evo

2

sirca

3

loft

4

ferrovial

5

nederlandse staatsloterıȷ

6

urbansplash

7

golla®

seymourpowell

8

9

1. Atelier LaDurance
Denim fashion brand,
France
*Designed by Boy
Bastiaens/Stormhand,
2002*
Timelessness and stylish
Gallic unfussiness for this
exclusive denim label.

2. Folksam
Insurer, Sweden
*Designed by Stockholm
Design Lab, 2001*
With roots in Swedish
trade union and
cooperative culture
and a name that sprang
from the merger of
its two insurance
branches (*Folket*
[people] and *Samarbete*
[cooperation]), Folksam
is one of the country's
largest insurers and
investment managers.
Its identity, in a high-
contrast serif face,
has a homely, modest,
uncorporate air.

3. Goldlog
Rock band, Norway
*Designed by
KalleGraphics, 2005*
American Typewriter,
tightly tracked, lends a
gentle, DIY feel to the
identity for a folk-
influenced band.

4. Kaspar
Luxury stationery brand,
Switzerland
*Designed by Hotz & Hotz
(Roman Imhof, Herbert
Seybold), 2006*
For a business dealing
in products such as
notebooks bound in
full-grain leather and
writing cabinets made of
cow's horn, a hand-drawn
logotype that attempts
to fuse the sophisticated
character of serif type
with the soft, fluent look
of handwriting in ink.

5. Kemistry Gallery
Graphic design gallery, UK
*Designed by Proud
Creative, 2005*
Understatement with, in
the ligature between 's'
and 't', a quiet flourish for
a wordmark that mustn't
shout louder than the
work on show.

6. People Tree
Fair Trade fashion brand,
UK/Japan
*Designed by Practice
+ Theory (Andreas
Pohancenik), 2007*
People Tree designs
exclusive fashion for
manufacture by 50
Fair Trade groups in 15

countries, employing local
skills and creating jobs in
marginalized communities.
Its wordmark was created
to work across a range of
applications, from stitched
labels to catalogues to
the brand's website.

7. Pearson Lyle
Photographic agency, UK
*Designed by Dowling
Duncan (Rob Duncan,
John Dowling), 2009*
An elegant slab serif
that creates character
but keeps a low profile
alongside the company's
clients' work.

8. Ragne Sigmond
Photographer, Denmark
*Designed by
KalleGraphics, 2007*

9. Canon
Imaging and optical
products, Japan
Designed by Canon, 1956
The Canon name, like
Sony, was originally a
product brand before
being adopted as the
corporate name. In
1934, Precision Optical
Instruments of Tokyo
prototyped Japan's first-
ever 35mm camera with
a focal-plane shutter, and
christened it Kwanon –
the Japanese name for
the Buddhist goddess of
mercy. When the camera
entered production, the
trademark it bore was the
closest Western word
to Kwanon: Canon. The
accompanying wordmark
was a spindly, hand-
drawn affair, with a large,
oval 'C' and an 'a' with a
distinctive, sloping stem.

In 1947 as Canon
cameras won over
photographers
worldwide, the company
adopted the name. Six
years later the logo was
redrawn with thicker
strokes, and the 'C' and
'n's gained their first,
tentative serifs. The
letters were bulked up
further in 1956 to create
Canon's idiosyncratic,
semi-serif wordmark:
the 'C' made smaller and
more circular, the serifs
and terminal on the 'a'
harmonized, and the 'o'
given its angled stress.

**10. The McNay Art
Museum**
Regional art museum,
USA
*Designed by C&G
Partners (Emanuela
Frigerio), 2008*

The McNay, in San
Antonio, celebrated its
50th anniversary by
adding a major new wing,
designed by Jean-Paul
Viguier, to the original
19th-century mansion
museum. A new identity
uses a classical font,
Minion, but adopts the
modern way of referring
to the museum.

11. Tomorrow
Retirement financial
services, UK
*Designed by KentLyons,
2007*
Some typefaces go
through peaks and
troughs of popularity.
Souvenir, with its quirks
and curves, was huge in
the 1970s in advertising
and on soft-rock album
covers, then looked on
in horror throughout the
1980s and 1990s.
Now, though, designers
are rediscovering
Souvenir and putting it
to novel use, such as in
this rebrand of retirement
specialist GE Life,
commissioned by owner
Swiss Re. Maybe it struck
a distant chord with
the 1970s generation:
the rebrand was such
a hit with retirees that
Tomorrow was quickly
snapped up by LV=.

Atelier LaDurance®
LES BAUX DE PROVENCE

1

Folksam®

2

Goldlog

3

Kaspar

4

Kemistry Gallery

People Tree

5

6

PearsonLyle

Ragne Sigmond

7

8

Canon

9

theMcNay

Tomorrow™

10

11

Google™

12. Google
Search engine, USA
Designed by Ruth Kedar and Sergey Brin, 1999
Ruth Kedar was an assistant professor of design at Stanford University in California when a friend introduced her to a pair of computer-science PhD students, Sergey Brin and Larry Page. The research project the pair had been working on – a search engine that ranked websites by the number of pages that linked to them, not by the repetition of search terms on a page – was starting to attract serious interest from technology investors, and they asked Kedar to help them to give it an identity.

The pair had a name for the search engine – one that they hoped would suggest its grasp of vast volumes of information. It was the largest number they knew the name of: one followed by 100 zeros, known as a googol. Their misspelt number had a playfulness they liked, and it stuck.

Brin had created a multicoloured wordmark in a simple graphics program with a standard bold serif font and an exclamation mark. Kedar was asked to refine the logo into something that suggested complexity but that was not visually complex.

After experiments involving Garamond, web motifs, crosshairs, overlapping 'o's, magnifying glasses and all upper-case letters, Kedar ended up with just the word itself, set in the quirky Catull typeface, with different coloured letters and shadows on each that 'floated' the logo on the search page. Finally, she revived Brin's original primary colours progression, complete with a green 'l' to convey unpredictability. The logo that saw Google through its boom years was born.

The only change since then was made on 6 May 2010, when the logo adopted more vibrant shades of the same colours and the drop shadow was brought much tighter into the letterforms.

Keeping its logotype simple, free of any form of illustration or symbolism, has, ironically, allowed Google to take liberties with its identity on a regular basis. Branding wisdom urges consistency, but in Google's case the liberties it takes are its trademark, because they play on the logotype's universal recognizability. Its 'Google Doodles', designed to mark anniversaries and major events, help keep the simple Google logotype – seen by more than a billion unique vistors every month – from being boring.

13. Rupert Sanderson
Luxury shoe designer, UK
Designed by Johnson Banks, 2000
For a shoemaker to the stars, an aesthetic designed to be 'undesigned', creating an air of authenticity and craftsmanship by recalling the innocent era before graphic designers and 'the brand'.

14. Scotland + Venice
Arts funding partnership, UK
Designed by Graphical House, 2009
Scotland + Venice is the umbrella identity for the bodies that fund Scotland's participation in the Venice Biennale art festival. A wordmark that employs an amended form of Baskerville and a minimalist '+' captures the contemporary nature of the art and the historic context of Venice.

15. Soda Reklamebyrå
Advertising agency, Norway
Designed by Mission Design (Karl Martin Sætren, Gary Swindells), 2004
A splash of Rockwell for Soda.

16. SugarSin
Confectionery shop, UK
Designed by &Smith, 2011
A typewriter-esque face with round, lollipop-style terminals for a 'non-traditional' sweet shop for adults and children.

Rupert Sanderson

13

Scotland +Venice

14

Soda™

15

SugarSin

16

1. Molton Brown
Premium beauty brand, UK
Designed by Farrow, 2011
Molton Brown started out in 1973 as a hair salon at 58 South Molton Street in London's Mayfair, mixing its first products in the room upstairs using nettles and camomile. After 38 years, the business felt that the original logotype, with its hand-tooled capitals and white highlights, was in need of modernization and simplification. Farrow stripped away the outline, leaving just the highlights, and drew a new logotype based on this skeleton of shapes. This use of natural ingredients has led to a modern, more refined mark that still bears the stamp of the original.

2. MC Partners
Recruitment consultant, UK
Designed by Rose, 2007
A City of London recruitment firm skilled at making 'mutually compatible' introductions and connections – hence the ligatures on the 'R's.

3. Northsea Capital
Private equity advisor, Denmark
Designed by We Recommend (Martin Fredricson, Nikolaj Knop), 2007
Pure type with integrity for one of the largest independent private-equity advisors in northern Europe.

4. Arup
Multidisciplinary construction consultancy, UK
Designed by Pentagram (David Hillman), 1985
In construction, the name 'Arup' is synonymous with innovation and ingenuity – so why add anything else?

5. Tiffany & Co.
Jewellery and silverware retailer, USA
Designed by Pentagram (Paula Scher), 1995
A redrawing of the Tiffany & Co. logotype that subtly revives the air of impeccable craftsmanship, taste and exclusivity.

6. Taryn Rose International
Luxury shoe designer, USA
Designed by Elixir Design (Jennifer Jerde, Nathan Durrant), 2005
A wordmark for a fashion-shoe business founded in 1998 by orthopaedic surgeon Dr Taryn Rose. Serif fonts with small capitals are favoured by luxury and heritage brands, particularly in North America, for giving a stamp of refinement and craftsmanship.

7. Norton & Sons
Bespoke tailor, UK
Designed by Moving Brands, 2006
Norton & Sons is as steeped in history and tradition as any brand. A Savile Row tailoring firm dating back to 1821, it has kitted out the likes of Winston Churchill, Cary Grant, Frank Sinatra, David Niven and three US presidents. As Moving Brands delved into Norton's history in the early stages of a contemporary rebranding directed at young gents, a designer queried the inverted 'S' on the shopfront signage. It was found to be the result of an uncharacteristically hasty repair after the shop suffered bomb damage in the 1940s. The quirk has been kept and an equally idiosyncratic, notched small-caps typeface adopted, to capture classic English eccentricity in a logotype.

8. Rigby & Peller
Corsetry retailer, UK
Designed by Springer & Jacoby, 2002
Rigby & Peller's bespoke lingerie and expert bra-fitting service have earned it a distinguished female clientele over the years, including HM Queen Elizabeth II. For decades, its only store was in South Molton Street, opened in 1939 by Mrs Rigby and Mrs Peller. In the last few years, it has reached out to a younger, more fashion-conscious market. Its 2002 brand revitalization created a new logotype that removed the impression that its products were only for

elderly ladies with deep pockets by unclipping the name from its Royal Warrant crests.

9. The New York Palace
Luxury hotel, USA
Designed by &Smith, 2009
The identity of a Madison Avenue landmark, which combines the spectacular Villard Mansion of 1882 with a 55-storey tower block from the late 1970s.

10. GSA Venture Partners
Venture capital fund, USA
Designed by Area 17 (Sara Berks), 2010

11. Via Snella
Male fashion brand, Sweden
Designed by We Recommend (Martin Fredricson, Nikolaj Knop), 2008
A confident, classical identity designed to create a solid base on which the brand can develop over seasons and years, and with which it can widen its international distribution.

MOLTON BROWN
L O N D O N

1

MCPARTNERS

2

NORTHSEA CAPITAL

3

ARUP

4

TIFFANY & CO.

TARYN ROSE

5

6

NORTON & SONS

7

RIGBY & PELLER
LONDON

THE
NEW YORK PALACE

8

9

GSA Venture Partners

VIA
SNELLA

10

11

SONY

12. Sony Corporation
Conglomerate, Japan
Designed by Yasuo Kuroki, 1961; modified by Sony, 1973
Sony's belief in the value of a simple, memorable, consistently presented brand name was fundamental to the company's rise to global eminence from a radio repair shop in a bomb-damaged Tokyo department store.

Masaru Ibuka and Akio Morita came up with the name as a way of branding their line of transistor radios, which started in 1955 with the TR-55. 'Sony' suggested products that were sound-related or 'sonic' (from the Latin origin 'sonus'), but also echoed the English word 'sonny', meaning boy. It was short, bright and easily said in any language, and 'sonny boy' was also used in 1950s Japanese to connote smart, presentable young men. A cartoon character known as Sony Boy featured in advertising for the firm's increasingly successful pocket radios.

So well received was the combination of compact product design and a Western-friendly brand, that the company – until this point known as Tokyo Tsushin Kogyo KK – adopted the Sony name in 1958. For a Japanese business to brand itself with a logotype of Roman letters and not kanji characters was almost unheard of at the time, as was Sony's desire for a name that did not restrict it to any one industry.

The first Sony logo was a hard-to-read wordmark with an angular 'S', squashed into a box. When it came to creating a large neon sign in downtown Tokyo in 1961, Sony publicity designer Yasuo Kuroki redrew the name as a stretched-out serif wordmark, and it stuck. Apart from some slight filling out of its letterforms to add a little extra visual weight, and despite a competition in 1981 to find a replacement, the logotype has remained unchanged for more than 50 years.

13. I/Object
Online fashion and homewares retailer, Belgium
Designed by Coast (Frederic Vanhorenbeke), 2010
Sustained! I/Object sells furniture, fittings, gadgets and gifts sourced from around the world. Its high-contrast serif font complements the of-the-moment nature of the merchandise.

14. Fabbrica
Italian restaurant, Canada
Designed by Concrete (Diti Katona, John Pylypczak, Edmond Ng), 2010
A super slab serif recalls post-war Italian type – or spaghetti westerns? – for this Toronto eaterie, set up by Canadian celebrity chef and entrepreneur Mark McEwan.

15. Foodparc
Gourmet food hall, USA
Designed by Mucca Design (Matteo Bologna, Andrea Brown), 2010
For this high-tech food hall on Sixth Avenue designed by *Blade Runner* and *Aliens* set designer Syd Mead, Mucca sought an identity that was 'a whimsical blend of the organic and the technological'.

16. Kopiosto
Artists' and writers' copyright organization, Finland
Designed by Hahmo (Pekka Piippo), 2005

I/OBJECT

13

FABBRICA

14

FOODPARC

15

KOPIOSTO

16

1. Amlin
Insurance and
reinsurance underwriting
group, UK
*Designed by OPX (Bill
Bickerstaff, David
Bennett, Adam Johnson),
2010*
Mixing small caps
with lower case, this
wordmark was designed
for typographic impact
across a wide range of
applications, from pens
to rugby sponsorship
hoardings.

2. iD
Electronic payment
system, Japan
*Designed by Good
Design Company
(Takuya Tomohara,
Manabu Mizuno), 2005*
iD allows consumers
to pay for goods and
services contactlessly
by waving a 'Osaifu-keitai'
(mobile wallet) handset
over a compatible reader.
Like credit cards, it is
based on post-payment,
and in its first five years
it gained more than
15 million subscribers
in Japan.

3. Puntari
Elderly care home,
Finland
*Designed by Hahmo (Erik
Bertell, Hanna Hakala,
Antti Raudaskoski), 2010*

4. Friendship Works
Children's mentoring
charity, UK
*Designed by hat-trick
(Gareth Howat, Jim
Sutherland, Alex
Swatridge), 2010*
Friendship Works gives
support to children in
London by providing
adult mentors who
encourage, listen and
guide them towards
adulthood. The adult-
and-child 'Ff' gives
the organization a
distinctively human but
professional face.

5. Arboretum Kalmthout
Arboretum and gardens,
Belgium
*Designed by Studio Hert
(Bart Rylant), 2009*

6. Virgin Galactic
Suborbital spaceflights
service, UK
Designed by GBH, 2006
Like the Erco logotype
(see p.22), the wordmark
for Richard Branson's
stratospheric tourism
venture uses a range
of weights to represent
light and dark. The

retro-futuristic font, titled
Elevon, was the work of
London type designers
Dalton Maag.

7. Green Park
Organic fashion brand,
UK
*Designed by B&W Studio
(Lee Bradley, Andrew
Droog), 2007*
A fashion line dominated
by combats and hoodies,
with a logo to catch the
eye of skateboarders.

**8. Constitutional Court
of South Africa**
Constitutional court,
South Africa
*Designed by Mister
Walker (Garth Walker),
2004*
The site chosen for
South Africa's new
constitutional court
in 1994 was that of an
apartheid-era prison
whose rubble was
recycled into the new
building. Originally
created for the court's
way-finding system, the
font of its official identity
comprises characters
based on documented
cell-wall graffiti by
apartheid prisoners, and
prison signage. A case of
letters speaking volumes.

9. architectsAlliance
Architectural practice,
Canada
*Designed by Concrete
(Diti Katona, John
Pylypczak), 2000*
A pure, modern
approach, with
the emphasis on
the 'Alliance', for
this 40-strong
multidisciplinary
practice.

10. Kilvil
Sports equipment
retailer, Andorra
*Designed by Summa
(Tilman Solé, Eduardo
Cortada), 2005*
Mixed case goes
down well with people
who go downhill well,
if this wordmark for
an extreme-sports-
equipment shop in the
Pyrenees is anything
to go by.

11. oki-ni
Online fashion retailer, UK
*Designed by Tomato
(Simon Taylor), 2004*
Founded in 2001, oki-ni
works with established
brands and innovative
designers to make
available exclusively
limited-edition fashion.

1

2

3

4

arboretum
KALMTHOUT

V1RG1N GaLacT1C

5

6

Green
park™

7

CONSTITUTIONAL
COURT
OF SOUTH AFRICA

aA

8

9

KiLVIL

OKI-ni

10

11

1. Bidfreight Port Operations
Portside logistics, South Africa
Designed by Mister Walker (Garth Walker), 2006
For South Africa's amalgamated portside logistics and stevedoring operations, a logotype of large and small letterforms inspired by shadows cast by letters on the sides of corrugated steel shipping containers.

2. Mini Museum Mürren
Museum, Switzerland
Designed by Atelier Bundi (Stephan Bundi), 2009
The Mini Museum Mürren is a very small museum indeed – just a few shop windows, in fact – in and about Mürren, a small village in the Swiss Alps.

3. SOM
Telecommunications operator, Andorra
Designed by Summa (Tilman Solé, Daniel Bembibre), 2009
SOM, the new brand for Andorra's sole telecoms operator (*Servei de Telecommunicacions d'Andorra STA*), is an acronym that also means 'we are' in Catalan, and seeks to identify the business with its paying customers.

4. SoundCircus Kees Kroot
Recording studio, The Netherlands
Designed by The Stone Twins (Declan and Garech Stone), 2007
The logotype for SoundCircus changes all the time, following different waveforms on different applications and incorporating slogans such as 'The Greatest Sound Studio on Earth featuring Kees and his Amazing Twiddling Knobs'.

5. Pueblo Chico
Theme park, Spain
Designed by Summa (Josep Maria Mir), 2000
Pueblo Chico (Little Town) is a park in Puerto de la Cruz, Tenerife, where the story of the Canary Islands is told in miniature, with scale models of streets, plazas, landmarks and monuments.

6. RTVE
Public broadcaster, Spain
Designed by Summa (Tilman Solé, Rocío Martinavarro, Joern Oelsner), 2008
For the first update of the *Radio y Televisión Española* (RTVE) brand in decades, Summa placed special emphasis on the 'e', which stands for 'Española' (Spanish) and recurs in all RTVE's TV-channel and radio-station brands. Its custom typography strives to suggest 'a balance between the human and the technological'.

7. HEMU
Academy of Music, Switzerland
Designed by >moser, 2010
The *Haute Ecole de Musique* (HEMU) in Lausanne is renowned for the eminence of its faculty members; amplifying the last two letters of the logotype stresses the importance of serious musical study.

8. Low-Income Investment Fund
Social investor, USA
Designed by C&G Partners (Steff Geissbuhler), 2010
LIIF is about people helping people: connecting low-income communities with capital markets to get social projects for housing, education and childcare off the ground.

1

2

3

4

PUEBLOCHICO

TENERIFE

5

6

HE**MU**

7

8

1. Association of Art Historians
Professional body, UK
Designed by REG Design (Emily Wood, Ruth Sykes), 2005
Two fonts by a favourite subject of art historians – Eric Gill (1882–1940) – convey the association's twin concerns. Joanna, a typeface influenced by those of Robert Granjon from the 16th century, represents art from all periods of history, while Gill Sans symbolizes contemporary practice.

2. ESADE
Business school, Spain
Designed by Summa (Wladimir Marnich, Eduardo Cortada), 2008
Ranked the world's foremost business school by *The Wall Street Journal* in 2006 and 2007, ESADE is a little less conservative than other international schools in its branding. The second 'E', picked out in a bold sans serif, denotes education, ethics and enterprise – the three fields in which students should aim for excellence.

3. Historic House Trust
Preservation partnership, USA
Designed by Doyle Partners (Stephen Doyle, August Heffner), 2006
The Historic House Trust is a consortium of 23 houses and buildings in New York City, offering insights into the history of the city. The combination of typefaces in the logotype alludes to the diversity on offer.

4. Fresh Co.
Grocery retailer, Canada
Designed by Rethink, 2010
A new discount grocery store brand launched in 2010 by Sobeys, one of Canada's largest supermarket chains, Fresh Co. is designed to be fresh as well as low in price. The logotype uses the Bree typeface to convey 'fresh' and the more functional DIN to represent the bargain price point.

5. Joly Beauty
Cosmetics brand, China
Designed by Hesign International (Jianping He, Jun Dai, Lin Yu), 2008
A logotype of many faces, designed to reflect the many sides to oriental beauty.

6. TOJO
Furniture and housewares retailer, UK
Designed by Graphical House, 2010
A double logotype conveying the range of design on offer in this Glasgow store. A heavily abstracted mark reduces the letters to their simplest forms while an elegant classical rendering offers a diametrical contrast.

7. International Creative Union Center
Creative arts centre, China
Designed by Hesign International (Jianping He), 2008
A monogram to represent the multiplicity of disciplines and directions at this state-run centre for artistic training and cultural activities.

8. Danish Fashion Institute Academy
Network organization, Denmark
Designed by Homework (Jack Dahl), 2009
In design terms, Denmark is perhaps better known for its furniture than its fashion. The Danish Fashion Institute aims to rectify that, encouraging innovation and promoting Denmark as 'a fashion brand in itself'.

1

ESADE

2

3

FRESHCO.

4

J0ly Beauty
精艺妆品

5

TOJO.

6

ICUC

7

Dafi/Academy

8

9. Muscular Dystrophy Campaign
Charity, UK
Designed by Spencer du Bois (John Spencer), 1998
Influenced by the attitudes of muscular dystrophy sufferers encountered during the brandng process, John Spencer created a logotype that directly conveys the progressive weakening and wasting effects of the disease in the type contrast between the strong and and the 'dystrophic'.

10. Take Ten
Change management consultancy, The Netherlands
Designed by Burobraak (Arjan Braaksma), 2008
Change made tangible through type.

11. Martin Prosperity Institute
Think tank, Canada
Designed by Hambly & Woolley (Frances Chen, Barb Woolley), 2007
Part of the University of Toronto, this think tank studies the role of 'sub-national factors' in global economic prosperity. The diversity of research and expertise at the institute led to a multifaceted logotype.

12. Oliver & Bonacini Restaurants
Restaurant group, Canada
Designed by Gottschalk + Ash International (Udo Schliemann, Michael Kirlew), 2008
Peter Oliver and Michael Bonacini teamed up in 1993 to open Jump in Toronto's Bay Street, and their portfolio of restaurants has grown steadily since. Oliver is the business half of the partnership; Bonacini is the chef.

13. Avid Reader
Independent bookstore, Australia
Designed by Inkahoots, 1997
Eclectic reading from this Brisbane bookstore.

14. Kino Cinema
Art-house cinema, Australia
Designed by Sadgrove Design (Brian Sadgrove), 1985

15. Hulton Archive
Picture library, UK
Designed by Pentagram (Angus Hyland), 2000
In 2000, Getty Images embarked on a project to digitize its entire collection of 15 million historic British press images, and called it the Hulton Archive. This meeting of historic images and modern technology is captured in the logotype.

16. Gr(eat)
Delicatessen, Denmark
Designed by Homework (Jack Dahl), 2008
Somewhere to eat green: a Copenhagen deli with a special respect for the environment in its food and packaging.

9

10

11

12

13

14

Hulton | Archive

15

great.

16

1. MoreySmith
Interior design
consultancy, UK
*Designed by Cartlidge
Levene, 2007*
Ten years after it had
designed MoreySmith's
original identity,
Cartlidge Levene redrew
the logotype as a dot-
matrix font. It was then
repeated and offset,
creating a fluid identity
and new opportunities
for tactile applications,
such as thermography
and laser cutting.

2. Living Beauty
Skincare concession, UK
*Designed by SEA (Bryan
Edmondson), 2004*
The clinical and the
organic meet in this
identity for Selfridges'
skincare concession.

3. Marawa the Amazing
Hula-hoop artist,
Australia/UK
*Designed by Mind Design
(Holger Jacobs, Romilly
Winter), 2010*
A logotype based on
revue theatre display
fonts that makes the
job of putting Marawa's
name up in lights
straightforward, should
that ever be necessary.

4. Cupcake
Spa and crèche, UK
*Designed by Mind Design
(Holger Jacobs, Craig
Sinnamon), 2008*
Composing Cupcake's
identity of dots leaves
open the option of using
multiple colours and
creating a 'Smarties'
effect to catch the eye
of young children.

**5. North / South /
East / West**
Photographic/musical
project, UK
*Designed by Give Up Art
(Stuart Hammersley),
2009*
For a series of
collaborative projects
between recording
artists from four different
parts of the world, a
typeface with characters
created from a grid
of tiny crosses, each
one representing the
compass of cardinal
points.

6. Speirs + Major
Lighting design
consultancy, UK
*Designed by
Bibliothèque, 2010*
A logotype that is a
construction of light,

typography and solid,
perforated materials for a
company that illuminates
the built environment.

7. Cha Cha Moon
Chinese noodle bar, UK
Designed by North, 2008
Cha Cha Moon in
London's West End
creates high-quality
fast Chinese food.
Noodles are, literally,
its trademark.

8. Bespoke Careers
Design recruitment
agency, UK
*Designed by 1977 Design
(Paul Bailey), 2004*
Bespoke, in London's
design heartland of
Clerkenwell, is identified
by a logotype based on
its own, appropriately
custom-designed
typeface, with letters
built around perfect
circles.

9. JBPR
Public relations agency,
UK
*Designed by Studio
Tonne, 2010*

10. Six Wines Eight
Wine retailer, UK
*Designed by Hyperkit,
2007*
Six Wines Eight stocks a
changing selection of 48
wines (6x8=48). Hyperkit
developed a vine-like grid
that generated a bespoke
typeface and logotype.

11. Dalton Maag
Type design studio, UK
*Designed by Mode (UK)
(Phil Costin, Ian Styles),
2002*
Dalton Maag's craft is
steeped in centuries of
tradition, but its identity
reflected the need to
appeal to the company's
principal audience of
graphic designers. The
logotype, based on early
Modernist type, uses
only the abbreviation
'DaMa' – the signature
appended to all Dalton
Maag font file names
(i.e .DaMa).

1

2

MARAWA

3

cupcake

4

North/South
East/West

5

6

Ohn Ohn moon

7

bespoke

8

ubpr_

9

six
wines
eight

10

11

BREE

12

12. Bree Collection
Bagmaker, Germany
Designed by Büro Uebele Visuelle Kommunikation (Sabine Schönhaar, Andreas Uebele), 2008
Logos that survive untouched, in their original state, for decades are rare. Even those logotypes that seem as if they have been around forever have usually required occasional refinements to strokes or serifs, or adjustments to the spacing of characters, to keep pace with changing tastes – of customers or company members – and typographic trends.

The Bree label was brought into the world in 1970 by a young couple, Wolf Peter Bree and his wife Renate, who had a vision of creating fashionable, functional bags from high-quality traditional materials. Its logotype was the height of fashion: looking high-tech but a little gauche, as if they had been drawn by a robot arm, the capital letters each filled the same square unit and comprised only straight-line strokes that seemed to be of uniform thickness. At the centre of the 'B' and the 'E's, these lines doubled back on themselves.

Almost 40 years later, the logotype was updated as part of a modernization programme. Stroke endings and the corners of characters were softened and curved, and a series of detailed refinements of individual letters were carried out to create a balanced optical effect, and to retain the impression that the logotype was grid-based, like its predecessor.

The changes addressed the elements of the logo that were mathematically correct but optically wrong. For example, because horizontal strokes look thicker to the human eye than vertical strokes of equal width, the verticals of the logotype were made marginally thicker. The width of the letters varies in the new logotype, and the spaces between them have been optically adjusted. The close parallel lines at the centre of the 'B' and 'E's have been thinned to create more space between them, and also raised slightly because their mathematical centre is too low for the rest of each letterform.

These and other tiny tweaks have given the logotype a new lease of life, although most of the shoppers passing through Bree's doors may be too distracted to notice any difference.

13. Vanity
Women's clothing brand, Mexico
Designed by Lance Wyman, 1972
One of many identities designed by Lance Wyman for Mexican enterprises following his acclaimed design of the graphics for the 1968 Mexico Olympic Games.

14. Nimmin
Power diet brand, Switzerland
Designed by Atelier Bundi (Stephan Bundi), 2010

15. Channel 9 TV
TV broadcasting channel, Australia
Designed by Sadgrove Design (Brian Sadgrove), 1975
A timeless TV channel logo from Australia that English watchers of the 1980s Ashes series will be familiar with. It remains essentially intact despite having been messed about continually, with makeovers in blue, silver and gold, in 3-D, with a high-chrome effect, a bevelled edge and the nine dots removed.

For any logo designer, watching your creation suffer in the hands of others can be a painful experience. Brian Sadgrove, who has designed identities for numerous Australian corporations, takes a philosophical view, comparing it to 'worrying about an extremely wayward child. You can't do anything about it, so don't get attached, whatever you do.'

16. Parc Central del Poblenou
Public park, Spain
Designed by Serracatafau (Quim Serra, Adriana Alós), 2007
A 'green lung' in Barcelona, designed by Jean Nouvel, the park is a lush oasis for the community with dense vegetation and a perimeter wall covered in Mediterranean plants. A grid system of nodes and connectors provides the base for the logotype, the signage and drawings of abstract gardens.

13

14

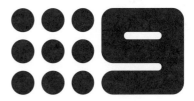

15

16

17. OQO
Chinese bar/restaurant,
UK
*Designed by SEA (Bryan
Edmondson), 2005*
A north-London bar with
a backward 'Q', known for
its quirky Chinese tapas.

18. Ogee74
Bathroom fittings
supplier, UK
*Designed by Studio8 (Zoë
Bather, Matt Willey, Steve
Fenn, Alex Ecob), 2010*
Ogee74 imports luxury
bathroom fittings and its
main market is architects
and interior designers. To
catch their eye, its circle-
based logotype features
an 'ogee curve' (related
to the S-shaped 'line
of beauty' in art), which
describes the profile
of a particular form of
architectural moulding: a
convex curve that flows
into a concave curve,
with parallel ends.

19. IDTV
Independent TV
production company,
The Netherlands
Designed by Lava, 2008
For a groundbreaking
Dutch TV producer, Lava
created a flexible identity
system based on four
different pixel designs,
whose combination at
different scales leads
to a host of different
logotype/background
permutations. The
system is also capable
of generating closely
related new identities for
subsidiary activities.

20. Show And Tell
Annual film event,
Australia
*Designed by Mark
Gowing Design, 2008*
'Show And Tell' is an
annual event run by
Hopscotch Films to
promote its forthcoming
film releases. Its logotype
is composed of the
geometric counter-forms
found in the Hopscotch
logo (see p.75), creating
an artful, engaging visual
link between the two.

21. c+c workshop
Design studio, Hong
Kong
*Designed by c+c
workshop, 2005*
A logotype that is often
remade using everyday
objects.

22. Unit Architects
Architectural practice,
UK

*Designed by Johnson
Banks, 2009*
For a practice that
specializes in modular
solutions, a wordmark
based on a six-unit
square grid.

**23. Whitney Museum
of American Art**
Museum, USA
*Designed by Pentagram
(Paula Scher), 2000*
It is the minimalist,
orthogonal architecture
and stepped facade of
the building, designed by
Bauhaus master Marcel
Breuer (1902–81), that
informed the museum's
logotype.

**24. Gertrude
Contemporary**
Art gallery, Australia
*Designed by Fabio
Ongarato Design (Fabio
Ongarato, Daniel
Peterson, Meg Phillips),
2010*
A strong, commanding
identity for an art
institution known for
challenging convention
as well as for nurturing
new talent. This logotype
was the foundation for a
bespoke typeface that
exerts the same non-
conformist personality
across a range of
contexts.

**25. aut. architektur
und tirol**
Architecture centre,
Austria
*Designed by Bohatsch
und Partner (Zita
Bereuter, Walter
Bohatsch), 2004*
Formerly the
Architekturforum
Tirol, the centre took
up residence in an
appropriately impressive
architectural landmark
in 2002: the Adambräu
building, designed by
Lois Welzenbacher
in 1927, and an
outstanding example
of the International Style.
The modular logotype
developed in the wake
of the institute's move
takes inspiration from
the building's section
and floor plans.

**26. Australian Centre for
Contemporary Art**
Contemporary art
gallery, Australia
*Designed by Fabio
Ongarato Design (Fabio
Ongarato, James Lin,
Yarra Laurie), 2004*
ACCA is the only major
public art gallery in

Australia focused on
commissioning rather
than collecting, and its
rust-red steel building in
Melbourne's Southbank
arts precinct has become
a city landmark. Its
logotype forms part
of a flexible 'graphic
language', allowing for
changes from show to
show and the generation
of new, related typefaces
within the same grid
system.

**27. Hans Sipma
Photography**
Digital photographer,
Canada
*Designed by Rethink,
2008*
LCD letters from a
digital camera interface
for this award-
winning advertising
photographer.

28. MEA Accountants
Accountancy
consultancy, Australia
*Designed by Mark
Gowing Design, 2008*
More strokes than strictly
necessary suggest
wealth and luxury for
accountancy firm Mark
Edmunds Associates,
and its contemporary
sophistication provides
a stark contrast to the
company's competitors.

17

18

19

20

21

22

23

24

25

26

27

28

29. Smith Partners
Property development
consultancy, USA
*Designed by Thirst
(Rick Valicenti), 2009*
For Rick Valicenti, the
founder of Thirst, design
is always personal,
whether there is a client
involved or not. The
studio is known for its
playful, experimental,
uncompromising
approach to commercial
work, and reports
candidly – and often
amusingly – on its hits
and misses with clients.
Some customers have
stayed with Thirst for
more than a decade;
some don't last more
than a week.

The images Thirst
creates never follow a
consistent style, and are
never easily forgotten.
Valicenti's typography
is just as intolerant of
convention, 'good taste'
and fashion. He enjoys
designing identities –
'It's always fun to serve
as mirror and reflection'
– and sees it, just as
he sees other areas of
practice, as an intuitive
process, in which the
designer responds
directly to contact with
the 'decision-makers' in
a business, rather than a
committee. The identity
for Smith Partners is,
says Valicenti, 'close
to my heart'. It reflects
the back-to-basics
approach of his recent
typography (also seen in
the identities for Thirst
and Peter Ellis New
Cities, on this page), in
which letterforms are
composed of simple
lines connecting points
in a grid. This underlying
system offers almost
endless possibilities.
Valicenti compares the
process with 'making a
constellation'. 'Whenever
I sit to draw these gridded
letters,' he says, 'it is
always a personal thrill to
see the form unfold. Even
when an initial sketch is
rendered, surprise lurks
at the other side of the
process.

'The Smith Partners
identity was almost
pure designer intuition
as there is no font
that can create this
composition off the
shelf.' Each letterform
was constructed and the
words 'built' in a manner

'reflective of how Smith
Partners develops its
modern architectural
buildings from steel
and glass'. Citing Paul
Rand's famous but now
discarded logotype
for Yale Press as an
inspiration, Valicenti
says that when the Smith
Partners identity was
complete, he 'delighted
in how it appeared to live
simultaneously in the
past and the present'.

30. Circus
Club/restaurant, UK
*Designed by Mind Design
(Holger Jacobs, Andy
Lang), 2009*
The identity for this
burlesque-themed club
and restaurant takes
many forms. The club
interior's many mirrored
surfaces led to the idea of
basing the construction
of the wordmark on
the view through a
kaleidoscope. The
internal pattern depends
on the application; these
reference Surrealism,
Art Deco, *Alice in
Wonderland* and other
themes.

31. Thirst
Design studio, USA
*Designed by Thirst
(Rick Valicenti), 2008*
Another example of
Valicenti's back-to-
basics typographic
approach, this mark for
his own Chicago-based
studio is about creating
original connections with
clients, collaborators and
forms of communication
and expression.

32. Peter Ellis New Cities
Urban design
consultancy, USA
*Designed by Thirst
(Rick Valicenti), 2010*
The wordmark for this
firm focused on India is
inspired by the urban
grid: infrastructure gives
rise to identity.

33. Acqua Design
Bathroom fittings retailer,
Italy
*Designed by milkxhake
(Javin Mo), 2008*
The geometric loops of
washbasin mixer taps lay
behind the letterforms of
this wordmark.

30

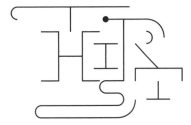

31

32

33

34. Asylum
Blog, USA/UK
*Designed by Area 17
(David Lamothe), 2007*
Half circles and parallel
stems provide the curves
for the identity of this
'men's news blog'.

35. Amazee
Online networking
platform, Switzerland
*Designed by Mixer
(Erich Brechbühl), 2007*
Amazee is an Internet
platform that helps
groups of like-minded
people discuss projects,
find funding and get
them off the ground.
Paper clips hold projects
together, so they became
the building blocks of the
logotype.

**36. Savviva Lifestyle
Management**
Lifestyle management,
Belgium
*Designed by Denis Olenik
Design Studio, 2010*

37. Kerik
DJ, Switzerland
*Designed by Mixer
(Erich Brechbühl), 2010*
A voluble logotype
composed of a few basic
forms for this Swiss DJ's
club nights and events.

38. Massif
Flame-resistant clothing
brand, USA
*Designed by Sandstrom
Partners (Sally Morrow,
Shanin Andrew), 2010*
Set up by two search-
and-rescue veterans,
Massif produces fire-
resistant clothing for a
new audience of military
and aviation personnel,
whose confidence in the
brand was not enhanced
by its old logo: a wacky
illustration of a St
Bernard. Its replacement
offers a more reassuring
message of strength,
reliability, performance,
teamwork... and
badass-ness.

39. Popular Front
Branding agency, USA
*Designed by Cue (Alan
Colvin, Nate Hinz), 2007*
A digital agency that
grew into a full-service
one, Popular Front has
an identity that feels
confident and precise,
with breaks in the
modular letterforms that
hint at motion and the
firm's digital core.

**40. Museo Italiano
Cultural Centre**
Cultural centre, Australia
*Designed by Design By
Pidgeon (David Pidgeon),
2010*
An alphabet based on
the angular, brightly
coloured shapes
that characterized
the Memphis design
movement of early
1980s Milan. Museo
Italiano Cultural Centre
explores Italian culture
in Melbourne.

41. Suttergut
Property developer,
Switzerland
*Designed by Hotz & Hotz
(Thomas Barmettler,
Roman Imhof), 2010*
Suttergut's custom-
drawn logotype, based
on modified capitals from
the Gridnik typeface,
creates an industrial
aesthetic with historic
echoes of 19th-century
sign painting, reflecting
its context: the former
site of an agricultural
machinery factory.
Gridnik derives from a
single-weight typewriter
face created by Wim
Crouwel in the late 1960s.
The Foundry, which has
made the face available,
christened it after the
name Crouwel's friends
knew him by in the 1960s:
Mr Gridnik.

42. Stadium
Sporting goods retailer,
Sweden
*Designed by Stockholm
Design Lab, 2006*

43. Lyons
Architectural
practice, Australia
*Designed by Cornwell
Design, 2005*
Lyons is one of Australia's
leading architectural
practices, known for its
highly expressive, non-
linear facades. Its identity
displays the same
interest in the geometric
manipulation of forms.

44. Social Traders
Social enterprise
promoter, Australia
*Designed by Fabio
Ongarato Design (Fabio
Ongarato, Maurice Lai),
2009*
Social Traders works
with the Australian
government to
encourage business
support for community
groups. The folds and
turns of its ribboning
logotype are meant as

a visual motif for the
paths and journeys that
give rise to new social
enterprises.

45. The Jarman Award
Film prize, UK
*Designed by KentLyons
(John Cefai), 2009*
The Jarman Award is an
annual film prize given by
Film London and inspired
by the avant-garde film-
maker, Derek Jarman
(1942–94). Jarman's
iconic black timber-clad
house on the pebble
beach at Dungeness
provided the inspiration
for the branding.
KentLyons designed a
logotype that could be
constructed out of similar
black timber boards,
with the cross bars of the
'A's in yellow beading to
add vibrancy. The logo
was then made up in
metre-high (3-foot-high)
letters and photographed
on London's very own
beaches – the Thames
at low tide.

34

35

36

37

38

popular front

39

MUSEO
ITALIANO
CULTURAL
CENTRE

40

SUTTERGUT

41

42

Lyons

43

SOCIALTRADERS'

44

JARMAN

45

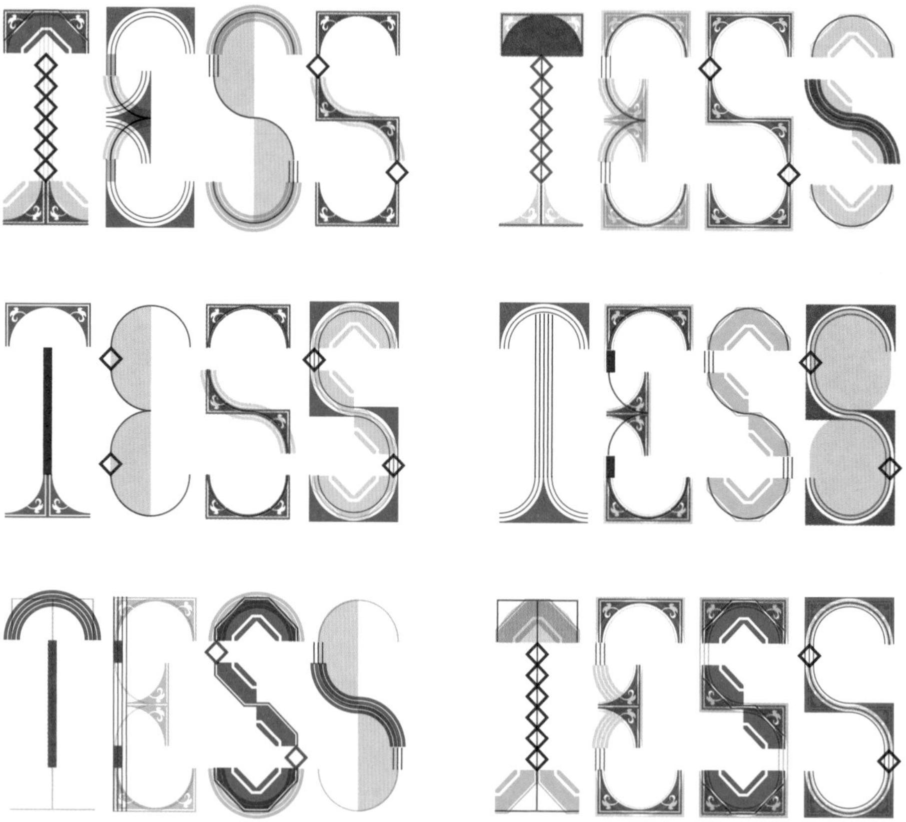

46. TESS Management
Model agency, UK
Designed by Mind Design and Simon Egli, 2009
The notion that corporate identity 'solutions' are singular and can only be reached, like answers to mathematical problems, through a long, logical process – including market research, positioning, structural planning – has been called into question in recent times. The consultancies that once preached the gospel of the single logo talk today about the need for brands to respond to a world of constant change, to a multiplicity of media and audiences. They are creating identities with the flexibility to reflect and document the world around them, in the quest to be all things to all people.

The flexible identity also appeals to those who reject the modernist concept of designer as 'problem-solver', with the job of seeking out the one true identity of an organization. These companies provide clients with variations on a visual theme – changes of colour, pattern, imagery or typography that allow the identity to be customized to suit a particular application or audience.

One such design studio is London-based Mind Design, led by Holger Jacobs. The firm never uses the word 'branding', and celebrates the scope for inspiration from chance visual encounters that textbook branding methods close off. 'We have never claimed to offer a guaranteed problem-solving solution,' says Jacobs. 'Our approach to identity design is more intuitive and based on inspiration rather than logic. Many of our designs could have looked completely different but they simply turned out that way and felt right at the time.'

Founded by Tori Edwards (TE) and Sian Steel (SS), the London-based model agency TESS Management required a confident female identity.

Jacobs looked to key periods of women's liberation, such as the 1920s and 1970s, and the visual styles of those times, then teamed up with Swiss designer Simon Egli to develop a modular identity system based on a range of simple outlined letter shapes overlaid with Art Deco-inspired ornaments and shapes. The system was capable of generating endless logo combinations, but a set of six colour and six black-and-white versions were chosen for general use.

47. dropyx
Creative network, Germany
Designed by Six (Darren Firth), 2009
dropyx links design clients to creative agencies and designers in its network. Its logotype features altered letterforms with circular bowls, while overprinted ascenders and descenders hint at the overlapping relationships in the dropyx process.

48. Studio RBA
Architectural practice, Italy
Designed by milkxhake (Javin Mo), 2006

49. Typopassage
Micro-museum, Austria
Designed by bauer – konzept & gestaltung (Erwin Bauer, Michael Herzog), 2009
With its own 'micro-museum with and about lettering', bauer wishes to show experimental typographic design from concept to final font with exhibitions focusing on a series of international designers. The logo for the space started life as a series of solid rectangles standing on end to represent each letter, similar to a barcode. Moulding the corners of the shapes to intimate, thin joining strokes made a vital difference to its legibility.

50. Come Enjoy
Tae-kwon-do competition, Hong Kong
Designed by c+c workshop, 2008
Shi-jak! Tae-kwon-do belts do backflips for this tournament logotype.

47

48

49

50

1. Bruised
DVD distributor, Australia
Designed by Mark Gowing Design, 2010
Bruised, part of Hopscotch Entertainment, distributes film DVDs, specializing in male-orientated sports and action titles.

2. Atelier 210
Arts venue, Belgium
Designed by Coast (Ingrid Arquin), 2010
A logotype that makes its presence felt, for an arts venue without the budget to do it any other way.

3. Tubestation
Video production company, Australia
Designed by Naughtyfish (Paul Garbett), 2010
Inflated inner tubes inspire a pumped-up logotype.

4. Upplevelseindustrin
Non-profit association, Sweden
Designed by We Recommend (Martin Fredricson, Nikolaj Knop), 2007
Uppleveleindustrin (literally, 'Swedish creative industries generator') promotes the creative industries in Sweden, including design, advertising, film-making, fashion and music.

5. NOBA
Kitchen furniture maker, Norway
Designed by KalleGraphics, 2008

6. Avvio
Online hotel booking systems, Ireland
Designed by Creative Inc (Mel O'Rourke, Garrett Murphy), 2009
Avvio's previous identity focused on the company's technology and systems. Its new one takes a different tack, highlighting the warm feelings its systems create between hotel and guest.

7. Crisis
Homelessness charity, UK
Designed by 300million (Martin Lawless, Nigel Davies, Nick Vincent, Natalie Bennett, Kerry White), 2008
Every person in the UK has a right to his/her own home, says Crisis. Its identity aims to reflect the charity's focus on the individual while appearing uncorporate, gritty and disruptive, but at the same time, authoritative.

8. ABB Group
Power and automation technologies, Switzerland
Designed by Pentagram (Alan Fletcher), 1987
The merger of ASEA of Sweden and BBC Brown Boveri of Switzerland in 1988 produced an engineering supergroup, and the world's leading supplier of electrical power generation plants. Alan Fletcher's brutalist monogram, held together by its criss-crossing power lines, remains unchanged and just as contemporary today, after numerous acquisitions, expansions and technological advances in the field.

9. Slowly
Cafe, Hong Kong
Designed by Tommy Li Design Workshop, 2008
The heavyweight typography is for a cafe that encourages customers to ease off the pace in their lives. Maybe the speed of service leaves something to be desired.

10. Von Rotz
Bakery and patisserie chain, Switzerland
Designed by Hotz & Hotz (Judith Knapp, Roman Imhof), 2009
Displaying a very un-Swiss relish for excess, the Von Rotz identity reflects the chain's rustic, wholehearted, additive-free approach to its craft.

1

2

TUBESTATION +

3

4

NOBA®

5

avvio

Crisis

6

7

ABB

8

SLOWLY
BY DA DOLCE

VON ROTZ

9

10

11. Black Panda
DJ, Denmark
Designed by Me! Me! Me!
(Tom Nielsen, Mads
Katholm), 2010

12. Life + Times
Lifestyle website, USA
Designed by Area 17
(Rumsey Taylor), 2010
Jay-Z's guide to all things
life-enhancing, with
dinner-party-friendly
content organized under
art, technology, music,
sports and leisure.
There's a healthy helping
of Mr Z himself in there,
too. As you'd expect, the
identity is, ahem, bitchin'.

13. Brussels Electronic
Music Festival
Music festival, Belgium
Designed by Coast
(Frederic Vanhorenbeke),
2009

14. Ceri Hand Gallery
Contemporary art
gallery, UK
Designed by Uniform
(Marcus McCabe), 2008
A monogram for this
Liverpool gallery that
could also be read as
exhibition spaces, in plan.

15. NCM Interiors
Interior design service,
UK
Designed by Dowling
Duncan (John Dowling,
Rob Duncan), 2008
Again, letterforms
become spaces; the
logotype as interior.

16. Della Valle
Bernheimer
Architectural practice,
USA
Designed by Pentagram
(Eddie Opara), 2007
The work of British-born
Eddie Opara, who joined
Pentagram in 2010, is
generally characterized
by its visual richness
and sophisticated
complexity; this
monogram goes against
type.

17. Only
Advertising agency,
The Netherlands
Designed by The Stone
Twins (Declan and Garech
Stone), 2008
Inspired by the
architectural forms found
in Only's extraordinary
glass-and-concrete
office building, which
is built on piers in
Amsterdam harbour.

18. Motherboard
Online technology
magazine, USA
Designed by Area 17
(David Lamothe), 2008
www.motherboard.tv
explores the
intersections between
technology, humanity
and art. Its logotype took
inspiration from memory
chips; its final iteration is
more approachable and
human but retains a techy
edge.

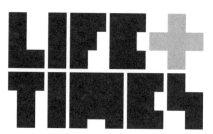

11

12

13

14

15

16

17

18

1. à point books
Publisher, Israel
Designed by Dan Alexander & Co. (Dan Alexander, Michael Koll), 2006
Foody stains are the battle scars of the best (i.e. the most used) cookbooks. Designer Dan Alexander and chef Yair Yosefi met in a Parisian boulangerie and discovered a mutual love of baking. à point books, the publishing house they set up, is the result of their 'obsessive collection of fonts, calories and cookbooks'.

2. Afrique Contemporaine
Scientific journal, France
Designed by Studio Apeloig (Philippe Apeloig), 2010
Afrique Contemporaine is a quarterly academic review of scientific research relating to the African continent. Finding engaging subjects for front-cover photography is a challenge, so Philippe Apeloig created a logotype that occupies almost half the cover on its own. Every other letter is coloured to give each edition an identity of its own.

The high-tech stencil design relates to both science and African painted lettering. Apeloig created two further alphabets based on the same design, pushing the limits of their legibility by progressively increasing the width of the vertical 'slots' that bisect each character. Combining and mixing the three alphabets on other literature creates typographic images that resemble scientific code or a gene sequence.

3. Brand & Value
Brand strategy consultancy, Germany
Designed by SWSP Design (Georg Schatz), 2007

4. Big Talk
DJ management agency, UK
Designed by Give Up Art (Stuart Hammersley, Adam Morten), 2010
Although most of its clients are in the UK underground music scene, Big Talk was keen to move on from the clichés of graffiti, tags and macho typography. The stencil font is a nod to the genre's accepted graphic styling, but the serif font and lower-case letters keep a lid on things.

5. Blokk Architects
Architectural practice, UK
Designed by Proud Creative, 2006
A name for a new architecture firm in Wales that, in its simplicity, is linguistically ambiguous and international. The logotype represents construction in a universal, fundamental way, recalling sets of wooden building blocks. The letterforms can be dismantled and stacked up, as if in a box.

6. De Webfabriek
Website design agency, Belgium
Designed by Studio Hert (Bart Rylant), 2009
Industrial-grade stencilling for De Webfabriek (The Web Factory), a strongly environmental website design agency.

7. Façade
Plastics recycler, The Netherlands
Designed by Me Studio, 2009
Façade finds new uses for recycled advertising billboards, including plastic products to which text is applied using stencils and spray cans.

8. Midi
Restaurant, Belgium
Designed by Coast (Ingrid Arquin), 2010
An unpretentious canteen in Brussels' K-nal centre with a 1980s retro vibe.

9. Assin
Fashion retailer, Australia
Designed by Fabio Ongarato Design (Fabio Ongarato, Simone Elder), 2004
A high-end fashion store in Melbourne and Sydney whose stripped-back, monochrome aesthetic, industrial materials and streetwise stencilling are a counterpoint to the immaculate tailoring of the goods on the rail.

1

2

3

4

Blokk

5

De Webfabriek

FAÇADE

6

7

MIDI

8

ASSIN

9

10. Factset Research Systems
Financial data provider, USA
Designed by Chermayeff & Geismar, 1996

11. Plywood
Rock band, Norway
Designed by KalleGraphics, 2005

12. Resilica
Kitchen worktop manufacturer, UK
Designed by Studio Tonne, 2009
Resilica, on England's south coast, hand-makes bespoke kitchen worktops from 100% recycled glass waste, in almost any colour. The logotype references a low-cost recycling aesthetic, and can be die-cut into the packaging of the samples that are frequently mailed out.

13. Opera North
Opera company, UK
Designed by North, 2010
Not the operatic arm of the design agency, but an edgy, contemporary, award-winning opera company based in the north of England. The bands that run through the logotype suggest integration – of audience and performance, of performers and company, of productions and seasons – and provide the basis for a stage-curtain effect, with imagery appearing from within and behind the lettering.

14. Palau Foundation
Art conservation foundation, Spain
Designed by Summa (Wladimir Marnich, Ellen Diedrich), 2003
A strong visual rhythm, reminiscent of books on a shelf, for the foundation that conserves and exhibits the library and art collection of Josep Palau i Fabre (1917–2008), the writer, poet and playwright regarded as one of the world's authorities on the life and work of Pablo Picasso.

15. Biketreks
Bicycle retailer, UK
Designed by B&W Studio (Lee Bradley, Alex Broadhurst), 2010
Hints of cogs and pedals in the 'e's of this wordmark for a high-end mountain-bike shop in Cumbria.

16. Japlab
Recording studio, Switzerland
Designed by Mixer (Erich Brechbühl), 2008

17. Daiwa
Angling equipment manufactuer, Japan
Designed by Samurai (Kashiwa Sato, Tomoatsu Kasahara), 2009
A wordmark intended to express the precision technology of Daiwa's rods and reels and, in the arrow next to the 'D', the value of innovation and creativity.

10

11

12

13

palau

14

Biketreks ©

15

16

17

SAN
-TA-
REL-
-LI-
ANO
CO

18. Santarelli and CO
Advertising agency, France
Designed by Studio Apeloig (Philippe Apeloig), 2010
Philippe Apeloig follows a unique path in modern typography. Turning a blind eye to passing fads in graphic design, he gives life to letterforms by treating them as the material of artistic expression, and words and syllables as components with the potential to be choreographed and coaxed into an endless variety of compositions, each with its own unique internal tensions.

Apeloig learned his trade under two revolutionary figures in design, both pioneers of computerized typography: Wim Crouwel at Total Design in Amsterdam and April Greiman. In primitive digital type, he began to see letters as sets of shapes and spaces that could be manipulated and abstracted. In grids and systems, he perceived the liberation of letterforms, and the opportunities for giving them 'authentic feeling and an emotional dimension' influenced by his love of live art, such as contemporary dance and theatre.

His identity for Santarelli and CO demonstrates the dynamism Apeloig brings to the static logotype. The client is a 'post-digital' advertising agency established by Christine Santarelli and Christopher Oldcorn (CO). 'The company name plays with and subverts established codes,' says Apeloig. 'That made me want to create a cutting-edge form based on traditional structures.'

'I wanted to combine the languages of the tag and the totem, taking an age-old "primitive" element and bringing it into the digital era – like the company's vision of bringing the ancient universal ideals of truth, good and beauty into the contemporary era. I wanted something "digital", like a tag – something to decode, like a stamp with which to sign their work.

'I imagined a game of graphic construction, a visual assemblage in motion that evokes their profession: the construction of ideas to create communication concepts, for media in perpetual reinvention. Mobile like thought – simple forms, allowing us to create "dancing" elements balanced by a totem structure that gives a very strong feeling of equilibrium in the overall composition.'

19. Softbox
Interface solution services, Switzerland
Designed by Hotz & Hotz (Roman Imhof), 2003
The disconnected strokes and meeting points of the logotype (based on the Courier Sans typeface) allude to the interfaces that are Softbox's business.

20. Solo Mobile
Mobile phone network, Canada
Designed by Rethink, 2004
Constructed from a limited set of 'connectors', which became the basis for campaigns and applications across the brand to promote it to its target audience of constantly connected teens.

21. The Acting Company
Touring theatre company, USA
Designed by Thirst (Rick Valicenti, John Pobojewski), 2010

22. The Lab
Recording studio, Denmark
Designed by Homework (Jack Dahl), 2009

19

20

21

22

1. Teplitzky's
Restaurant, USA
Designed by Mucca Design (Matteo Bologna, Steve Jockisch, Meg Paradise), 2008
A 24-hour diner-inspired restaurant that is part of The Chelsea Hotel in Atlantic City, Teplitzky's takes its name from the family-owned kosher hotel that stood on the same corner in the 1950s. The painted-sign look hails from that post-war period.

2. Harrods
Department store, UK
Designed by Minale Tattersfield (Marcello Minale Snr, Brian Tattersfield), 1967; revised by Minale Tattersfield, 1986
The luxury department store was taking a luxury approach to its identity in the 1960s, employing a wealth of signature styles and colour variations. Minale Tattersfield drew the now widely recognized signature and defined the green-and-gold colour scheme, making sure the system was stuck to by providing a comprehensive set of guidelines for its application. Almost 20 years after it first brought harmony to Harrods, Minale Tattersfield was asked to make the only significant change to the identity by integrating the store's location.

3. Saveurs Nobles
Artisan food retailer, Switzerland
Designed by Hotz & Hotz (Roman Imhof, Samir Ganouchi), 2004
The blacked-out loops and terminals of this signature-style wordmark add an extra, individual flavour.

4. La Strada
Café, Russia
Designed by Transformer Studio, 2008

5. Danfoss
Heating, refrigeration and air-conditioning supplier, Denmark
Designed by Danfoss, 1952
Danfoss, which today turns over the equivalent of $3.5 billion, started life in Mads Clausen's parents' attic in 1933, where the graduate engineer started making valves for refrigerators. The Danfoss name ('Dan' for Denmark, 'foss' for refrigerant) was trademarked in 1940 and applied to products, while the company traded under Dansk Køleautomatik- og Apparat-Fabrik. After the war, as the company grew its business outside Denmark, it made life a great deal easier for its customers by switching its name to Danfoss.

6. Fridcorp
Property developer, Australia
Designed by Cornwell Design, 2010
In the sea of solid, rather staid property developer identities, Fridcorp wanted to associate itself closely with its flamboyant CEO and the distinctive style of the residential developments under his direction.

7. Fluid
Personal financial services, UK
Designed by Buddy (David Jones, Mark Girvan), 2010
The flowing, single line of this logotype reflects the effortless ease with which, according to Fluid, customers can access its services.

8. Cath Kidston
Home furnishings retailer, UK
Designed by Cath Kidston, 1993
Cath Kidston was once a single shop selling hand-embroidered tea towels and repainted furniture to the well-to-do residents of London's Holland Park. The cursive logotype harks back to those homespun origins, and to the days when our mothers knitted matching teacups, tote bags and phone cases.

9. Halcón Vineyards
Winemaker, USA
Designed by Nathan Durrant Design (Nathan Durrant, Anneka Foushee), 2010
High up in the cool, rocky mountain tops of northern California is Halcón Vineyards, a winery that bottled its first product in May 2011. The name (Spanish for 'hawk') calls to mind the vineyard's location and the loose, signature-style script holds a sense of artistry. There's also a hint of hawk in the 'H'.

10. Hoptimist
Cartoon figurine producer, Denmark
Designed by Me! Me! Me! (Tom Nielsen, Mads Katholm), 2010
Furniture designer Gustav Ehrenreich gave the world the Hoptimists in 1968: colourful cartoon figures with little legs and heads that bobbed about on springs. Today, his son Jørn is reviving production of the toys with the creative input of designer Lotte Steffensen. The new identity reflects the Hoptimists' quirky personalities, replacing the shouty, all-caps sans-serif logo of old.

1

2

3

4

5

6

7

8

9

10

11. Campbell Soup Company

Food processing company, USA
Designed by Campbell's, 1898; revised by Lippincott & Margulies, 1946

The Old Masters painted still lifes of fruit and vegetables; Andy Warhol (1928–87) painted Campbell's soup cans. His 32 'portraits' of different soup varieties in 1962 immortalized one of America's most familiar consumer products. Its label was the epitome of high-volume packaging design at the time, conveying its information with the minimum of means: one colour, one logo and no more words than were absolutely necessary.

That label had been around, in essence, for more than 60 years. The Campbell Soup Company launched its condensed soup line in 1897, with labels that were orange and blue, but switched just a few months later. While attending a university football game, a certain Herberton L Williams (later the company's treasurer and assistant manager) was struck by the arresting visual qualities of the Cornell team's bright red-and-white strip. It was his recommendation that led to the Campbell's colour scheme.

The logotype was based on the signature of founder Joseph Campbell. It was thought it would appeal to the housewife of the time, offering a stamp of authenticity and also giving the sense that the soup in the can was based on a home-made, handwritten recipe.

Over the following decades, the red-and-white can and curly signature branded themselves indelibly into the American consciousness. By 1946, though, the label had become cluttered with extra information and Campbell's asked Lippincott & Margulies' packaging design planning board to take a fresh look. L&M redrew the rather spindly signature, giving the letters more body and air, and removing peculiarities such as an extraneous ascender on the 'p'. The gold medal in the centre of the label was reduced in size and the flavour name given more prominence.

The label has changed substantially since Warhol rendered it on canvas, but the colour scheme and the signature logo remain.

12. Lusben

Yacht refitting and repair company, Italy
Designed by SVIDesign (Sasha Vidakovic), 2010

The scripted letterforms hail from the mid 20th century, when Lusben began refitting luxury yachts in Viareggio, and offer a reminder of the company's heritage.

13. Nowhere Resorts

Luxury house rental service, Japan
Designed by Good Design Company, 2009

Nowhere Resorts hires out three very different homes along the coast of the Izu Peninsula, all designed by Yasutaka Yoshimura, husband of Nowhere's founder Michiyo Yoshimura. Each house is branded 'Nowhere but…' (e.g. 'Nowhere but Sajima'), and the aim is to provide places to get away from the city and unwind – just like the logotype.

14. Lea Singers

Chamber choir, UK
Designed by 300million (Martin Lawless, Tom Mesquita), 2011

A looping logotype, expressing the choir's spirit of accessibility and the notion of singers in the local community (of Harpenden, near St Albans) coming together in an artistic way.

15. litl

Webbook brand, USA
Designed by Pentagram (Abbott Miller), 2009

The litl webbook combines the functions of a laptop and a TV. It has no hard drive, applications or files of its own, but runs on web-based applications and flips over backwards for TV-like viewing of programmes, pictures and video. Its selling points of simplicity and fun for the family are captured in Abbott Miller's spiralling logotype.

12

13

14

15

16. Hand me Down
Vintage clothing brand,
UK
*Designed by Studio
Paradise (Samuel Moffat,
Jade Abbott), 2007*

17. ElAstIC
Creativity workshops,
USA
*Designed by Thirst
(Rick Valicenti, John
Pobojewski), 2009*
ElAstIC (a strained
acronym for Eliminating
Assumptions to Increase
Creativity) is the brand
for an ongoing series of
seminars designed by
Chicago architectural
firm 4240 to stretch the
creative faculties of
business leaders and
entrepreneurs. Two
continuous lines bend
their way into the seven ·
letterforms.

18. Ivy
Entertainment venue,
Australia
*Designed by Cornwell
Design, 2008*
With ivy tumbling down
its sides, this award-
winning $150-million
leisure complex on
Sydney's George Street
is described by developer
Justin Hemmes as 'a
living, breathing urban
oasis fusing nature with
contemporary glamour'.
Elegantly over the top,
perhaps, like its logotype.

19. Krrb
Online classified
advertising, USA
*Designed by Area 17
(Arnaud Mercier), 2010*
Handwriting infers
person-to-person
interaction, and this
cursive wordmark
suggests a friendly
community feel to
this website.

20. Hopscotch Films
Film distributor, Australia
*Designed by Mark
Gowing Design, 2002*
A logotype that
encapsulates the
independent film-
maker's craft: to
represent the humanity
of storytelling. It began
life as a handwritten
wordmark, before being
honed and refined into
an harmonious, pleasing
end product.

21. Angels Motel
Rock band, Norway
*Designed by
KalleGraphics, 2010*
So much did the

band's singer like the
typeface designed for
his solo album (*Cable
Script*, designed by
KalleGraphics' Karl
Martin Sætren) that he
asked for a matching logo
for his band.

22. Fenwick
Department store
chain, UK
Designer unknown
The origins of the
Fenwick wordmark are
lost in the mists of time,
it would seem, but it
is likely to have been
based on the signature
of John James Fenwick,
who opened his first
outlet, a 'mantle-maker
and furrier' shop, in
Northumberland Street,
Newcastle, in 1882.

23. io
Well-being centre,
Switzerland
*Designed by >moser,
2009*
Well-rounded,
balanced… just as you
might expect to be
feeling after a therapy
or two at this Lausanne
city-centre spa.

24. iwa
Insurance underwriter,
South Africa
*Designed by Mister
Walker, 2010*
A looping, lower-
case logotype to
replace the Edwardian
monogram of old and to
accompany a truncation
of the company name
from deeply un-
catchy International
Underwriters and
Administrators.

25. We Jane
Marketing agency,
The Netherlands
*Designed by Me
Studio, 2007*
A company that does
what it calls 'female
marketing' – 'insights,
ideas and concepts from
a feminine perspective'
– works with a subtly
feminine ribboned logo
in a range of colours.

16

17

18

19

Hopscotch

20

Angela Motel

21

Fenwick

22

io

23

iwa

24

25

26. Zildjian
Cymbal maker, USA
Designed by Gunn Associates (Dave Lizotte), 1976
Designers are frequently asked to develop identities that capture the 'heritage' of a brand: to hint at past associations or achievements while maintaining a contemporary air. Rarely, however, do they face the task of trying to embody in a single word almost four centuries of corporate culture, spanning two continents.

The Avedis Zildjian Company is the USA's oldest family-owned business – older, in fact, than the USA itself. And its origins lie a long way in every sense from its current home in Norwell, Massachusetts. Avedis Zildjian was an Armenian alchemist in 17th-century Constantinople (now Istanbul), searching for a way to create gold by mixing base metals and hoping to unlock a door to untold wealth. During his experiments, he discovered an alloy of copper, tin and traces of silver with unique sound qualities, and in 1618 began making cymbals that quickly became known for their clarity, power and sustain.

The alloy recipe was passed down through the generations, and Zildjian cymbals came to the attention of European composers. Berlioz, Wagner and others expressly stipulated the use of Zildjian cymbals in their works.

By the early 20th century, the USA was the Zildjian Company's largest market and the firm relocated to Quincy, Massachusetts, under the leadership of Avedis III. The first American cymbal factory opened at the dawn of the Jazz era.

By the mid 1970s, Zildjian realized that, while its products were receiving massive exposure from use by such drummers as Ginger Baker, Phil Collins and Buddy Rich, none of its cymbals displayed its name. David Lizotte's logotype design changed all of that, capturing the exoticism and artistry of the company's past with script based on calligraphy from the Ottoman era. The wordmark felt authentic and connected with the dark art of cymbal-making, long ago and somewhere far, far away. At a time when rock bands were extending their musical influences and drum kits were expanding in new directions, Zildjian had hit a chord.
Avedis Zildjian Company – All rights reserved

27. Alpenmilch Zentrale
Office accommodation provider, Austria
Designed by bauer – koncept & gestaltung (Erwin K Bauer), 2004
The hand-drawn font recalls the past life of this building in central Vienna as a large dairy.

28. The Chelsea
Hotel, USA
Designed by Mucca Design (Matteo Bologna, Steve Jockisch, Meg Paradise), 2008
For the first non-gaming, luxury hotel name on Atlantic City's boardwalk since the 1960s, Mucca Design looked to that era and the days of the original Jet Set for inspiration when creating The Chelsea's identity.

29. The Creative Group
Design and marketing recruiter, USA
Designed by Hatch Design (Joel Templin, Katie Jain, Eszter T Clark), 2010

30. Christopher Lee
Visual merchandising consultant, Hong Kong
Designed by gardens&co, 2004
The copyright icon stands for the client's first name, as well as for the ownership of his creative ideas.

Alpenmilch Zentrale

27

the Chelsea

28

29

30

31. Electric Works
Office accommodation
provider, UK
*Designed by Peter and
Paul (Paul Reardon,
Peter Donohoe, Peter
Horridge), 2008*
An open-all-hours office
space in Sheffield aimed
at creative and digital
businesses, Electric
Works includes Vitra-
furnished shared areas
and a three-storey helter-
skelter. Its spiralling
monogram glows with
allusions to this unique
feature and electric
filaments.

32. Lankabaari
Handcraft retailer, Finland
*Designed by Studio Emmi
(Emmi Salonen), 2008*
Lankabaari ('yarn bar')
in Turku sells everything
related to knitting,
weaving and sewing.

33. Cunéo
Classical conductor,
Australia
*Designed by Frost
Design, 2011*
Australian conductor
Ollivier-Philippe Cunéo
is a bandleader aiming to
become a brand leader,
commissioning this
identity with an eye on
raising his international
profile. The continuous
line, tracing loops, angles
and straight strokes
suggest the motions of
the conductor's baton
in the air as it guides
the orchestra through
passages of music. The
acute accent reinforces
the connotation.

**34. Gibson Guitar
Corporation**
Musical instrument
manufacturer, USA
Designed by Gibson, 1951
The Gibson signature,
seen on guitars played by
the likes of Eric Clapton,
Jimmy Page and The
Edge, first appeared
on mandolins made to
the designs of Orville
Gibson in Kalamazoo,
Michigan, in the 1900s.
It remained a wobbly,
uneven affair, with a
florid 'G' and bulbous
'b', until 1951, when the
letters were redrawn with
a consistent x-height
and vertical strokes of
uniform thickness, much
as it is today.

**35. Fashion World Talent
Awards**
Professional awards,
Hong Kong

*Designed by Tommy Li
Design Workshop, 2009*
The measuring tape, tool
of the fashion trade,
is a perfect fit for this
awards logotype.

36. RooX
Telecommunications
platform provider, Russia
*Designed by 300million
(Martin Lawless, Nigel
Davies, Natalie Bennett,
Kerry White), 2010*
A brand that claims to
have no limits.

37. Moulinex
Small household
appliances provider,
France
*Designer and date
unknown*
In the early 1930s, John
Mantle, an Englishman,
experienced a potato
mousseline made by his
wife that was so lumpy
he decided to invent a
mechanical device that
would ensure it was
never repeated. His
hand-operated food
processor – named
'Moulin Vegetable', as the
rotary action resembled
the motion of a windmill
– was a huge hit with
housewives, selling two
million units between
1933 and 1935. In 1957
he renamed his business
Moulinex, and it is likely
the scripted logotype,
with its corkscrewing
'M', originates from this
period. Today, Moulinex
the brand is owned
by French appliances
giant SEB.

**38. Fashion Human
Rights**
Human rights initiative,
USA/India
*Designed by de.MO
(Giorgio Baravalle), 2010*
Fashion Human
Rights is a project by
American NGO Alba
Collective to connect
rural craftswomen and
micro-entrepreneurs in
Gujarat with international
designers and brands,
so that their skilled work
earns an income that can
benefit their families and
communities.

39. Wellicious
Yoga wear, UK
*Designed by SVIDesign
(Sasha Vidakovic), 2001*

40. Tank Stream Bar
Bar, Australia
*Designed by Cornwell
Design, 2001*
Part of Merivale Group's

Establishment leisure
development, the
colonial-flavoured Tank
Stream Bar is named
after the water source
from which Sydney's
early settlers refreshed
themselves.

**41. Tampereen
Ammattikorkeakoulu
(TAMK)**
*Designed by Hahmo (Erik
Bertell, Jenni Kuokka,
Pekka Piippo, Antti
Raudaskoski), 2009*
Tampere University of
Applied Sciences offers
a range of business-
oriented science
degrees and MBAs.
The typography of its
logotype suggests a
rule of education: that
things become clearer
through study.

31

32

33

34

FWTA

r*o*oo*o*

35

36

Moulinex

37

wellicious

38

39

tank

TAMK

40

41

1. Ash St Cellar
Wine bar, Australia
Designed by Cornwell Design, 2008
Shades of pen-and-ink sketching and woozy artists at corner tables for this 'European-style' wine bar in Sydney's Ivy development.

2. Black Sun
Hair care brand, Italy
Designed by Brunazzi & Associati (Andrea Brunazzi), 2004

3. Blue Gallery
Art gallery, UK
Designed by Atelier Works (Ian Chilvers), 2000
A departure from the typical, muted typographic identities of contemporary art galleries, this mark appears in any colour – except blue. Art is never obvious, after all.

4. Design Academy Eindhoven
Design school, The Netherlands
Designed by The Stone Twins (Declan and Garech Stone) and DAE students, 2010
An abstracted 'E' holds the academy name, handwritten in numerous versions by students, who are also invited to write their own messages and slogans in the white bars.

5. Duke
Band, UK
Designed by Form (Paul West, Arran Lidgett), 2007
Tag-style type for a hip-hop/dance act from Gloucester.

6. Erskine
Website designer, UK
Designed by Funnel Creative, 2007

7. Festland
Band, Germany
Designed by Claudius Design (Stefan Claudius), 2006
The covers of all of Festland's releases feature paintings by the band's chief lyricist, who is also a miniaturist. Adorning the artwork, the band logo resembles an artist's signature.

8. Just Moved
Residential removal firm, Canada
Designed by Transformer Studio, 2009
A back-of-the-envelope solution for a no-frills service.

9. Lara Gut
Professional alpine skier, Switzerland
Designed by >moser, 2010
One of Europe's top downhill skiers and a competitor in Super-G races, Lara Gut has wasted no time in launching her own brand: a super 'G' and small 'l', combined dynamically to suggest ski tracks in the snow.

10. Knickelkopp
Handmade bags company, Germany
Designed by Claudius Design (Stefan Claudius), 2007
'Knickelkopp' was the name given to the owner's childhood drawings of heads by her grandmother, and the logo's rough-around-the-edges look recalls those early signs of creativity.

1

2

3

4

erskine

5

6

festland

7

el

8

9

knickelkopp™

10

GREENPEACE

11. Greenpeace
Non-governmental environmental organization, The Netherlands (HQ)
Designer unknown, early 1980s
In an organization that grew out of the late-1960s West-Coast peace movement to fight the might of over-powerful polluting conglomerates, resistance was strong towards adopting something as 'corporate' as a logo. In its early years, there was no single, agreed way of writing or visually representing 'Greenpeace'. Some activists would set the word in Times Roman, while others would simply use whichever font came to hand from the Letraset sheets lying around the office (or ship). Some opted for a symbol: a peace sign, an ecology icon and a Native American symbol were all in use.

It was only when Greenpeace International was established in the late 1970s and its campaigns started hitting the headlines globally that the non-conformity of the organization's publicity was finally conceded to be undermining its credibility. The question of finding a unifying symbol or logotype became a recurring agenda item in planning meetings. But whenever the subject came up it usually led to an impassioned – and inconclusive – argument.

The issue was finally settled one day in Paris in the early 1980s. Greenpeace International co-founder Rémi Parmentier recalls: 'We were out of Letraset sheets and the local stationery shop was closed. A publication needed a Greenpeace logo, so a fellow who had been making posters and stickers ran around the corner to a bar and asked an artist friend to write out "Greenpeace" for him. The guy drew quickly with a fat felt-tip pen on a beer mat, and the "graffiti logo" was born.' By no means the first globally recognized image to emerge from a Parisian cafe, the scribble was adopted by office after office and ship after ship, and went on to become one of the most recognized pieces of writing in the world.

'Whenever I see that logo today,' says Parmentier, 'especially in remote places like Antarctica and the Amazon, I remember that artist with a pen in one hand and a beer in the other.'

12. Mellow Mushroom
Restaurant franchise, USA
Designed by Mode (USA) (John Pietrafesa, Maxim Vakhovskiy, Alex Westray), 2010
Mode replaced the locally generated logos and type treatments across Mellow Mushroom's 100 or so pizza restaurants with a set of loose, informal wordmarks that could be applied across the chain's vast menu of collateral and merchandise.

13. Multilingua
Language school, Russia
Designed by Transformer Studio, 2010
Students of English, German, French and Spanish contributed their own handwriting to create a series of highly individual wordmarks.

14. Museum voor Communicatie
Museum, The Netherlands
Designed by Lava, 2009
The Museum for Communication in The Hague opened in 2008 to document and showcase the development of communication technologies. The identity invites visitors, curators, artists and designers to convey different facets of the museum in a spontaneous way by appending the name of an exhibition, the museum's address or website, their own name, a sign or a personal message.

15. thestreethearts.com
Fashion blog
Designed by Heydays, 2009
Graffiti for a blog that documents the creativity and fashion sense of people on the streets of cities around the world.

12

13

14

15

16. Sweet Little Things
Children's photographer,
Australia
*Designed by Naughtyfish
(Paul Garbett), 2008*
Sweet things or Swamp
Things?

17. Teppanyaki
Japanese bar and grill,
Australia
*Designed by Cornwell
Design, 2008*
Painted with a Japanese
calligraphy brush,
this mark connotes
something traditional
and hand-prepared; in
this case, the cuisine of
the teppan hot plate.

18. The Open Museum
Museum, Israel
*Designed by Dan
Reisinger, 1985*
The Open Museum is an
outdoor exhibit in Kibbutz
Negba that tells the story
of the state's earliest
days through remnants of
Israel's armed struggles.
Its monogram, like a
hurriedly daubed mark of
defiance, combines the
initials both in English and
Hebrew: 'O' and 'M'; 'mem'
and 'peh'.

19. Mad Cow
Restaurant, Australia
*Designed by Cornwell
Design, 2008*
A name that evidently
doesn't have the same
connotations in Australia
as it does in the UK. Mad
Cow is based on the
traditional American
steakhouse and, like
Teppanyaki above, is
part of the Ivy leisure
development in Sydney.

**20. Werner Sobek
Engineering & Design**
Engineering consultancy,
Germany
*Designed by Büro
Uebele Visuelle
Kommunikation, 2007*
For a high-tech structural
engineering consultancy
with offices around the
world, a humble signature
serves to represent the
founder's values and
mindset, and lends an
anonymous professional
practice a human face.

21. pHuel
Skills and leadership
developer, Australia
*Designed by SML
(Kelly Weber, Vanessa
Ryan), 2007*

22. yoomee
Digital media provider, UK
*Designed by Peter and
Paul (Paul Reardon, Peter
Horridge), 2009*
The name (a rebranding
of andymayer.net)
and signature-style
mark reflect yoomee's
emphasis on people
before technology in its
work, developing 'social
media for social change'.

23. Moderna Museet
Museum, Sweden
*Designed by Stockholm
Design Lab, SWE (Greger
Ulf Nilson) and Henrik
Nygren Design, 2003*
As personal and
engaging as an artwork,
this signature – provided
by Robert Rauschenberg
– is a fittingly
contemporary take on
identity for Sweden's
national museum of
modern art.

24. Yde & Toklum
Fashion design, Denmark
*Designed by Homework
(Jack Dahl), 2007*
Two designer signatures
for the price of one, this
marked a collaboration
between Ole Yde and
Cecilie Toklum.

16

17

18

19

WRZNRZ SDBNA .

20

yoomee

21

22

MODERNA MUSEET

23

24

1. Arc Biennial
Art and design festival,
Australia
*Designed by Inkahoots,
2005*

2. AsBuilt
Architectural practice,
Belgium
*Designed by Coast
(Frederic Vanhorenbeke),
2010*
Rendering the two
letters in outline makes
this an engaging,
almost architectural,
conjunction of forms.

3. UIP
Architectural practice,
Japan
*Designed by Ken Miki &
Associates, 1999*

4. Pacific Place
Leisure complex,
Hong Kong
*Designed by Mode (UK)
(Phil Costin, Darrell
Gibbons, Filipe Valgode,
Richie Clarke), 2009*
A new identity to mark
Thomas Heatherwick's
regeneration and
extension of this retail,
residential and office
complex, originally
opened in 1988.

**5. Kwaku Alston
Photography**
Celebrity portraiture,
USA
*Designed by de.MO
(Giorgio Baravalle), 2008*
A mark that implies
Alston's heavyweight
photographer status,
but whose reduction to
a minimum of lines for
readability ensures no
distraction from
the pictures.

6. Brand New Alliance
Brand entertainment
specialist, Australia
*Designed by SML
(Vanessa Ryan, Tania
Fausti), 2007*

7. Tukes
Safety and chemicals
agency, Finland
*Designed by Hahmo (Erik
Bertell, Jenni Kuokka,
Pekka Piippo, Anttli
Raudaskoski), 2010*

8. Kaya
Rope and harness
manufacturer, Turkey
*Designed by Chermayeff
& Geismar, 2009*
For this maker of
high-quality climbing
ropes and harnesses,
Chermayeff & Geismar
developed a bespoke,
rope-inspired typeface,

with each letter
composed of a single
length.

9. Blanc Kara
Hotel, USA
*Designed by Coast
(Frederic Vanhorenbeke,
Ingrid Arquin), 2011*
Coast lists the reference
points for this identity –
for a boutique hotel
in Miami Beach – as
'Paris/Art Deco/Marion
Cotillard/White/Varnish/
Black/Sun/Timeless'.

1

2

3

4

kwaku

5

6

tukes

KAYA

7

8

BLANC KARA

9

1. Central School of Speech & Drama
Drama school, UK
Designed by Studio8 (Matt Willey, Zoë Bather), 2010
The Central School of Speech & Drama (CSSD), part of the University of London, has a star-studded past, counting among its alumni Laurence Olivier, Vanessa Redgrave, Judi Dench, Kathleen Turner, Julie Christie and Harold Pinter. Working with type foundry Dalton Maag, Studio8 developed a bespoke typeface named 'Fogerty' – after the school's founder Elsie Fogerty – that recalls traditional neon-tube-lit theatre signs. Its shape is based on lettering in the original sign at the Embassy Theatre in London, home of the CSSD since 1957.

2. The Press
Coffee and juice bar, USA
Designed by Mucca Design (Matteo Bologna, Andrea Brown, Erica Heitman-Ford), 2010

3. Vivid Research
Market research agency, UK
Designed by Studio Special (David Lovelock), 2010
An inline logotype for an insights company. Letterforms based on the Typ1451 typeface are modified to do what all good research does – invite scrutiny.

4. Rothfield
Print management, Australia
Designed by Cornwell Design, 2009

5. Surus
Online music platform, UK
Designed by Give Up Art (Stuart Hammersley, Matt Jenkins), 2010
Surus was the last of the 37 elephants Hannibal of Carthage took across the Alps. Its connection to e-commerce fulfilment is unclear.

6. FireWater
Film editing service, UK
Designed by Give Up Art (Stuart Hammersley), 2004
Scalextric-inspired type for a company that specializes in cutting footage for motorsport industry clients.

7. Bettys
French restaurant, Hong Kong
Designed by North, 2010
A traditional French restaurant with an English-sounding name, dressed in tartan, located in Hong Kong. It seems to have its cultural wires crossed, but the Brittany region of France has a strong Celtic tradition: the word 'tartan' is thought to have come from the French 'tiretain', and the Breton tartan provides the starting point for this identity.

8. Crown Metropol
Hotel, Australia
Designed by Fabio Ongarato Design (Fabio Ongarato, Daniel Peterson, Meg Phillips, Matt Edwards), 2010
With an identity whose typography draws on connotations of sophisticated Art Deco establishments of the 1930s, the Crown Metropol in Melbourne is Australia's largest hotel, with 658 rooms.

9. Hemtex
Home textiles retailer, Sweden
Designed by Stockholm Design Lab, 2010
Replacing strokes with strands adds depth and texture to what would otherwise be a bland sans-serif wordmark.

1

2

3

4

SURUS

FiRe WaTer

5

6

BETTYS

7

CROWN METROPOL

8

HEMTEX®

9

10. Tricolette Yarns
Knitting yarn retailer, UK
Designed by KentLyons (Shammi Umeria), 2010
The three strands of 'tricolette' (a type of knitting yarn) weave a wordmark with echoes of the Woolmark symbol for this St John's Wood yarn shop.

11. FirstCut Studio
Music composition agency, Australia
Designed by Mark Gowing Design, 2010
FirstCut creates music for film, television, theatre and advertising. Its canvas, the five-line musical stave, provides the raw material for its identity.

12. Znips
Hair and beauty salon, UK
Designed by Mind Design, 2009
Locks of hair and custom lettering from a 1980s punk fanzine inspired the styling of this logo for a salon in Victoria, London.

13. Haptic
Architectural practice, UK
Designed by Bob Design (Mireille Burkhardt, Tom Green), 2010
This young London-based practice puts the emphasis on a shift away from the '"optical" to the "haptical"', while its logo invites the viewer to get feely, too.

14. Regional Acting Studio
Drama workshops, Australia
Designed by Inkahoots, 2008
A spirit of improvisation – and stage sets under construction? – animates this identity for the annual season of touring workshops from Queensland Theatre Company.

15. Sounds Like Brisbane
Record label collective, Australia
Designed by Inkahoots, 2010

16. Vincenzo
Hair salon, Switzerland
Designed by Hotz & Hotz, 2006
A showy logo for a flamboyant hair stylist, Vincenzo D'Adamo, and one intended to display his preference for geometric styles and his obsession with detail.

17. Parfumerie Leni
Perfumery, Austria
Designed by Practice + Theory (Andreas Pohancenik), 2008
Parfumerie Leni is a Viennese institution, open since the 1940s and steeped in stories. Its 2008 logo started out as a simple logotype based on the original neon sign above the door and evolved into a multilinear design in a number of weights and sizes, with more of an appeal to younger customers.

18. The Margarets
Band, Norway
Designed by KalleGraphics, 2007

19. Mark Warner
Tour operator, UK
Designed by SomeOne (Therese Severinsen, Gary Holt), 2008
A logo whose folds and flutterings suggest the ability to 'be active, and at the same time relaxed'. The sails of a boat and towels on the beach, maybe.

10

11

12

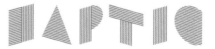

13

REGIONAL
ACTING
STUDIO

14

SOUNDS
LIKE
BRISBANE

15

VINCENZO

16

Leni

17

18

mark warner™

19

1. 2 Longwalk
Office accommodation provider, UK
Designed by Blast (Giff, Paul Tunnicliffe, Andy Mosley), 2010
Following IVG's refurbishment of this 5,000 sqm (54,000 sq ft) office building at Stockley Park, a logo of three overlapping '2's represents the building's physical evolution.

2. Blurrr
Performance art festival, Israel
Designed by Dan Alexander & Co., 1997
Rendering indistinct the barriers between art and urban public life, the Blurrr Biennial sends around 20 international artists out into Tel Aviv to perform at different sites.

3. Coolera, wind & drinks
Cocktail bar, Spain
Designed by Estudio Diego Feijóo (Diego Feijóo), 2009
Definitely shaken, possibly stirred, at this cocktail bar in Colera, an area of northern Catalonia with unusually high winds.

4. Double Good Windows
Window manufacturer, UK
Designed by Atelier Works (Quentin Newark), 2007
Triple-glazed and super-airtight, this company's windows do double good: by saving energy used in heating they are good for your bank balance and good for the environment. The logotype conveys double-thickness window goodness.

5. Klar!
Fashion consulting agency, Denmark
Designed by Designbolaget, 2010
Danish for 'It's clear!', being brought into focus.

6. MAK Center
Art and architecture centre, USA
Designed by Made In Space, 2005
The MAK Center at the Schindler House in Los Angeles (sister institution of Vienna's MAK Museum) continually switches focus between art and architecture, and between the two- and three-dimensional – something that could also be said of Made In Space, April Greiman's LA studio.

7. SMP Partners
Trust and fund administrator, UK
Designed by Uffindell (Nigel Hillier, Gary Deardon), 2007

8. Strum
Music workshops, UK
Designed by hat-trick (Jim Sutherland, Gareth Howat), 2001

9. Über Gallery
Contemporary art gallery, Australia
Designed by Fabio Ongarato Design (Fabio Ongarato, Andrea Wilcock, James Lin), 2004
A wordmark with no defined edges for a gallery in Melbourne founded on the notions of accessibility, collaboration and 'art unlimited'.

10. Tate
Art galleries, UK
Designed by Wolff Olins, 1999
Wolff Olins' creation of the Tate brand and unification of several disparate gallery experiences – covering 500 years of British and international art – was based on a set of logos that shift in and out of focus – recognizable but in a perpetual state of transformation. This idea of dynamism became part of the attitude that was, and is, shared by Tate Britain, Tate Modern, Tate Liverpool and Tate St Ives.

11. Water By Design
Water conservation agency, Australia
Designed by Inkahoots, 2009
A suitably liquid logotype for an organization promoting capacity building and water-sensitive urban design in south-east Queensland.

1

2

wind & drinks

3

4

K L A R !

5

6

SMP

7

8

ÜBER

9

10

11

1. Altitude Music
Music production
company, UK
*Designed by &Smith,
2010*

**2. Viewpoint
Photography**
Commercial photography
service, UK
*Designed by Taxi Studio
(Spencer Buck, Ryan
Wills, Luke Manning),
2007*
A brand mark with depth
aplenty.

3. Dutch Uncle
Illustrators' agency, UK
*Designed by 1977 Design
(Paul Bailey, Chloe Pillai),
2005*
An agent for a number of
well-known illustrators
from around the world,
Dutch Uncle shows its
playful side with a mark
that puts itself forward,
but never further than its
clients' work.

4. The Kx
Not-for-profit arts
publication, UK
*Designed by Practice
+ Theory (Andreas
Pohancenik), 2010*
The Kx is a guide, online
and in print, to culture in
and around the King's
Cross area of London.
A lighter weight is
used in the magazine's
masthead.

5. MONU
Event venue, Singapore
*Designed by &Larry
(Larry Peh, Adora Tan),
2010*
MONU, a huge
contemporary events
space within a striking
WOHA-designed building
in downtown Singapore,
calls itself a 'spatial
canvas'. The paint spatter
pattern on the logo's
letterforms allude to the
creative possibilities the
space offers.

6. Future Designs
Bespoke lighting systems
provider, UK
*Designed by Dowling
Duncan (John Dowling,
Rob Duncan), 2004*
A game of shadows in
this mark for a designer
of lights and lighting
systems.

7. Boyd Baker House
Historic property,
Australia
*Designed by Design By
Pidgeon (David Pidgeon),
2007*
Taking an aerial view of

the property's gently
pitched square roof
and courtyard as the
starting point, this
logotype celebrates
one of Australia's most
important post-war
houses, designed by
Robin Boyd in 1967 for
English mathematician
Dr Michael Baker.

8. Sorg Architects
Architectural practice,
USA
*Designed by Pentagram
(Eddie Opara), 2008*
A Washington, D.C.-
based, mother-and-
daughter-owned
architectural studio
specializing in US
embassy buildings,
Sorg asked Eddie
Opara (then at Map
Studio) for an identity
that wasn't feminine (or
masculine), but focused
on its main themes of
organization, modularity
and transformation.
The folded forms of
the mark play with
perspective, almost
transforming on the
page, before your eyes.

9. House of Propellers
Exhibition space, UK
*Designed by Hyperkit,
2009*
With a name and an
engraved-lettering-style
logotype that suggest
a peculiar old specialist
shop that never seems
to be open, House of
Propellers is anything
but. Rather, it is a space
hosting quick-change
exhibitions by artists and
designers, open to all.

10. Infinite Sum
Design and
manufacturing
consultancy, USA
*Designed by Thirst (Rick
Valicenti), 2010*
The bottom (straight) line
is the shortest distance
between two points in
this typically angular
Rick Valicenti-designed
wordmark.

**11. Trinity Laban
Conservatoire of Music
and Dance**
Music and contemporary
dance school, UK
*Designed by Johnson
Banks, 2010*

1

2

3

4

FUTURE

5

6

BOYD BAKER HOUSE

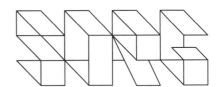

7

8

HOUSE OF PROPELLERS

9

infinite sum.

10

11

R O T O

A R C H I T E C T S

12. RoTo Architects
Architectural practice,
USA
*Designed by Made In
Space, 2000*
The 3-D logotype is
very much the territory
of April Greiman, a
designer who trained in
Switzerland at the highly
influential Schule für
Gestaltung Basel. She
went on to pioneer the
application of early Apple
Macintosh computers
and software in graphic
design, exploring the
extra dimension they
brought to this previously
flat world.

Greiman saw the new
digital technology as
the key to a release of
creativity and to greater
subjectivity in design.
'Design must seduce,
shape and, perhaps most
importantly, evoke an
emotional response,'
she has said. She once
exhorted designers to
'think with the heart'
with a poster for *Design
Quarterly* magazine
featuring a life-size nude
self-portrait overlaid with
items and statements of
personal significance.

Her work in print and
video helped to inspire
something of a digital
design revolution in the
early 1990s, opening the
door to new, intuitive
forms of composition
with image, type and
space for a generation of
younger designers. Since
that time, Greiman has
consistently challenged
the traditional
boundaries between
disciplines, and in
particular between
design, art and
architecture.

Her identity for
RoTo Architects, the
practice of architect
(and husband) Michael
Rotondi, is a highlight
of Greiman's work in
the field of branding. It
had a modest objective:
to bring to the fore the
correct spelling of the
architect's surname,
which was frequently
misspelt as 'Rotundi'.
(A rotunda is a round,
domed classical building
– about as far as it is
possible to get from the
angular, postmodern
structures Rotondi is
known for.) Note the
underline of the '<u>o</u>'. More

significantly, the identity
conjured up ideas of
space, planes and a
concern with the division
of space. The repeated
'o' creates a progression
within the logo, like
that seen in a building
facade. Equally effective
in print and digital
applications, it achieves
an unconventional
3-D quality that many
architects' identities
would love to emulate.

13. Briffa Phillips
Architectural practice,
UK
Designed by Hand, 2009
Architectural elements
twisted and fused to
form a monogram of
lower-case initials and
an impossible, Escher-
like structure. The
'unbuildability' of the logo
was well received.

**14. Asia Pacific Interior
Design Awards**
Awards scheme,
Hong Kong
*Designed by Tommy Li
Design Workshop, 2010*
More apparently
impossible structures
in this wordmark, which
uses small cubes in
different arrangements
to convey the theme of
'Shape your space'.

15. Peter Freed
Advertising and editorial
photographer, USA
*Designed by C&G
Partners (Steff
Geissbuhler), 2006*

16. Tickety Boo
Environmental
consultancy, UK
*Designed by Elmwood
(Steve Shaw), 2010*
Tickety Boo advises
clients on how to reduce
waste by avoiding
shoddy product design,
excessive packaging
and inefficient services.
Its brand announces
its presence through
a distinct absence of
substance.

13

14

15

16

1. 45 Park Lane
Hotel, UK
Designed by &Smith, 2010
A five-star London hotel
whose identity and decor
hark back to an Art-Deco
heyday of glamour and
exclusivity.

2. 64 Knightsbridge
Office accommodation
provider, UK
Designed by GBH, 2001
More Art Deco just down
the road from Park Lane,
in these luxury serviced
offices behind the
Georgian facade of the
former Danish Club.

3. Gott's Roadside
Restaurant, USA
*Designed by Elixir Design
(Jennifer Jerde, Nathan
Durrant, Scott Hesselink),
2010*
This family-run, Bay Area
eatery was previously
the well-loved Taylor's
Automatic Refresher, and
reopened with an identity
that pays homage to
1950s burger-stand
vernacular.

4. bFelix
Furniture manufacturer,
Hong Kong
*Designed by gardens&co
(Wilson Tang, Jeffrey
Tam), 2008*
A strong Art-Deco
sensibility in this identity
for a maker of 1920s- and
1930s-style European
furniture.

5. Joe and Co.
Hair salon, UK
*Designed by Hyperkit,
2010*
Traditional barbershop
patterns – red-and-
white striped poles and
black-and-white checked
lino floors – come to
mind in the geometric
letterforms of this logo
for a retro salon in Soho,
London.

6. The Edison
Office development, UK
*Designed by Mode (UK)
(Phil Costin, Darrell
Gibbons, Filipe Valgode),
2010*
A contemporary
interpretation of Art Deco
to reflect the origins of
this refurbished office
building in London's
Marylebone district,
with interior detailing by
architect David Adjaye.

7. Mint Furniture
Furniture brand, UK
*Designed by Loovvool
(Hannes Unt), 2010*

A bespoke contemporary
furniture and joinery
service with an identity
that's more 1930s than
2010s.

8. NL-Ruhr
Arts festival, The
Netherlands
Designed by Lava, 2010
A cultural festival
involving Dutch artists
and performers touring
the Ruhr area of Germany
to celebrate the region's
spell as European Capital
of Culture, used as its
banner a logo based
on the Dutch number
plate – a common sight
in the Ruhr, apparently,
on Dutch cars towing
caravans.

9.Vinifiti
Wine importer, Czech
Republic
*Designed by Toman
Graphic Design (Jiri
Toman), 2008*

10. Naturopathica
Skin and beauty brand,
USA
*Designed by Elixir Design
(Jennifer Jerde, Scott
Hesselink), 2009*
A rebrand that involved
developing a more
asymmetric and
rectilinear replacement
for Naturopathica's
previous arched logo (to
fit a new packaging style),
while still evoking the
old brand's apothecary
foundations.

11. On Pedder
Fashion accessories
provider, Hong Kong
*Designed by Fabio
Ongarato Design, 2006*
Shades of 1970s
designer labels
(and earrings) in the
contrast between the
long ascenders and
descenders and the
generous loops of the
'O' and 'n'.

12. Jerde
Architectural practice,
USA
*Designed by Elixir Design
(Jennifer Jerde, Nathan
Durrant), 2003*
For the former Jerde
Partnership, a banknote-
style font was chosen
as the appropriate way
to reflect the financial
returns generated
by its work in urban
revitalization schemes
and large-scale mixed-
use developments.

1

2

3

4

JOE AND CO.

THE EDISON

5

6

MINT

NL-RU 20/10 HR

7

8

vinifiti

NATUROPATHICA

9

10

Onpedder

JERDE

11

12

To add? Or to take away? For the artistic, quirky, fragrant or flamboyant by nature, a flourish (or several) of line or letterform can speak volumes. For others, less is more: cropping, reduction or abstraction commonly conveys a feeling for shape, space and form, or can equally suggest emergence or decay.

FINOVINO

STUDIO
DAMINATO

More or Less

r t r&k ch r		⊤⊤_⊒	DAVIS	*New York*	PLEASANT STUDIO
⊐ICⴹ™	CS/\	LA mAISON DE PHOTO	Norton		EAT•N
	MODE ZONEN	WESTERN UNION	)OMMΛ	DIRECTORY	

1. Anida
Property agency, Spain
Designed by Summa (Tilman Solé, Sandra Dios), 2004
When BBVA Inmobiliaria entered the top ten of Spanish estate agents, its parent group, BBVA, rebranded it Anida, meaning 'to nest'. The extended 'n' makes a safe haven for the remainder of the word.

2. Allie Giles
Artist, UK
Designed by Guild of Sage & Smith (Neil Tinson), 2006
The ink spots that serve as swollen finials on the 'A' and 'e' refer to Giles' medium, and the thousands of tiny strokes of the pen with which she builds each image. The flourishes hint at the whimsical nature of her subject matter.

3. AJM Productions
Music recording and production agency, UK
Designed by &Smith, 2009

4. King's Cross Social Club
Music and events venue, UK
Designed by 1977 Design (Paul Bailey, Elizabeth Gatt, Chloe Pillai), 2009
A retro name and a decorative style influenced by fashion labels and 'high-end, aspirational bands' for this venue close to London's King's Cross Station.

5. Firescape
Rock band, USA
Designed by Claudius Design (Stefan Claudius), 2006

6. Pleasant Studio
Photographic studio, UK
Designed by Studio Emmi (Emmi Salonen), 2007
A studio for hire and a logotype that both include original Victorian features.

7. Deborah Hodgson
Folk singer, UK
Designed by Hand, 2009
Hand drawn and curly-quirky for this diminutive modern folk singer.

8. L'Anima
Restaurant, UK
Designed by Mode (UK) (Phil Costin, Darrell Gibbons), 2008

L'Anima translates as 'soul'. At this Italian restaurant in the City of London, it refers to the menus of the chef Francesco Mazzei, whose creative flair is the subject of the logotype.

9. Corilon Violins
Violin restorer, Germany
Designed by Lockstoff Design (Susanne Coenen, Nicole Slink), 2010
Letterforms, musical notes and f-holes fuse into a harmonious composition for this leading restorer of violins, violas and cellos.

10. Flow
Mineral water brand, Israel
Designed by Dan Alexander & Co. and Yotam Hadar, 2007

11. Hecker Phelan & Guthrie
Interior design consultancy, Australia
Designed by Cornwell Design, 2004
A growing international reputation demanded an identity that reflected the decorative flamboyance of this Melbourne consultancy's work for restaurant and retail clients.

1

2

3

4

FIRESCAPE

5

6

Deborah Hodgson

7

8

corilon

9

inflown

10

11

12. The Gorbals
Restaurant, USA
Designed by The Partners (Ryan Adair), 2009
From the south bank of the Clyde to South Spring Street, Los Angeles… The Gorbals, a restaurant with an eclectic, cosmopolitan menu, takes its unlikely name from Glasgow's similarly multicultural tenement district, where chef Ilan Hall's father was raised.

13. Horse Feathers Home
Home furnishings company, Canada
Designed by Hambly & Woolley (Bob Hambly, Dominic Ayre), 2008
The opening flourish is meant, 'like the swish of a horse's tail', to scoff at the relevance of the true meaning of 'horsefeathers' (i.e. rubbish).

14. Strange Beast
Multimedia production company, UK
Designed by SomeOne (Laura Hussey, David Law), 2008
Younger and edgier than its big sister Passion Pictures, Strange Beast wants to be seen as a living, changing creative organism.

15. Kaiser Sound Studios
Recording studio, The Netherlands
Designed by The Stone Twins and Niels 'Shoe' Meulman, 2008
Kaiser's typography was inspired by signwriting on the windows of Amsterdam's 'brown bars', and executed by graffiti legend Niels 'Shoe' Meulman.

16. Lilium
Florist, Canada
Designed by Hambly & Woolley (Bob Hambly, Frances Chen), 2009

17. New York
Magazine, USA
Designed by Pentagram (Luke Hayman), 2004
Founded in 1968 by Milton Glaser and Clay Felker, and known as *The New Yorker*'s arch-rival, *New York* had lost its edge by the late 1990s. Its 2004 redesign under British-born Luke Hayman and editor-in-chief Adam Moss helped to restore the magazine's former radical reputation. Hayman revived and refined the original, flamboyant logotype, introduced new typefaces and put the emphasis on strong, witty covers.

18. Miquelrius
Stationery manufacturer, Spain
Designed by NOMON DESIGN, 1999
The first spiral-bound Miquelrius logotype appeared in the 1940s – a highly calligraphic, handwritten wordmark. This was redrawn in the years that followed, but while it remained cursive, the mark's legibility was always an issue. In 1999, the letters were separated and the troublesome loops of the joined-up 'l' and 'r' dispensed with once and for all.

19. Flow Life Coaching
Life coaching service, South Africa
Designed by Mister Walker, 2010

20. M2b
Maternity fashion, UK
Designed by Together Design, 2009
Inspired by magazine mastheads (by the *New York* logotype, maybe?), this mark's swashes include a particularly pregnant terminal on the '2'.

21. Ole Lund
Fashion art director, USA
Designed by A2/SW/HK, 2010

22. Independent State
Art exhibition, UK
Designed by Funnel Creative, 2009
A hand-drawn typeface for an art event in Frome, Somerset that included work by Bob and Roberta Smith, Edwina Ashton and Matt Stokes.

Los Angeles

12

13

14

15

Purveyor of Fine Flowers

16

17

18

mothercare

19

20

21

22

23. Norton Motorcycles
Motorcycle
manufacturer, UK
*Designed by Carter Wong
Design (Phil Carter) and
Geoff Halpin Design,
2010*
An invitation to review
the identity of a historic
brand always presents
designers with mixed
emotions: excitement at
the challenge of a high-
profile opportunity, and
anxiety at the possibility
of making a high-profile
hash of it. Throw in a
fanbase of eagle-eyed
heritage fanatics and
the trepidation can
start to outweigh the
anticipation.

When asked to fine-tune
the Norton Motorcycles
wordmark, Carter Wong
wisely headed for the
archives. A small army
of detail-obsessed
Norton aficionados might
have stopped a radical
redesign in its tracks, but
Carter Wong based its
refinements on Norton's
second logotype (of
many), designed at the
dining table in 1913
by founder James
Lansdowne Norton
and his daughter Ethel.
The designers were
delighted to find that the
Nortons' mark crossed
the 't' with a long 'swash'
from the top of the 'N'
– an idea they had been
considering also.

Norton logotypes from
1924 onwards featured
a double-crossed 't',
possibly to prevent
the letter from being
read as an 'I'. Master
typographer Geoff Halpin
helped to redraw the
mark, doing away with
awkward bulges and
shapes, adding weight
to the 'swoosh' and
creating balance in the
spaces and weight of
strokes. The signature
go-faster 'o's were kept,
but instead of tilting the
entire letterform, as in
the original, Carter Wong
simply turned the counter
of each 'o', to generate a
modicum of motion.

24. Pizza Nova
Restaurant chain, Canada
*Designed by Concrete
(Diti Katona, John
Pylypczak, Tom
Koukodimos), 2006*

25. Dickens 2012
Cultural festival, UK
*Designed by KentLyons
(Jon Cefai), 2010*
A flourish of the pen
from Dickens' signature
to underline this
international celebration
of the writer's work,
to mark the 200th
aniversary of his birth.

26. Saks Fifth Avenue
Department store, USA
*Designed by Pentagram
(Michael Bierut), 2007*
Saks had got through
dozens of different logos
by the time Michael
Bierut was invited to
create something with
the potential to be iconic
and instantly identifiable
from across Fifth
Avenue or any street.
Bierut modelled a new
identity on a signature
designed in 1973 by Tom
Carnese, which in turn
had been based on one
from 1955. Redrawn with
the help of typographer
Joe Finocchiaro, the
retro-looking mark was
then applied to bags,
packaging, signage
and advertising in an
ultra-contemporary way.
The black square was
divided into an 8x8 grid,
with almost every tile
containing an abstractly
poetic stroke, swirl or
swash. And the 64 tiles
can be rearranged within
the grid in an almost
infinite number of ways.
Not quite infinite, but,
according to a physicist
friend of Bierut's, a
number many times
greater than the number
of electrons in the known
universe.

27. Satoko Furukawa
Acupuncturist, Japan
*Designed by Good
Design Company, 2010*
Delicacy, art and
precision, for a therapy
that demands those
qualities.

24

25

26

27

1. Yrkeshögskolan Göteborg
Professional training school, Sweden
Designed by Lundgren+Lindqvist, 2010
A dotted line represents the school's openness – everyone is welcome – and policy of making room for new ideas and initiatives from students. On slate signs around the school, class numbers are written in chalk.

2. iLIVETOMORROW
Creative workspace, Hong Kong
Designed by milkxhake (Javin Mo, Jan Cheung), 2010
A logotype whose gaps invite creative interaction, much like the workspace it represents, a meeting place for artists, designers, architects and manufacturers.

3. Estudio
Studio rental agency, Hong Kong
Designed by c+c workshop, 2008

4. Mini McGhee
Textile designer, UK
Designed by Graphical House, 2010
An identity simple enough to accompany any future collections, underpinned by a single stitch, the simplest component of the designer's work.

5. Annie
Singer, Norway
Designed by Form (Paul West), 2008

6. Amanda Wakeley
Fashion designer, UK
Designed by Pentagram (John Rushworth), 2000
Dramatic, simple, expertly constructed, like Wakeley's creations.

7. Anthony Nolan
Charity, UK
Designed by Johnson Banks, 2010
Previously known as the Anthony Nolan Trust, this blood cancer charity matches donors on its bone marrow register to those in need.

8. MICA
Art school, USA
Designed by Pentagram (Abbott Miller), 2007
Maryland Institute College of Art was founded in 1826, making it the oldest accredited art school in the USA. The switch of name to MICA was concluded by the introduction of this identity, whose use of a traditional typeface (a slab serif of the kind popular at the time of the college's foundation) is balanced by a contemporary linear framework, reflecting the contrast between the college's 1904 Beaux-Arts main building and its crystalline 2003 counterpart across the street.

9. m/studios
Architectural practice, UK
Designed by Untitled (David Hawkins, Glenn Howard), 2010
A classical Italianate wordmark, set in lower case and bracketed between fine keylines, represents m/studios' founder: an Italian designer of contemporary buildings, Alvise Marsoni.

10. RadLyn
Medical device company, USA
Designed by Cue (Alan Colvin), 2006
The central feature of this mark is a reference to the company's flagship product: a 'rapid airway device' to simplify intubation in difficult cases. The logotype symbolizes the product, but also positions the company – which was founded by a doctor at the University of Cincinnati Hospital – as a credible presence in the medical devices field.

11. Western Union
Financial services and communications company, USA
Designed by Lippincott, 1980s
With its 150-year dominance in money transfer and messaging services threatened by new technologies and with its branding in disarray, Western Union was boosted by a bold, streamlined logotype whose vertical rules became the basis for a unified identity system, in which the names of individual services are displayed to the right.

12. Studio Daminato
Architectural practice, Singapore
Designed by &Larry (Larry Peh), 2008
A thin vertical stroke signifies both the division of space and the joining of ideas.

Yrkeshögskolan Göteborg ©

1

ilive
i tomorrow
_livetomorrow

2

_ ESTUDIO

3

MINI McGHEE

4

5

6

7

8

9

10

11

12

1. Negro Rojo
Restaurant, Spain
Designed by Mario Eskenazi, 2003
A split-level logotype for a Barcelona restaurant with a dual personality. At street level is Negro (Spanish for 'black'), an urban restaurant, and in the basement is Rojo ('red'), a Japanese canteen.

2. inter-view
Cultural exchange project, Switzerland
Designed by Kambiz Shafei, 2009
Designed for an ongoing video project by Milan Büttner recording the views of Swiss and Chinese writers about each others' cultures, this wordmark refers to the insights captured through the gap that divides its two cropped halves.

3. Vision Publishing
Publisher, USA
Designed by CDT Design, 2005

4. Creative Industries Development Unit
University research unit, UK
Designed by The Chase (Chris Challinor, Ben Casey, Mike Rigby), 2001

5. The Association of Photographers
Professional association, UK
Designed by The Partners (Janet Neil, Jack Renwick, Martin Lawless, Dominic Wilcox), 2002
The bold typeface conveys a contemporary air of authority for this respected and prestigious professional body, while the framed crop focuses attention on the detail of the mark.

6. Blonde + Co
Creative media agency, USA
Designed by PS New York, 2010
A mark that appears with various orientations and crops, reflecting the bold, full-on nature of the agency's personality.

7. Hotel Omm
Hotel, Spain
Designed by Mario Eskenazi, 2003
Omm, a sound that 'has no beginning and no end' – and, it has to be said, no meaning – is represented by this open-ended mark, which is extended by adding letters at different points in the hotel. The hotel restaurant is called Moo…

8. Urban Strategies
Urban planning firm, Canada
Designed by Hambly & Woolley (Barb Woolley, Emese Ungar Walker), 2004
A crop that implies a pushing of boundaries within the urban planning field.

9. GMW
Architectural practice, UK
Designed by CDT Design, 2003
A mark that creates a cutting edge by turning and cropping the letterforms.

10. Kevin Boniface
Author, UK
Designed by Music (Anthony Smith), 2008
A 'K' that is a cropped 'B' for Kevin Boniface, who captured the comedy of being a Huddersfield postman in his book *Lost in the Post.*

11. Fashion Fringe
Annual fashion contest, UK
Designed by Pentagram (John Rushworth), 2006
Fashion Fringe is an annual project to give promising young British designers a glimpse of the big time.

1

2

3

4

AOP

BLONDE co

5

6

DOMMM

URBAN
STRATEGIES
INC   .

7

8

K

9

10

11

12. Brooklyn Academy of Music
Performing arts centre, USA
Designed by Pentagram (Michael Bierut), 1995
Between them, Pentagram's Paula Scher and Michael Bierut have changed the face of culture in New York. Scher has designed identities for the Public Theater, the Metropolitan Opera, New York City Ballet and the New York Philharmonic. Bierut has rebranded the Morgan Library & Museum, the Museum of Arts & Design and the Tenement Museum, among others.

Cultural institutions in major cities like New York have learned how to compete with big brands for visibility and disposable dollars. Since opening in 1861, the Brooklyn Academy of Music (BAM) has grown into a major urban arts centre. Home to the Brooklyn Philharmonic, it also hosts an opera house, a theatre, a four-screen cinema, art shows and live music.

In the 1980s, the success and profile of its edgy Next Wave Festival started to eclipse that of BAM's work in the classical field. The diverging design directions taken to promote these different activities presented a confusing overall picture. What was BAM all about? The solution to BAM's identity issues appeared almost by accident. When Michael Bierut designed the 1995 Next Wave brochure he made the most of a small cover by setting the two words at large sizes in a simple sans serif (News Gothic) and bleeding them off the bottom and sides of the cover. Not only did this give the words extra presence and impact, it also created space for other imformation and imagery.

The logotype, and the broader identity concept of type that was too big for its given space, appealed to BAM's management. It expressed the notions of emerging talent and big ideas on the cultural

horizon, which had the potential to speak equally powerfully to classical and avant-garde audiences. Bierut applied the idea to the identity, and BAM hasn't looked back since.

13. The Futures Company
Research and forecasting consultancy, UK/USA
Designed by Neon Design (Dana Robertson), 2008
The merger of two research consultancies – Henley Centre Head Light Vision (UK) and Yankelovich (USA) – under a new name led to a logo that hints at what's ahead, just out of sight.

14. Bookfactory
Photobook printer, Switzerland
Designed by Bob Design (Mireille Burkhardt, Alexis Burgess), 2006

15. Tama Art University
Art school, Japan
Designed by Good Design Company, 2010
A wordmark that doesn't seem to mind breaking the rules, just as any good art school shouldn't.

16. Mouse Awards
Online advertising awards, UK
Designed by Johnson Banks, 2008

the
futures
company

13

BOOKFACTORY

14

TAMA
ARTU
NIVE
RSIT
Y

15

16

1. BrainagencyMedia
Media agency, Germany
*Designed by SWSP
Design (Georg Schatz),
2009*

2. Dendy Cinemas
Cinema chain, Australia
*Designed by Sadgrove
Design (Brian Sadgrove),
1994*

3. First Booking
Make-up and styling
agency, Denmark
*Designed by
Designbolaget, 2008*
A follow-up to the
agency's previous
wordmark, in which the
place of the 'i' in 'First'
was taken by a '1'. The
two kinds of talent –
make-up artists and
stylists – are represented
by the two characters: a
black '1' and a white 'i'.

4. Cinema Nova
Arthouse cinema,
Australia
*Designed by Sadgrove
Design (Brian Sadgrove),
1992*
Tricks with shadows and
negative space create
intriguing letterforms for
this Melbourne cinema.
Try making a 3-D sign out
of this.

5. Eaton
Power management
technology company,
USA
*Designed by Lippincott
& Margulies, 1971*
In 1971, Eaton, Yale &
Towne became Eaton,
and gained a timeless,
multilayered logotype
that gives a sense of its
numerous divisions and
services.

6. Perplex
Music production
company, The
Netherlands
*Designed by Me Studio
(Martin Pyper), 2007*

7. Tess Hurrell
Photographer, UK
*Designed by Studio
Special (David Lovelock),
2007*
A mark that highlights the
nature of Hurrell's work,
which finds unrecognized
beauty in the everyday.

8. Engage
Digital design agency, UK
*Designed by
Bibliothèque, 2008*
A typographic expression
of engagement. The stem
and crossbars of the 'E'
are deconstructed into

a series of panels that
allow for varying levels
of abstraction.

1

2

FIRST BOOKING

3

4

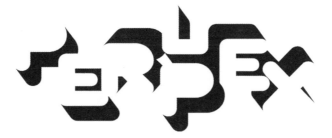

5

6

7

8

9. FedEx

Courier service, USA
Designed by Landor Associates (Lindon Leader), 1994
What makes a logo likeable? If it is the ability to reward repeated viewing with a minimum of means, the FedEx logotype delivers likeability to the max. The arrow between the 'E' and the 'x' never fails to raise a smile when it is revealed to the unaware.

Fred Smith founded Federal Express in 1971 after famously putting forward his concept for a high-speed, nationwide door-to-door delivery service in a student paper at Yale University. By mid 1973, the company was operating an overnight service with a fleet of Dassault Falcons that connected 25 US cities. By the 1990s, it served around 200 countries.

When it was asked to evolve the Federal Express identity, Landor found in research that there were issues with the word 'Federal'. In the USA, it was associated by some customers with government, and in non-English-speaking countries, it was just plain difficult to say. It was recommended that the brand switch to the shortened name that many regular customers were using, anyway: FedEx. It was easier and quicker to say, and conveyed a greater sense of technology, speed and innovation.

For the new logo, Landor retained the old brand's signature purple and orange, and created and reviewed more than 200 designs before reaching a shortlist of six for presentation to senior management in Memphis in April 1994. One of these was borne of an observation by Lindon Leader, senior design director at Landor, that between the 'E' and 'x' lay the hint of an arrow – a symbol that would neatly embody the key FedEx attributes of speed and precision. To perfect the arrow's geometry, Leader crafted a new set of letterforms that blended characteristics

from Univers 67 (Bold Condensed) and Futura Bold, and included a raised x-height (i.e. larger lower-case letters relative to upper-case ones).

The final typographic composition appeared so natural that many failed to see the arrow in the logotype. At the presentation, Fred Smith spotted it immediately. But what he also recognized was that knowledge of this hidden sign would be given and received like a punchline or a gift, and that this almost unique quality – the logo that keeps on giving – would rub off well on the brand. Importantly, even those in ignorance of the arrow would still see a powerful, compact, confident wordmark, highly visible in city streets on vans and packages.

Smith and his board gave the identity the go-ahead and resisted, thankfully, pressure from some to make the arrow more obvious. After all, if you give the game away, the game is over.
The FedEx Logo is a registered trademark of Federal Express Corporation. Used by Permission. All Rights Reserved.

10. McGarry & Eadie

Water management engineering company, Australia
Designed by Inkahoots, 2010
A grid of valve-like partial circles conjure up an overlapping 'M' and 'E'.

11. The Milton Agency

Film and TV crafts agency, UK/USA
Designed by Magpie Studio (David Azurdia, Ben Christie, Jamie Ellul, Tim Fellowes), 2009
The Milton Agency represents behind-the-scenes production skills in make-up, hair and costume design. Less visible than the stars, perhaps, but no less important.

12. Hanzehof

Theatre, The Netherlands
Designed by Teldesign (Peter Post), 1996
A billowing stage curtain announces this theatre and concert hall.

13. For

Charity, The Netherlands
Designed by Me Studio (Martin Pyper), 2008
Previously known as Computers For Africa, this charity's name change paves the way for the exchange of a wider range of products and knowledge.

10

11

12

13

1. Anorak
Advertising agency,
Norway
*Designed by Heydays,
2010*
A typographic expression
of Anorak's belief that its
clients are just as much
a part of every project as
the agency.

2. Ashburton
Investment manager, UK
Designed by ASHA, 2008
The removal of three
downstrokes and
the fusion of those
characters with their
neighbours creates a
mark that is easier to read
in small spaces – such as
investment listings – than
its predecessor, and
demonstrates the brand
positioning of 'seeing
things differently'.

3. Directory
Direct marketing
magazine, UK
*Designed by SVIDesign
(Sasha Vidakovic), 2007*
A trade magazine that's
all about getting a
message from one side
to the other as directly
as possible.

4. Bite
Cosmetics company,
Canada
*Designed by Concrete
(Diti Katona, John
Pylypczak, Ryan
Couchman), 2010*
Lip products made
entirely with natural,
organic, food-grade
ingredients – good
enough to lick, if not to
eat – for a brand that
emphasizes performance
and style, rather than
'natural', for the fashion-
conscious customer.

5. Finovino
Wine importer, Serbia
*Designed by SVIDesign
(Sasha Vidakovic), 2008*
A logotype that, like
wine, is sensed first then
finished with the brain.

6. Eden Island
Property development,
Dubai
Designed by Hand, 2007
One of the islands in
'The World', the artificial
archipelago made with
dredged sand off the
coast of Dubai, with a
logo that also appears to
be emerging from liquid.

7. Davis Evolution
Property developer,
Australia
*Designed by Cornwell
Design (Anthony Nelson,
Nuttorn Vongsurawat),
2010*
A custom typeface,
apparently still in
formation, expresses
the evolving nature of
this company's lifestyle
developments.

8. Gallery Litvak
Contemporary art
gallery, Israel
*Designed by Studio
Apeloig, 2009*
A Tel Aviv gallery
that specializes
in contemporary
works in glass and
experimentation in form.

9. Restaurant Sternen
Restaurant, Switzerland
*Designed by Hotz & Hotz
(Roman Imhof, Erich
Moser), 2009*
Letterforms based on
Baskerville Old Face
reflect the traditional
nature of the French
cuisine at Sternen ('Star'),
while their vanishing
strokes suggest a
contemporary culinary
interpretation.

10. Mordisco
Restaurant, Spain
*Designed by Mario
Eskenazi, 2010*
In Spanish, *el mordisco*
is 'the bite', a name that
led to a typeface with
chunks taken out of it
for this laid-back
Barcelona eatery.

1

2

3

4

FINOVINO

eden

5

6

DAVIS

7

GALLERY
LITVAK

Sternen*

WALCHWIL

8

9

10

11. INREV
Professional association,
The Netherlands
*Designed by Teldesign,
2001*
The aim of the European
Association for
Investors in Non-Listed
Real Estate Vehicles
(INREV) is to increase
the transparency and
accessibility of non-
publicly listed real-estate
funds.

12. Ivan Hair Salon
Hair salon, Greece
*Designed by G Design
Studio (Michalis
Georgiou, Alexandros
Gavrilakis), 2009*

13. Kubota Corporation
Heavy equipment
manufacturer, Japan
*Designed by Pentagram
(Colin Forbes), 1989*
A regular, mechanical
excision of the
letterforms suggest
precision and rhythm for
this 120-year old maker
of agricultural machinery,
pipes, pumps and
vending machines.

14. Mode Zonen
Trade promoter, Denmark
*Designed by Homework
(Jack Dahl), 2010*
The job of *Mode Zonen*
('Fashion zone') is to put
Denmark on the global
fashion-industry map.
Some creative cutting
expresses the fashion
connection, and brings
the letters 'D', 'E' and 'N'
to the fore.

15. Raw Space
Contemporary art gallery,
Australia
*Designed by Inkahoots,
2005*

**16. Motor Neurone
Disease Association**
Charity, UK
*Designed by Spencer
du Bois (John Spencer),
2009*
While motor neurone
disease (MND)
disconnects sufferers
from their bodies and
lives, the association
aims to reconnect them,
with family, friends and
quality of life.

17. Rondo Media
TV production agency,
UK
*Designed by Elfen (Aaron
Easterbrook, Guto
Evans), 2009*

18. GF Smith
Paper manufacturer, UK
*Designed by SEA (Bryan
Edmondson), 2005*
An update of a mark first
drawn in 1969.

19. Oyuna Cashmere
Fashion and homewares
brand, UK
*Designed by Thomas
Manss & Company, 2003*
The muted aesthetic
of designer Oyuna
Tserendorj, expressed in
a pared-down wordmark.

20. Saratoga Associates
Landscape architecture
and engineering firm,
USA
*Designed by Chermayeff
& Geismar (Emanuela
Frigerio), 2004*

INREV

11

ivan.hair salon

12

Kubota

13

MODE
ZONEN

14

15

mnda

RONDO

16

17

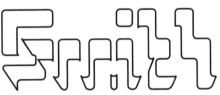

Paper from GFSmith

18

oyuna

SARATOGA
ASSOCIATES

19

20

21. Silver Plate
Recording studio,
Norway
Designed by
KalleGraphics, 2005

22. Roam Digital
Digital hardware provider,
Australia
Designed by Mark
Gowing Design, 2010
A simple, confident mark
to help give a portable
devices start-up a kick-
start in a market crowded
with multinational rivals,
and to remain crisp and
clear at very small sizes.

23. Tuveri
Directory publisher, Italy
Designed by Brunazzi &
Associati, 1988

24. Dialog In The Dark
Social entertainment
group, Japan
Designed by Good
Design Company, 2005
A mark for the Japanese
franchise of a 'social
entertainment' launched
in Germany in 1989, in
which sighted people
experience the everyday
world of the blind through
a series of darkened
rooms and settings.

25. Face
Cycling events, UK
Designed by Tomato
(Jason Kedgley), 2007

26. Victoria Beckham
Fashion label, UK
Designed by SVIDesign
(Sasha Vidakovic), 2009
Eliminating the break
between the two words
and the cross strokes
of the 'A's creates a
rhythmic repetition,
and a new angle on a
brand name we are all
familiar with.

27. Steam
Restaurant, Australia
Designed by Inkahoots,
2010
Hot type generates rice
and rising steam for this
Asian restaurant on the
Mornington Peninsula
near Melbourne.

28. At What Cost
Travelling exhibition, USA
Designed by de.MO
(Giorgio Baravalle), 2009
The sense of an
unfinished, precariously
balanced project in this
wordmark for a travelling
outdoor exhibition on
human trafficking, forced
labour and child labour.

21

ROAM

22

TUVERI®

23

DIALOG
IN THE
DARK

24

25

VICTORIA BECKHAM

26

27

HUMAN TRAFFICKING |

| FORCED LABOR |

| CHILD LABOR

28

1. 3DW
Architectural
visualization, UK
*Designed by
DesignStudio, 2010*
An elemental mark that
gently unfolds when
animated, and provides
a stamp of ownership
on the company's 3-D
architectural renders.

2. From Scratch
Cultural think tank,
Belgium
*Designed by Coast
(Frederic Vanhorenbeke),
2010*

3. Ad Kinetsu
Advertising agency, Japan
*Designed by Ken Miki &
Associates, 2010*
An 'A' and a 'D', two
directions, alternative
courses of action.

4. Atelier Pedro Falcão
Graphic design studio,
Portugal
*Designed by Atelier
Pedro Falcão, 2010*
Three characters
reduced to make one.

5. Vumi
Online career portfolio
system, Australia
*Designed by Inkahoots,
2010*
Strong shapes and
colours for a young job-
seeking audience who
use the system to create
digital resumés and invite
potential employers to
'view me'.

6. Lean Alliance
Management training
company, Germany
*Designed by Thomas
Manss & Company, 2005*
No sign of waste in this
wordmark for a company
teaching the ways of
lean manufacturing. The
abstracted letterforms
are based on Walter
Haettenschweiler's
never-published
Africaine typeface.

7. Orso
Sign manufacturer,
Greece
*Designed by G Design
Studio (Michalis
Georgiou, Diamantis
Arabatzis), 2009*
Sign-like simplification
taken to extremes in this
signmaker's logotype.

8. Cwmni Da
Television production
company, UK
*Designed by Elfen (Aaron
Easterbrook, Guto
Evans), 2008*

Focusing solely on the
'Good' (*Da*) of 'Good
Company', this wordmark
embodies the youthful,
fun nature of the
company's output.

9. Capital Partners
Property developer,
Kazakhstan
*Designed by Pentagram
(Michael Gericke), 2006*

10. DACS
Not-for-profit
rights management
organization, UK
*Designed by 300million
(Martin Lawless, Nigel
Davies, Katie Morgan,
Helen Stergious), 2008*
A mark that had to
be authoritative and
professional while
remaining contemporary
and unconventional
enough to appeal to
DACS' (formerly the
Design and Artists
Copyright Society)
members, who include
the likes of Damien Hirst
and Banksy.

**11. Olmo Reverter
Photography**
Photographer, UK
*Designed by Studio
Paradise (Samuel Moffat,
Jade Abbott), 2010*
The name of this
London-based Spanish
photographer is one that
can be distilled down
to the three most basic
geometric shapes.

12. Komono
Fashion accessories
company, Belgium
*Designed by Coast
(Ingrid Arquin), 2009*

1

2

3

4

5

6

7

8

9

10

11

12

**13. FaulknerBrowns
Architects**
Architectural practice, UK
*Designed by A2/SW/HK,
2007*
An identity that gets
creative with spaces: the
counters in the letters
of the basic wordmark
– the 'A's, 'R's, 'B' and
'O' – undergo constant
rearrangement in print
and digital applications.

14. FramePage
Editorial photography
agency, Finland
*Designed by Hahmo
(Erik Bertell, Jenni
Kuokka, Pekka Piippo,
Antti Raudaskoski), 2009*
An ingenious tweak of the
camera's viewfinder mark
creates a monogram for
FramePage, a start-up
by photographer Hanna
Raijas.

15. Nine Point Nine
Architectural practice,
Australia
*Designed by Studio
Paradise (Samuel Moffat,
Jade Abbott), 2010*
A multilevel logo. At
first sight, a grid of dots
suggests a floorplan or
column layout. But the
logo depicts the name in
the simplest terms (nine,
point, nine) and also spells
it (9.9), if the two blocks of
nine dots are joined up in
the right order.

16. Hans Freymadl
Multidisciplinary designer,
Australia
*Designed by Naughtyfish
(Paul Garbett), 2009*
A monogram that reflects
the restrained aesthetic
of this architect, interior
designer and furniture
designer.

17. Henderson Leyland
Rare book specialist, UK
*Designed by Bateson/
Studio (John Bateson,
Tom Miller), 2010*
A three-stage logotype
for a Kent company
specializing in collectable
posters and art and
design books. From a row
of book spines to the full
logotype in two steps.

**18. Japan Design
Society**
Academic society, Japan
*Designed by Ken Miki &
Associates, 1993*
The 3-D shapes and
shadows found in the
stylized initials of this
mark hint at the group's
main concern: product
design.

19. Kajimoto Music Office
Concert promoter, Japan
*Designed by Samurai
(Kashiwa Sato, Yhoshiki
Okuse), 2009*
A logo whose numerous
arrangements and colour
combinations celebrate
the possibilities and
creativity of this classical
music event organizer.

**20. Digital Illusions
Creative Entertainment**
Computer game
developer, Sweden
*Designed by Stockholm
Design Lab, 2006*
A code-like mark for
DICE, part of the EA
Games Group, designed
to appeal to the
company's young
male market.

21. La Maison de Photo
Photographic prints
retailer, France
*Designed by Studio
Apeloig, 2009*
Another of Philippe
Apeloig's carefully
choreographed
logotypes, this time for
a seller of limited-edition
prints by landscape
photographers Patrick
Borie-Duclaud and
Nicolas Boudreaux.

22. Circa
Music label, Australia
*Designed by Mark
Gowing Design, 2010*
A logotype (and CD cover
titling system) designed
in an experimental,
rhythmic type-code
comprising a strict set
of modular parts, for an
avant-garde music label.

23. NBS
Technical information
publisher, UK
*Designed by OPX
(Frances Jackson, Simon
Goodall, Viola Muller),
2008*
NBS publishes
information and
specification systems
for the construction
industry. The electronic
aesthetic of its logo
reflects the increasingly
digital nature of its
product range.

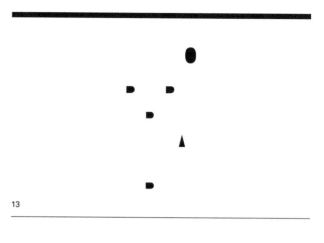

13

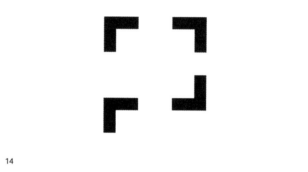

14

15

16

 HendersonLeyland

17

18

KAJIMOTO

19

 ™

20

LA
MAISON
DE PHOTO

21

22

23

24. Canterbury School of Architecture
Architecture school, UK
Designed by Graphical House, 2010
A mark that establishes a restrained identity for CSA within the University for the Creative Arts, whose faculties span south-east England.

25. Chartered Society of Physiotherapy
Professional association, UK
Designed by Spencer du Bois (John Spencer), 2010
Bending and flexing, the CSP's letterforms allude to shapes made by the human body.

26. AAYA
Restaurant group, Hong Kong
Designed by North, 2010
The odd letter out is actually the same character as the others, flipped, to give the second initial of owner Alan Yau, who transformed oriental dining in London with restaurants such as Wagamama, Yauatcha, Hakkasan and Busaba Eathai.

27. Studio Sam
Multidisciplinary designer, Australia
Designed by Design By Pidgeon, 2008
A set of movable triangles that spell the name of Sam (Samantha) Parsons and whose multiple variations express her adaptability in designing interiors, products and furniture.

28. UCLA Architecture & Urban Design
Architecture school, USA
Designed by Pentagram (Eddie Opara), 2007
An identity designed to capture the transformative, expressive nature of contemporary architecture with a series of letterforms that seem to fold and grow out of each other. Despite surviving only a year before UCLA overruled its Architecture & Urban Design school and rejected the identity, it lives on as an animation on the AUD website.

29. Title
Music and film retailer, Australia
Designed by Mark Gowing Design, 2006
An underground music and avant-garde film specialist, with a discerning audience and a logotype that invites the mind to do some of the work.

30. Reuter & Kucher Steuerberater
Tax consultancy, Germany
Designed by Büro Uebele Visuelle Kommunikation (Andreas Uebele, Beate Kapprell), 2004
For a firm whose skill is in reducing tax bills, a wordmark with a minimum number of letters. The fortuitous repeat of the 'r' allows the company's initials to hold the mark together in the centre.

31. Preston Kelly
Advertising agency, USA
Designed by Cue (Alan Colvin), 2007

32. Rotterdam Academie van Bouwkunst
Architecture and urban design school, The Netherlands
Designed by Total Identity, 2009
A mark that is manifested in many different materials and that, besides representing the two main initials of the academy, can also act as arrows, connection points and a framing device.

33. Visual Intelligence Agency
Moving image and cultural consultancy, UK
Designed by Studio Tonne, 2009

34. Peter Taylor Associates Limited
Architectural practice, UK
Designed by Mind Design, 2009
No shortage of room in this logotype, where the name has been written in full, then stripped of everything except the initials.

35. Seven Film Gallery
Film rental, Greece
Designed by Designers United (Dimitris Koliadimas, Dimitris Papazoglou), 2007

24

25

26

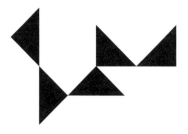

27

28

29

r   t r&k ch r

30

31

32

33

P   T   A   L

34

35

Rotating, reflecting, slanting and stacking words and portions of words can generate interesting dynamics, rhythms and hierarchies with plain or long names. Groups of letters are used as building blocks, orientated to suggest disruption, harmony, ascent, descent, space and structure.

APDI

I
U
A
V

SCiENCE MUSEUM

F\\ | FERGUSON WHYTE

TOR ON TO

7 50

SONIC EDITIONS

Bankside MIX

THE COMPANY BOOKS

HERREN ABIG

MARMALADE TOAST

Alter native Arrange ments

seven

SARAH DAVIES

MM

 VERTIGO

MoMA

Museums & Galleries NSW

BARNEYS NEWYORK

ELJ APO NÉS

WILHELM

Jamie Oliver

PEYTON AND BYRNE

actink

BEN SAUNDERS

SELF PUBLISH, BE HAPPY

certio

1. Appleton & Domingos
Architectural practice,
Portugal
*Designed by Atelier
Pedro Falcão, 2009*

2. Rethink
Charity, UK
*Designed by Spencer
du Bois (John Spencer),
2002*
A wordmark that
steers clear of trying
to symbolize the
sensitive and complex
issue of mental health.
Its orientation is an
encouragement to
change the way mental
illness is thought about.

3. Penoyre & Prasad
Architectural practice,
UK
*Designed by SEA (Bryan
Edmondson), 2009*
Some neat symmetry
and connections in this
mark to emphasize the
practice's collaborative,
joined-up approach and
group spirit.

**4. Vertical Garden
Design**
Landscape architecture
practice, Sweden
*Designed by Area 17
(Audrey Templier), 2010*
A suitably cascading
mark for a designer of
vertical gardens for
offices, shops and other
clients.

**5. National Library of
Ireland**
National library, Ireland
*Designed by Creative
Inc (Mel O'Rourke, Karen
Erdpohl), 2011*
A contemporary mark
with forms based on
the historic building's
Georgian features,
designed to broaden the
library's appeal among
the general public.

6. Louise Toohey
Architect's agent, UK
*Designed by Untitled
(David Hawkins, Glenn
Howard), 2004*
A monogram that
doubles as an excerpt
from an architectural
floorplan.

7. Dab Hand Media
Film production
company, UK
*Designed by Tomato
(Dylan Kendle), 2007*

**8. London Chamber
Orchestra (LCO)**
Chamber orchestra, UK
*Designed by CDT Design
(Mike Dempsey), 1989*

1

2

Penoyre &Prasad

3

VERTICAL GARDEN DESIGN

4

Leabharlann Náisiúnta na hÉireann
National Library of Ireland

5

6

7

LCO

8

9. British Library
National library, UK
Designed by Interbrand,
2002
Confident, trustworthy,
modern, the British
Library's logo is also
a nod, possibly, to the
orientation of book titles
on spines.

10. Home 3 Assistance
Home assistance
helpline, UK
Designed by CDT Design,
2008
A re-orientation of the
word highlights the
numeral: the '3' refers
to a three-way claims
helpline that connects
the homeowner, Home 3
and a tradesman who can
carry out the repair.

11. College of Built
Environments
Architecture school, USA
Designed by Studio/lab
(Hillary Geller), 2007
The new name of the
former College of
Architecture and Urban
Planning at the University
of Washington is stood
on end to echo the
modern skyline of Seattle
and the landscape's
former landmarks – totem
poles.

12. Museum Links
Cultural exchange, UK
Designed by Dowling
Duncan (John Dowling,
Rob Duncan), 2009

13. Octink
Display printer, UK
Designed by Felt
Branding (Scott Manning,
Tom Rogers), 2009
Intelligence, flexibility
and ink are the
associations Octink
hopes to make with its
new name (replacing
Allsignsgroup) and
tentacular ligature.

14. Metropolitan Wharf
Property development,
UK
Designed by SEA (Bryan
Edmondson), 2010
The original Victorian
roofline typography
that extends the length
of this riverside former
warehouse, put to work
for the building's new use
as office and retail space.

9

10

COLLEGE OF
BUILT ENVIRONMENTS

11

MUSEUM
LINKS

12

octink

13

METROPOLITAN WHARF
LONDON E1

14

MoMA

15. The Museum of Modern Art
Museum, USA
Designed by Chermayeff & Geismar, 1964; Matthew Carter, 2003; Pentagram (Paula Scher) and MoMA (Julia Hoffmann), 2009
As befits an institution of the original up-down city, and one whose signs have beckoned art lovers and tourists down the canyon of a crosstown street for decades, the MoMA identity has gone vertical.

One of the features of a system designed by Paula Scher and MoMA's Julia Hoffmann to refresh and strengthen the museum's 'institutional voice', the vertical placement echoes the logotype's most prominent application of recent years: on its side, on the facade. Scher is known for persuading New York institutions to embrace the popular, shortened versions of their names – the Whitney (Museum), the Met (Metropolitan Opera) etc. – and the MoMA realignment can be seen in the same light: as an affirmation of the way the institution is most commonly perceived.

The original, fully spelled-out identity was designed by Ivan Chermayeff in 1964, who chose the 'modern with roots' Franklin Gothic No.2 typeface to represent the museum. The system became an icon of institutional branding before the translingual, abbreviated form appeared in the 1980s. When Bruce Mau was asked to review alternatives to the Franklin Gothic identity, he advised MoMA to stick, not bust. The museum's mission and values had not really deviated: why change outwardly when it had not changed inwardly?

Mau did, though, spot that the digital version of Franklin MoMA was using contained defects that became glaring at large sizes. The letterforms were squatter and less elegant. Typeface designer Matthew Carter set the record straight,

returning to original metal type samples to plot the true contours of each letter.

The new system makes Carter's MoMA Gothic the font for all MoMA's typography, and makes prominent use of the museum's re-energized, reoriented logotype.

16. Intro Garde
Domestic security products, Switzerland
Designed by Nadine Kamber, 2010

17. Bankside Mix
Retail and leisure property, UK
Designed by GBH, 2009
A reflection of the new, strongly orthogonal architecture on London's Bankside, and possibly an arrow to point the way there.

18. Intermédiations
Mediation service, Switzerland
Designed by Atelier Bundi (Stephan Bundi), 2008

19. Xococava
Chocolatier, Canada
Designed by Concrete (Diti Katona, John Pylypczak), 2008
A Toronto shop celebrating the chocolate cultures of Spain and Mexico, *Xococava* ('choc cellar') is big on flavours and big on type, juggling letterforms (including a haloed 'c') on its packaging in loud, cross-cutting formations.

16

17

18

19

1. Booket
Paperback publisher,
Spain
*Designed by Summa
(Josep Maria Mir), 1997*
A book in a pocket for the
paperback arm of Grupo
Planeta.

2. FCE
University membership
association, Hong Kong
*Designed by CoDesign
(Eddy Yu, Hung Lam, Sum
Leung), 2010*
FCE stands for
the Federation for
Continuing Education in
Tertiary Institutions. Its
logo symbolizes personal
advancement through
lifelong learning, and
collaboration between
FCE's 14 partners.

3. Laidlaw Foundation
Charitable foundation,
Canada
*Designed by Hambly &
Woolley (Bob Hambly,
Barb Woolley), 2008*
The Laidlaw Foundation
promotes positive
youth development
through involvement in
the arts, environment
and community. It gets
individuals and groups
back on their feet, little
by little, as its logotype
illustrates.

4. Lill Rechtsanwälte
Solicitors' firm, Germany
*Designed by Thomas
Manss & Company, 2006*
A compact, stylish mark
that takes its cue from
the description of this
Berlin law firm by a law
trade magazine as a
'property boutique'.

5. Seven
Management recruitment
agency, UK
*Designed by B&W Studio
(Lee Bradley, Andrew
Droog, Adam Evans),
2009*
An edgy identity in more
ways than one, this mark
is always positioned
bleeding off the top-right
corner, creating the
illusion of a '7'.

6. The Burgiss Group
Investment software
company, USA
*Designed by Lance
Wyman, 2002*

**7. Breakthrough Breast
Cancer**
Charity, UK
*Designed by hat-trick
(Gareth Howat, Jim
Sutherland, Tim
Donaldson), 2009*

Breakthrough's mission
is to support research,
campaigning and
education that will help to
stamp out breast cancer.

8. Lokalt Företagsklimat
Annual regional
enterprise campaign,
Sweden
*Designed by We
Recommend (Martin
Fredricson, Nicolaj Knop),
2008*

9. Nau Capital
Macro investment
company, UK
*Designed by Atelier
Pedro Falcão, 2007*
A circle symbolizes the
movement of capital
around the world; an
upward tilt indicates the
direction of the results.

10. Wilhelm
Nightclub, Switzerland
*Designed by Mixer
(Erich Brechbühl), 2010*
A logo that leads
downstairs for this
basement club.

11. Tilt Design
Video graphics team,
UK/Australia
*Designed by Design By
Pidgeon, 1998*

1

2

3

4

seven

the Burgiss Group

5

6

BREASTHROUGH CANCER
BREAKTHROUGH

7

LOKALT SVENSKT NÄRINGSLIV SKÅNE HALLAND BLEKINGE
FÖRETAGSKLIMAT

8

9

WILHELM

TILT

10

11

1. Tossed
Salad bar chain, UK
Designed by Practice + Theory (Andreas Pohancenik) and LoveBranding, 2006

2. Calderdale Council
Local authority, UK
Designed by B&W Studio (Steve Wills, Lee Bradley, Alex Broadhurst), 2009
A logotype to promote working together across this region of Yorkshire, wrapping its message around the council's initials.

3. Martha Stewart Omnimedia
Media brand, USA
Designed by Doyle Partners (Stephen Doyle, August Heffner), 2006
The power of the name made a wordmark – rather than an emblem – the only option. A sense of Stewart's trademark 'handmade, home-made and artful' was conveyed by drawing the letterforms by hand, expertly but imperfectly. The circular arrangement is intended to stir warm, Martha-esque feelings of community.

4. Standard 8
Fabricator, UK
Designed by Browns (Nick Jones, Stephen McGilvray), 2005
Standard 8 makes bespoke installations and exhibition displays – its products are anything but standard. The same can be said of its logotype, which exists in eight different versions, each featuring eight numerals in a different typeface.

5. Trommpo
Children's clothing company, Uruguay
Designed by Buddy (David Jones, Mark Girvan, Sarah Mills), 2010
A name and mark inspired by *trompo*, the Spanish word for a spinning top.

6. Tuke & Bloom
Recycled glassware company, UK
Designed by Studio Special, 2010
A logotype that recycles the tradition of stamping the maker's name on the base of mould-made glassware, but one that also (with two ampersands) conveys the continuous circularity the company promotes.

7. Vertigo
Private yacht, Marshall Islands
Designed by North, 2010
Registered at Bikini Island, this yacht has its own logotype, suggestive of a sea compass.

8. Bob Schalkwijk
Photographer, Mexico
Designed by Lance Wyman, 1976

1

2

3

4

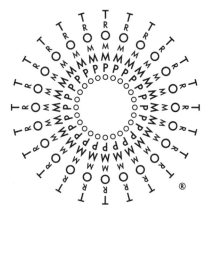

5

6

7

8

1. 750mph
Sound studio, UK
Designed by North, 2009
A name that is the
(approximate) speed of
sound, and a logotype
that separates the
number into two of its
component sounds – the
stock-in-trade of sound
engineers.

**2. American Cinema
Editors**
Honorary society, USA
*Designed by C&G
Partners (Steff
Geissbuhler), 2001*
A repetition that mimics
that of 35mm film – the
principal movie medium
in 2001 – with the arms
of the 'E's providing
the sprocket holes that
allowed editors to do
their job.

3. Ancillotto
Mixed-use development,
Italy
*Designed by milkxhake
(Javin Mo), 2009*

**4. Asociación
Profesional de
Diseñadores de
Iluminación**
Professional association,
Spain
*Designed by Mario
Eskenazi, 2010*
A logo and its shadow
for Spain's professional
association of lighting
designers.

5. Barneys New York
Department store chain,
USA
*Designed by Chermayeff
& Geismar (Tom Geismar,
Steff Geissbuhler), 1981*
Barneys' 1981 identity
was part of a gradual
move away from the
store's discount clothing
origins (it was founded
in 1923) to stock leading
designers and brands,
initiated by Barney
Pressman's son Fred. The
apostrophe was dropped
and the space between
the 'w' and 'y' reduced
to allow the two lines
to stack evenly and, in
so doing, put 'NY' at the
store's heart.

6. Aya Takano
Artist, Japan
*Designed by Homework
(Jack Dahl), 2010*

7. Beacon
Restaurant, USA
*Designed by Pentagram
(Paula Scher), 1999*
Paula Scher has designed
identities for a long series

of New York institutions,
including Tiffany & Co.
and the Metropolitan
Opera. This restaurant
on West 56th Street is
one of the smaller ones,
but built around a huge,
hearth-like wood-burning
oven.

8. Ben Saunders
Polar explorer, UK
*Designed by Studio8 (Zoë
Bather, Matt Willey, Steve
Fenn, Tom Pollard), 2010*
North or south – it's
always one or the other
for Ben Saunders.

**9. Arts for Health
Cornwall and Isles
of Scilly**
Art therapies
organization, UK
Designed by Two, 2009
A plain-speaking
logotype first created for
a pair of well-received
publications, whose
typography gave a
balanced, consistent
presentation to a diverse,
award-winning portfolio
of projects.

10. Casa Lever
Restaurant, USA
*Designed by Mucca
Design (Matteo Bologna,
Steve Jockisch, Christine
Celic Strohl), 2009*
For this Italian fine-dining
eatery – in the former
Lever House Restaurant,
with interiors by Marc
Newson – the logotype
and visual language
recall mid-20th-century
design and, specifically,
the output of Italian
Futurist Fortunato
Depero (1892–1960),
whose creations included
graphics, interiors and
the classic Campari
Soda bottle.

1

2

3

4

BARNEYS
NEWYORK

5

6

7

BEN
SAUNDERS

8

Arts for Health
Cornwall and
Isles of Scilly

CASA
LEVER

9

10

11. Chuck Choi
Architectural
photographer, USA
*Designed by C&G
Partners (Emanuela
Frigerio), 2009*
Another logotype (like
750mph, p.142) that
separates sounds by
stacking its constituent
parts; in this case, the
two words conveniently
sound like the
mechanical release of
a camera shutter.

**12. Claudine Colin
Communication**
Cultural public relations
firm, France
*Designed by Studio
Apeloig, 2008*
A stack of speakers to
get the message across
for this cultural PR firm.

**13. Museums & Galleries
NSW**
Cultural promotion and
support agency, Australia
*Designed by Mark
Gowing Design, 2007*
A tone of neutrality,
authority and
timelessness
characterizes this mark
for an agency giving
support to museums
and galleries in New
South Wales.

14. Columba
Financial event data
company, UK
*Designed by Carter Wong
Design, 2010*
Calendar-based event
data is central to
Columba's business,
and with seven letters,
the company name lends
itself to double as a
weekly calendar.

15. Covert Music
Artist management
agency, UK
*Designed by 1977 Design
(Paul Bailey, Chloe Pillai),
2009*

**16. Dansmakers
Amsterdam**
Contemporary
dance company,
The Netherlands
Designed by Lava, 2010
A logotype with its own
internal choreography,
with letterforms that
seem to morph into one
another, in formation.

17. Ellis Miller
Architectural practice, UK
*Designed by Cartlidge
Levene, 2008*
An architect's logotype
with strong structural
connections.

**18. Human Genome
Sciences**
Pharmaceutical
business, USA
*Designed by Landor
Associates (Beca Lee,
Paul Owen), 2010*
A departure from the
vacuous swirls, sails and
swooshes so beloved
of businesses in the
scientific sector in recent
years: a logotype that is
memorable for its relative
straightforwardness and
integrity.

19. Nest.co.uk
Online furniture retailer,
UK
*Designed by Universal
Everything, 2004*

20. Jamie Oliver
TV chef, UK
*Designed by SEA (Bryan
Edmondson), 2005*
A wordmark with on-shelf
presence for the TV
chef's legion of branded
goods, in a typeface with
the appropriate level of
'lovely-jubbliness'.

CHUCK
CHOI

11

12

**Museums
& Galleries
NSW**

13

14

15

16

Ellis Miller

17

HUMAN GENOME SCIENCES

18

19

21. English National Opera
National opera company, UK
Designed by CDT Design (Mike Dempsey), 1991
If you're looking for inspiration, get out of the office. That would seem to be the lesson from the making of many of the world's most memorable marks. An uncommon number, it would seem, were conceived while in transit: Milton Glaser came up with the 'I♥NY' logo in the back of a yellow cab; the Canadian National Railways 'CN' monogram was first sketched by Allan Fleming on a flight to New York. Like those two, Mike Dempsey's 'singing' logotype for English National Opera is often listed by designers as one of their favourite logos. And it was born on the number 38 bus.

Dempsey describes ENO's then-CEO Peter Jonas as 'brilliant' and 'extremely supportive'. Jonas admired Dempsey's recent work for the London Chamber Orchestra (p.133), but his expectations went higher. 'If you can come up with something as simple as the VW logo I'll be very pleased,' he advised Dempsey. The designer recalls the challenge of the ENO identity occupying him day and night, 'as with all design problems. They stay in my head 24 hours a day, nagging away until something starts to filter through.

'I generally keep a notebook and recall sitting on top of the 38 bus going to work and starting to doodle. I realized that the whole notion of opera is about the voice, the open mouth, and that gave me my visual clue. 'I showed it to both [Keith] Cooper (ENO's marketing director) and Jonas, and they responded enthusiastically from the moment they saw it, which was fortunate because it was the only idea I presented.'

Dempsey developed a complete branding and typographic system for ENO, and over a decade designed a series of startlingly original posters for the company. Cutbacks brought the work to an end, but the logotype remains. 'The important thing about the creative success of the project,' says Dempsey, 'was the fact that it was a great client. Both Cooper and Jonas wanted to make waves.'

22. Fonds Podium Kunsten
Performing arts fund, The Netherlands
Designed by Lava, 2010
A deliberately self-effacing, almost austere, logotype, only ever printed in black, intended to consume as little valuable arts funding as possible. As a set of steps up to a stage – or to new and higher levels for the arts – it stacks up neatly.

23. Herrenabig
Dining and events club, Switzerland
Designed by Hotz & Hotz (Roman Imhof, Kim Arbenz), 2009
Based on Century Gothic, this hand-drawn logotype for a group of male friends who organize events in Zurich is intended to echo the typography of early American jazz clubs.

24. Fischer Spooner
Electronica duo, USA
Designed by Homework (Jack Dahl, Enrico Bonafede), 2009

25. Le Vieux Manoir
Hotel, Switzerland
Designed by Hotz & Hotz (Thorsten Traber), 2009
Trad type, contemporary composition, for a new lakeside hotel at the former country estate of a French general.

FONDS PODIUM KUNSTEN PERFORMING ARTS COUNCIL

22

HERREN ABIG

23

24

LAC DE MORAT

25

26. Marmalade Toast
Cafe, Singapore
*Designed by &Larry
(Larry Peh, Lee Weicong),
2010*
A stylish, upmarket
cafe-cum-bistro opened
by the Marmalade
Group on Orchard
Road, Singapore, whose
name appears to be
simultaneously popping
out of toaster slots and
melting like butter.

27. Mattura
Winery consultant,
Argentina
*Designed by Ailoviu,
2009*

**28. Patrick Heide
Contemporary Art**
Contemporary art
gallery, UK
*Designed by Thomas
Manss & Company, 2008*

**29. Università IUAV di
Venezia**
University, Italy
*Designed by Studio
Apeloig, 2003*
Founded in Venice in
1940 as the Istituto
Universitario di
Architettura di Venezia,
IUAV is now the only
university in Italy to
cover all aspects of the
built environment, from
architecture to planning
to design and the arts.

30. Luna Design
Design consultancy,
Spain
*Designed by Estudio
Diego Feijóo, 2004*
A mark that highlights
Luna's emphasis on the
value of teamwork in its
projects.

31. Collectors Gallery
Vintage jewellery retailer,
Belgium
*Designed by Coast
(Frederic Vanhorenbeke),
2008*
A logotype that seems
to hang in strands, like a
vintage necklace.

32. DeTodo
Retail centre, Mexico
*Designed by Lance
Wyman, 1969*
The young Lance Wyman
made a name for himself
and created a vibrant new
look for the Olympics
when he designed the
identity for the 1968
Games in Mexico.
Afterwards he stayed on
in the country, designing
a string of identities.
This one, for a shopping
centre in Mexico City,

uses repetition, like the
Olympic identity, to
suggest abundance; *de
todo* is Spanish for 'of
everything'.

33. de.MO Books
Publisher, USA
*Designed by de.MO
(Giorgio Baravalle), 2010*
The design consultancy's
own imprint of thought-
provoking, beautifully
produced volumes of
journalistic photography
has a mark made for book
spines.

34. El Japonés
Restaurant, Spain
*Designed by Mario
Eskenazi, 1999*
El Japonés serves not
just Japanese but also
Asian dishes; its logotype
is based on the three-
lined trigrams found
in the *I Ching* (*Book of
Changes*), one of China's
earliest classic texts.

35. StartSkuddet
Student organization,
Denmark
*Designed by
KalleGraphics, 2010*

**36. Knabenchor
Gütersloh**
Boys' choir, Germany
*Designed by Thomas
Manss & Company, 2007*
More singing typography,
this time for a German
touring boys' choir. The
logotype provides a face
for the group and also
serves as affordable
advertising while on
tour; copies are printed,
poster-size, in advance,
and the concert dates are
applied locally.

37. RIBA Bookshops
Architectural bookshops,
UK
*Designed by OPX
(Frances Jackson, Britt
Gundersen), 2008*
Designed for the
bookshops of the Royal
Institute of British
Architects, both online
and in-store.

26

27

28

29

**Luna
una
na
a**

30

C O L
L E C
T O R
S **GA**
L L E
R Y

31

32

33

**E L J
A P O
N É S**

34

STAR
TSK
UDD
ET.®

35

36

**riba
book
shops.
com**

37

38. Science Museum
National museum of science and technology, UK
Designed by Johnson Banks, 2010
The Science Museum's identity originated in research on codes, puzzles and early digital typefaces, which led to a 3x4 grid of modular, slightly abstracted letterforms that demanded some decoding – one way of adding a little intrigue to two very generic words. There was only one problem: 'Science' has seven letters, not six. Without making the mark any less readable, the 'E' was altered to incorporate an 'i'.

39. St Mary-le-Bow Church
Church, UK
Designed by Untitled (David Hawkins, Glenn Howard), 2004
More than 900 years old, rebuilt by Sir Christopher Wren and the home of the famous Bow bells, St Mary-le-Bow in the City of London now competes with shopfronts and global brands for attention. The Revd George Bush realized that the church needed to employ contemporary visual language, too, to publicize its lunchtime and evening events.

40. Stara Piekarnia
Property development, Poland
Designed by logotypy. com (Wiktor Pawlik), 2010
Branding for a former industrial bakery in Wroclaw, south-west Poland, now converted into luxury apartments.

41. Statik Dancin'
Club nights brand, Belgium
Designed by Coast (Frederic Vanhorenbeke), 2008

42. The Colourhouse
Printer, UK
Designed by SEA (Bryan Edmondson), 2008
A stack of pages coming off the press?

43. The Restaurant at the Royal Academy of Arts
Restaurant, UK
Designed by Farrow, 2011
A distinctively classical logotype to reflect the surroundings, but one whose central alignment echoes that of Farrow's mark for Peyton and Byrne (see p.153) – the group behind this restaurant.

44. Museum of American Finance
Museum, USA
Designed by C&G Partners (Emanuela Frigerio), 2006

45. Mount Anvil
Property developer, UK
Designed by me&dave, 2010
Letters stacked brick-fashion for this builder-turned-developer.

46. Pilobolus Dance Company
Dance company, USA
Designed by Chermayeff & Geismar, 1982

47. The Wapping Project Bankside
Photography gallery, UK
Designed by Browns (Jonathan Ellery, Claire Warner), 2009
The Wapping Project, a rather wonderful exhibition space housed in a former hydraulic power station in London's East End, opened a photography gallery at Bankside, opposite Tate Modern in 2009. Its logotype makes the link between the two parts of town.

38

39

40

41

**Printed by
The Colourhouse**

42

R⚔A
THE
RESTAURANT
AT THE
ROYAL
ACADEMY
OF ARTS

43

MU$EUM
OF AMERICAN
FINANCE

44

45

P I L
O B O
L U S

46

THE WAPPING PROJECT
BANKSIDE

47

48. New Museum
Contemporary art gallery, USA
Designed by Wolff Olins, 2008
Simplifying the name of the New Museum of Contemporary Art allowed Wolff Olins to create a flexible identity that could act as a vessel for changing information, incorporating – between the two words – different messages about art, the museum and what's on.

49. The Company Books
Accountancy firm, UK
Designed by Atelier Works (John Powner, Lou Wood), 2006
Nothing to do with ancient symbology (or John Bonham's 'sign' from *Led Zeppelin IV*), but a good way of answering the client's brief to represent its integrated book-keeping services.

50. Self Publish, Be Happy
Self-publishing book promoter, UK
Designed by Untitled (Glenn Newark, David Hawkins), 2010
Type associated with the first printing revolution – letterpress – used to promote the latest: self-publishing.

51. Rainy City Stories
Online literary anthology, UK
Designed by Mark Studio, 2009
Rainy City Stories presents an interactive literary map of Manchester, one of the UK's wettest cities.

52. Ossie Clark
Fashion label, UK
Designed by SVIDesign (Sasha Vidakovic), 2007
A revival of a designer and a label that dominated fashion in the 1960s and 1970s, with a logotype that updates the kind of full, sinuous letterforms typical of that period.

53. National Youth Choirs of Great Britain
National youth choir, UK
Designed by Grade Design (Peter Dawson, Banlee Too, Paul Palmer-Edwards), 2008
A musical stave provides the platform for the full choir name.

54. Parrotta Contemporary Art
Contemporary art gallery, Germany
Designed by Büro Uebele Visuelle Kommunikation (Andreas Uebele, Beate Kapprell), 2006
A mark whose apparently random spacing of letters and blacking of counters suggests its own artistic interventions.

55. International Council of Museums UK
Professional association, UK
Designed by Mark Studio, 2008

56. Red Ladder Theatre Company
Theatre company, UK
Designed by The Chase (Kevin Blackburn), 2003

57. Peyton and Byrne
Bakery and restaurant group, UK
Designed by Farrow, 2006
An irresistibly restrained logotype for a client known for its seductive creations.

48

49

50

51

OSSIE CLARK

52

NATIONAL YOUTH CHOIRS GREAT BRITAIN

53

PARRO TTA
CONTEMPORARY
ART
STUTTGART
BERLIN

54

INTERNATIONAL
COUNCIL
OF MUSEUMS
UK

55

RED LADDER
THEATRE COMPANY

56

PEYTON
AND
BYRNE

57

58. Top Drawer
Retail trade event, UK
*Designed by KentLyons
(Shammi Umeria), 2010*
A stylish high-contrast
serif typeface (Caslon
Graphique) badges
this biannual event for
'design-led gifts, lifestyle
and fashion accessories'.

59. Toronto Magazine
Magazine, Canada
*Designed by Hambly &
Woolley (Barb Woolley,
Ross Chandler), 2008*
A magazine masthead
that highlights its
constituent letterforms,
like the boroughs or
neighbourhoods on
a city map, as well as
the shorthand for the
city and state: 'TO' for
Toronto; 'ONT' or 'ON'
for Ontario.

**60. University of
Westminster**
University, UK
*Designed by hat-trick
(Gareth Howat, Jim
Sutherland, Alex
Swatridge), 2009*
In the same vein as the
New Museum identity
(see p.152), this also
uses the name of the
institution to bookend
changing messages; in
this case, aspirations and
the names of individual
schools.

61. Walktall.com
Large-size footwear
retailer, UK
*Designed by Taxi Studio
(Spencer Buck, Ryan
Willis, Roger Whipp),
2009*

62. Sarah Davies
Television presenter and
model, Australia
*Designed by Couple,
2009*
For a multitalented
Miss World finalist who
now describes herself
as a 'TV presenter/
Master of Ceremonies/
Ambassador/Model',
a logotype that
incorporates the '/' into
its letterforms.

63. Usual Suspects
Experiential marketing
agency, The Netherlands
*Designed by The Stone
Twins (Garech and Declan
Stone), 2008*
Printed on rolls of
adhesive tape to brand
on-location events, this
identity hints at disguise,
codes and covert forces.

64. Toronto Life
Magazine, Canada
*Designed by A2/SW/HK
and Jessica Rose, 2010*

65. Big Science Read
Annual reading
campaign, UK
*Designed by Mark Studio,
2009*

top
drawer
London

58

TOR
ON
TO

59

UNIVERSITY OF
SHAPING
THE
FUTURE
WESTMINSTER

60

61

SARAH DAVIES

62

USUSUSUSUSUSUSUS
USUALSUSPECTSUSU
USUSUSUSUSUSUSUS
SUSUSUSUSUSUSUSL

63

TORONTO LIFE

64

big science read

65

1. Eye Place
Optometrist, Singapore
*Designed by &Larry
(Larry Peh, Ter Yeow
Yeong), 2006*
A mark for an 'optical
boutique' based on a
diagram of the workings
of the human eye, that
seems to say, 'If you can't
read the logo, maybe it's
time for a visit'.

2. Couple
Graphic design
consultancy, Singapore
*Designed by Couple,
2007*

3. Willem and Anne
Married couple,
The Netherlands
*Designed by Me Studio
(Martin Pyper), 2009*
Two names inextricably
linked in one wordmark,
which is also used turned
through 180 degrees.

4. Arteria
Performing arts network,
Spain/USA/Argentina/
Mexico
Designed by North, 2009

**5. The Dorchester
Collection**
Hotel group, UK
*Designed by Pentagram
(John Rushworth), 2006*
John Rushworth branded
this five-star hotel group
with a pair of abstracted
letterforms – a classic,
luxury-style monogram
that could also be seen
as a pair of heavy door
handles.

**6. Leong Ka-Tai
Photography**
Photographer, Hong Kong
*Designed by CoDesign
(Eddy Yu, Hung Lam),
2007*
Another lenticular-style
inversion.

**7. Turnaround for
Children**
Schools improvement
programme, USA
*Designed by Siegel &
Gale, 2009*
Turnaround works in New
York's most challenged
schools to treat safety,
social and learning
issues.

8. Magnusson Fine Wine
Wine storage and
consultancy, Sweden
*Designed by Stockholm
Design Lab, 2007*
A monogram for this
connoisseurs' service
designed to echo those
of luxury brands and
high-quality winemakers.

9. Viavai
Wine bar, Germany
*Designed by Büro Uebele
Visuelle Kommunikation
(Andreas Uebele, Beate
Kapprell), 2004*
A logotype-cum-symbol
composed of the letters
in the name Viavai.

10. JCL Records
Record label, UK
*Designed by Grade
Design (Peter Dawson,
Banlee Too), 2008*
A harmonious
composition for a
classical music label.

11. Millennium Models
Architectural model-
maker, UK
*Designed by Hyperkit,
2009*

**12. Joyce and Jonathan
Hui**
Married couple, Hong
Kong
*Designed by CoDesign
(Eddy Yu, Hung Lam, Ray
Cheung), 2010*

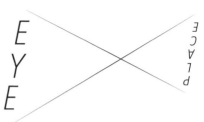

1

2

3

4

leong
ka
tai

5

6

7

8

9

10

11

12

randstad
uitzendbureau

13. Randstad Uitzendbureau
Temporary employment agency, The Netherlands
Designed by Total Design (Ben Bos), 1967
A pair of open arms? A pair of desks or computer screens? The stem and leaves of a plant? Or just an 'r' and its mirror image? The Randstad logotype is something different every time you look at it, and yet it is so simple. Its chameleon character, sophisticated simplicity and ageless modernity are reasons why it remains in use more than 40 years after its introduction.

It was the creation of Ben Bos, who worked at the pioneering Dutch design group Total Design (TD) for 30 years, doing the job of bringing beautifully concise identities into the world for corporate clients – and, with them, income into the studio – while his partners mixed commercial work with private design projects.

Randstad was a growing business, in an industry – temporary employment – that was in its infancy and still seen as not entirely above board. Frits Goldschmeding, the Randstad founder, wanted an identity that could convey respectability and professionalism – a mark with integrity, like the Mercedes Benz star or the droplet symbol TD had created for oil company PAM.

Bos found inspiration in the future, not the past. A year or so earlier, Bos's colleague (and, he has claimed, his idol) Wim Crouwel had developed the New Alphabet, a prototype computer typeface of light, square letterforms with bevelled corners. It was deliciously futuristic for its time.

Bos took the simplified 'r' and added body and character, adding weight to the strokes, rounding out their junction and increasing the bevel. What he was aiming for was a monogram that combined the precision to appeal to Randstad's (predominantly male) corporate clients with the softness that would attract (predominantly female) 'temps'.

He finally achieved a form he was happy with. But a single 'r' looked too unbalanced, 'too shaky'. It was only when Bos added a mirror image 'r' that the mark found its equilibrium, a centre, and a fund of visual associations.

It became the visual building block for a stream of striking exhibition stands, posters and publications, that kept Randstad with TD for an extraordinary 25 years. Meanwhile, the process of its conception seemed to point the way towards a new model for design companies, one that many still seek to emulate, in which commercial projects and private, research-type projects co-exist with mutually beneficial results.

14. Miso
Fashion label, UK
Designed by B&W Studio (Steve Wills), 2007

15. Saba
Restaurant, Ireland
Designed by Creative Inc (Mel O'Rourke, Kathryn Wilson), 2008
A mark for a Thai and Vietnamese restaurant in Dublin that mimics the iron fretwork in the interior with a ligature specially adapted from that between the 's' and the 't' in the Mrs Eaves typeface.

16. Third Light
Rock band, UK
Designed by Buddy (David Jones, Mark Girvan), 2009
Some typographic sleight of hand creates a mirror-image ambigram.

17. Tim Wood Furniture
Bespoke furniture maker, UK
Designed by Thomas Manss & Company, 1993
A modern monogram based on the initials 'TW', and providing a seal-like stamp of quality on stationery, literature and furniture.

14

15

16

17

1. John Jones
Art consultancy, UK
Designed by Browns (Jonathan Ellery, Claire Warner), 2009

2. Valtekz
Textile manufacturer, USA
Designed by Mode (USA), (John Pietrafesa, Ian Varrassi), 2007
All the hallmarks of a luxury brand for a manufacturer keen to appeal to interior designers, furniture makers and yacht and custom-car builders.

3. Graduates Yorkshire
Recruitment service, UK
Designed by Honey, 2009.

4. Hiscox
Insurance service, UK
Designed by Façade Design (Nick Havas), 1998
Heritage matters just as much as innovation in the specialist insurance areas Hiscox operates in, such as fine art, aerospace and the media. To reflect this, the identity redraws Gill Sans and a fleur-de-lys – a long-standing Hiscox family symbol – as an easily reproduced, contemporary mark.

5. Ferguson Whyte
Legal practice, UK
Designed by Graphical House, 2010

6. Certio
Vehicle certification centres, Spain
Designed by Summa (Tilman Solé, Olga Llopis, Roderic Molins), 2010
Certio centres examine and certify vehicles for roadworthiness, based on a cyclical process of maintenance, improvement and testing.

7. Kristin Morris Jewelry
Jewellery designer, USA
Designed by Mode (USA) (John Pietrafesa, Maxim Vakhovskiy), 2007

8. Sonic Editions
Online photography gallery, UK
Designed by Proud Creative, 2009
Sonic sells limited-edition classic music and movie industry images. Its combination of wordmark and monogram offers flexibility: one responds to the need for sophistication, the other can stand alone and badge affiliate relationships.

1

2

3

4

5

6

7

8

9. Architecture Centre Devon & Cornwall
Architecture centre, UK
Designed by Two, 2007
A name, an acronym and an abstracted monogram of the letter 'A', with two equal parts representing the two English counties.

10. Eye Develop
Property development and management service, UK
Designed by Brownjohn (James Beveridge, Andy Mosley, Tom Rogers), 2008

11. Good Measures
Change management consultancy, UK
Designed by Brownjohn (James Beveridge, Tom Rogers), 2009

12. Essence Pictures
Television production agency, Estonia
Designed by Loovvool (Hannes Unt, Robi Jõeleht), 2009

13. Holmes Mackillop
Legal practice, UK
Designed by Graphical House, 2009
A combination designed to position this firm, specializing in commercial law, as a boutique practice.

14. Diderot
Online wine reservation service, USA
Designed by Mode (USA) (John Pietrafesa, Maxim Vakhovskiy), 2007
A Venn-diagram-style double-D represents the interaction between wine connoisseurs and the service, which provides a single online location for previewing wine lists from high-end restaurants.

15. Ferrer Grupo
Pharmaceutical group, Spain
Designed by Talking (Fabián Vázquez, Gonzalo Sanchez), 2008

16. Ars
Highway service stations, Spain
Designed by Summa (Mario Eskenazi), 1995
A rebranding of the service-station group Ars is aimed at reversing the perception of Spain's motorway stops as uncared-for, soulless facilities with captive audiences.

9

10

11

12

13

14

15

16

A letter, a ligature, an accent. A full stop, a forward slash, an ampersand or colon. Colourful characters is a menagerie of single-letter marks, monograms and wordmarks in which typographic units of all kinds get the chance to beautify and signify.

CONGRESS

The Architecture Foundation

BAGS

R

art matters

text/ gallery.

SoüalBox

klartext

Colourful characters

    UEA

  HIVE&HONEY W

S4/C westzone° MF EAT. ByALEX®

1. Abbott Laboratories
Pharmaceuticals
company, USA
*Designed by George
Nelson Associates (Don
Ervin), 1958*
There aren't many logos
that last 50 years. The
comings and goings
of CEOs, managing
directors and marketing
chiefs, not to mention
fashions and companies
themselves, see to that.
In a scientific sector
like pharmaceuticals,
where corporations
are normally so much
at pains to convey their
latest advances and
innovation-focused
cultures, it is almost
unheard of for an identity
to last so long.

Given the longevity of the
Abbott 'a', it is surprising
and puzzling to find
that its creator is also
almost unknown, even
in design circles. The
Abbott mark wasn't the
only super-resilient logo
designed by Don Ervin.
At different design
groups, he was also
responsible for the
MetLife star, the
Mellon Bank 'M', the
Transamerica 'T', the
Conrail wheel and the
Cargill droplet-in-a-circle
– all strokes of mark-
making genius that made
a lasting impression on
American corporate
symbology.

The Abbott 'a' preceded
all of these and has
outlasted them all.
According to American
design historian Steven
Heller, Ervin claimed an
ancient inspiration for
this most modern of
marks, saying he derived
the sinuous, curling form
from the serpent that
wound itself around the
staff of Asclepius, the
Greek god of medicine
and healing.

Perhaps the reason
Ervin's prodigious talent
has not been more widely
recognized is that he
never struck out on his
own; he spent his career
working for people who
tended to be credited
with his achievements.
The Abbott identity
was one of his first
for George Nelson,
a giant of American
design, out of whose
shadow Ervin never
fully stepped (unlike

his contemporaries,
Robert Brownjohn,
Lance Wyman and Ettore
Sottsass). Lippincott &
Margulies, Siegel & Gale
and several other firms
also made full use of
Ervin's talents.

Ervin died in March 2010
in a road accident, aged
85, having spent his
retirement making and
racing cars for soapbox
derbies. May his 'a' for
Abbott live on.

2. Acocsa
Ceramic tile retailer,
Spain
*Designed by Estudio
Diego Feijóo, 2004*

3. Åhléns
Department store chain,
Sweden
*Designed by Stockholm
Design Lab, 1998*

**4. Anglesea Sports
& Recreation Club**
Sports club, Australia
*Designed by Design By
Pidgeon (David Pidgeon),
2010*
A case of designers
putting their oar in?

5. Alphabetee
T-shirt retailer, Australia
*Designed by Naughtyfish
(Paul Garbett), 2007*

2

3

4

5

6. Altitude Volvo
Car dealership, Australia
Designed by Design By Pidgeon (David Pidgeon), 2008
This Melbourne car dealership focuses on taking customer service to the highest level.

7. Ancoats Urban Village
Regeneration zone, UK
Designed by Mark Studio, 2008
Ancoats, a district of Manchester often described as the world's first industrial suburb, is distinguished by its grand, brooding mill buildings, whose large square windows are echoed in this monogram.

8. Barcelona pel Medi Ambient
Municipal environmental department, Spain
Designed by Mario Eskenazi and Diego Feijóo, 2009
Each of this suite of monograms for Barcelona City Council's environmental department contains an image relevant to a different team: leaves for parks, the sun for energy, clouds for cleaning (shown here), and so on.

9. Bloc
Music festival, UK
Designed by Give Up Art (Stuart Hammersley), 2010
A mark designed to act as a graphic element for creating background imagery and for holding text, images and pattern.

10. British Academy of Songwriters, Composers & Authors
Professional association, UK
Designed by Studio Dempsey (Mike Dempsey), 2008

11. Bolefloor
Hardwood flooring, The Netherlands
Designed by Loovvool (Hannes Unt), 2011
Bolefloor is the world's first industrial-scale producer of hardwood flooring with lengths that follow the curves of the tree's natural growth.

12. Beautiful Books
Publisher, UK
Designed by Studio Dempsey (Mike Dempsey), 2008

13. Broadgate
Mixed-use property development, UK
Designed by CDT Design, 1999
A broad and gate-like 'b'.

14. Bullionstream
Online trading platform, Germany
Designed by Six (Dan Bull), 2010
Bullionstream is a German start-up offering a digital platform for users to trade in the precious metals markets.

15. Bendis Financial
Leasing brokerage, Romania
Designed by Loovvool (Hannes Unt), 2010

16. The Brit Awards
Music awards, UK
Designed by Music (Anthony Smith, Craig Oldham), 2011
The outline of the new white trophy (to be customized by a different personality each year) forms the core of the new Brit Awards identity.

17. Caponata
Restaurant, UK
Designed by Atelier Works (John Powner, Lou Wood), 2008
The monogram for this Sicilian restaurant and music venue in London's Camden Town packs in references to both seasonal fare (colours) and music (the stave and distended finial).

6

7

8

9

10

11

12

13

14

15

16

17

18. The Central
Restaurant, Switzerland
Designed by Mixer (Erich Brechbruhl), 2009
You can't get more central in Lucerne than The Central.

19. Caviar Productions
Film and commercial production agency, Estonia
Designed by Loovvool (Hannes Unt), 2007

20. Crisp Media
Marketing and public relations agency, UK
Designed by Give Up Art (Stuart Hammersley), 2010
An agency intending to make waves, particularly in the hospitality sector, where monograms are popular.

21. Columbus
Retail centre, Finland
Designed by Hahmo (Antti Raudaskoski), 1996

22. Consortium for Street Children
Human rights network, UK
Designed by Purpose (Rob Howsam, Stuart Youngs, Piers Komlosy, Adam Loxley, Will Kinchin, Alice Reynolds), 2009
An international network working to make the voice of homeless youngsters heard, with a logotype that speaks for itself.

23. Creas Foundation
Social venture capital foundation, Spain
Designed by Estudio Diego Feijóo, 2009
A mark whose pie-chart-like spectrum of colours changes with every appearance, emphasizing the investor's interest in returns that aren't only economic.

24. Croydon Food Group
Industry networking group, UK
Designed by A2 Design, 2008

25. Corridor
Property developer, USA
Designed by Pentagram (Michael Gericke), 2010

26. Castleton
Signage manufacturer, UK
Designed by A2 Design, 2007

27. The Conspiracy Group
Branding agency, UK
Designed by &Smith, 2011

28. Conception Marketing
Marketing service, UK
Designed by The Chase (Ben Casey, Ivan Rowles), 2003

29. The Criterion Collection
DVD publisher, USA
Designed by Pentagram (Paula Scher, Julia Hoffmann), 2006
The hint of spinning film reels in this monogram for this New York-based publisher of contemporary and classic cinema on DVD.

18

19

20

21

22

23

24

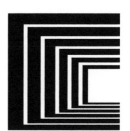

25

26

27

28

29

30. Dew Tour
Sports tour, USA
*Designed by Area 17
(Martin Rettenbacher,
Arnaud Mercier), 2008*
The Dew Tour is an 'action
sports tour', featuring a
series of events in which
athletes compete in
different skateboarding
and BMX disciplines.
The big 'D' takes its
curves from the ramps
of the tour.

31. Design Ranch
Design consultancy, USA
*Designed by Design
Ranch (Ingrid Sidie,
Michelle Sonderegger,
Michelle Martynowicz,
Jordan Gray), 2011*

**32. Diathlasis
Architectural Lighting**
Lighting design, Greece
*Designed by Designers
United (Dimitris
Koliadimas, Dimitris
Papazoglou), 2007*

33. Depken & Partner
Management
consultancy, Germany
*Designed by Thomas
Manss & Company, 2003*
A rotated ampersand,
doubling as the
initial 'D' lends a little
heritage to a young
firm of management
consultants.

34. East End Arts Club
Arts collective, UK
*Designed by Studio
Paradise (Samuel Moffat,
Jade Abbott), 2009*
All signs point to this
east London arts group
selling affordable prints
of their work.

35. Epromotores
Property agency, Spain
*Designed by Zorraquino
(Miguel Zorraquino, Miren
S Gaubeka), 2007*

**36. Engraved Stationery
Manufacturers
Association**
Professional association,
USA
*Designed by Chermayeff
& Geismar (Steff
Geissbuhler), 2007*

37. Expert Digital
Electronics retailer,
Romania
*Designed by Brandient
(Christian 'Kit' Paul), 2008*

**38. Edinburgh
International Festival**
Arts festival, UK
Designed by hat-trick
*(Gareth Howat, Jim
Sutherland, Alex
Swatridge), 2009*
Three pointers in
different directions:
drama, music and dance,
the three art forms at
the festival.

39. Feesability
Litigation budgeting
software, UK
*Designed by Ummocrono
(Fredrik Jönsson, Nina
Wollner), 2010*
Feesability produces a
web-based application
for compiling litigation
budgets – the first
system of its kind, hence
the milestone.

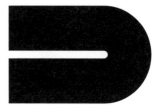

30

31

32

33

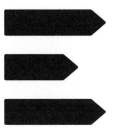

34

35

36

37

38

39

40. Friends of the Simon Stevin Institute for Geometry
Friends society, The Netherlands
Designed by Boy Bastiaens/Stormhand, 2008

41. The Forge
Music venue, UK
Designed by Atelier Works (John Powner, Lou Wood), 2008

42. Fluid Nail Design
Professional nail products supplier, Australia
Designed by Studio Paradise (Samuel Moffat, Jade Abbott), 2007
A liquid 'F' for this producer of nail varnishes, polishes and other products.

43. Friday
Personal services, Belgium
Designed by Coast (Frederic Vanhorenbeke), 2010
Friday is a concept for a range of 'morning-after-the-night-before' services, ranging from 'recovery water' to divorce lawyers.

44. Further
Design consultancy, UK
Designed by Further (James Beveridge, Ben Jeffery, Andy Mosley), 2009

45. Ai Fiori
Restaurant, USA
Designed by The O Group (Jason B Cohen, Eric Baker), 2010
Ai Fiori ('Among the Flowers') serves French and Italian cuisine at the Setai Fifth Avenue Hotel in New York.

46. G Design Studio
Design consultancy, Greece
Designed by G Design Studio (Michalis Georgiou, Alexandros Gavrilakis), 2006
Two partners, two ears.

47. The Guinness Partnership
Affordable homes partnership, UK
Designed by Spencer du Bois (John Spencer), 2008
A single letter to link 16 partner organizations around the UK.

48. Hakoltov
Content production and editing service, Israel
Designed by Yotam Hadar, 2008

49. Hand
Design consultancy, UK
Designed by Hand, 2010
Two pointing hands make an 'H' and symbolize the studio's ability to provide clear direction for brands.

50. Helen Brown Massage
Massage therapist, UK
Designed by Magpie Studio (David Azurdia, Ben Christie, Jamie Ellul), 2008
An initial made from the tools of Helen Brown's trade. A mark that shouldn't leave marks, maybe.

40

41

42

43

44

45

46

47

48

49

50

51. Hourigan International
Recruitment consultancy, Australia
Designed by SML (Vanessa Ryan), 2008
Hourigan offers a step up in the world to executives in the media and marketing industries.

52. Highly Solar Energy
Solar energy conversion technology provider, China
Designed by Hesign International (Jianping He), 2009

53. The Halcyon Hotel
Hotel, UK
Designed by Mytton Williams (Bob Mytton, Matt Michaluk, Keith Hancox), 2009
A stylish, contemporary monogram for a hotel in Bath, a city full of traditional places to stay.

54. Hostage
Film and commercial production agency, UK
Designed by The Chase (Stewart Price), 2006
Commercials for captive audiences.

55. Heinrup
Bag manufacturer, UK
Designed by *DesignStudio (Ben Wright, Paul Stafford), 2010*
Heinrup was established in 2010 by a Swedish Central Saint Martin's graduate, Anna Heinrup, with the intention of bringing out just one exclusive collection of men's and unisex bags each year. Its monogram reflects Heinrup's strong, simple, contemporary aesthetic, and the 'slow fashion' concept of creating timeless designs.

56. Hermes Mass Transit
Bus services, The Netherlands
Designed by Onoma (Roger van den Bergh), 1995
A good letter for buses, 'H'; the monogram can be flipped and used on both sides of the vehicle.

57. Harrow View
Mixed-use development, UK
Designed by Magpie Studio (David Azurdia, Ben Christie, Jamie Ellul, Will Southward), 2010
Harrow View is a large-scale development by Land Securities on the site of Kodak's former UK HQ – a heritage referred to in the scheme's identity.

58. Howe Baugeschäft
Construction company, Germany
Designed by Claudius Design (Stefan Claudius), 2007

59. Ian Chilvers
Designer, UK
Designed by Atelier Works (Ian Chilvers), 2001
In 2001, Ian Chilvers was asked to design a 3-D initial by a sign company wishing to demonstrate its prowess at manufacturing. He came up with this – then adopted it for himself.

60. Janelle
Essential oils company, Hong Kong
Designed by gardens&co (Wilson Tang), 2004

61. Jade Jagger for yoo
Interior stylist, UK
Designed by SomeOne (Laura Hussey, David Law, Simon Manchipp), 2007
A monogram intended to reflect Jade Jagger's 'flowing, organic interior design style', used in property developments by yoo, the partnership between Philippe Starck and John Hitchcox.

62. Katz PR
Public relations company, UK
Designed by Brownjohn (James Beveridge, Tom Rogers), 2008
Katz prides itself on teasing out newsworthy PR for its property industry clients.

51

52

53

54

55

56

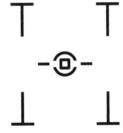

57

58

59

60

61

62

63. Kilver Dance Studio
Dance studio, UK
Designed by Taxi Studio (Spencer Buck, Ryan Wills), 2008
A dance studio founded by Shelley Dean (former choreographer to Kylie Minogue) and Roger Saul (co-founder of the Mulberry fashion label) puts its best foot forward. The studio is based at Saul's Kilver Court house and gardens in Shepton Mallet.

64. Kondyli Publishing
Publisher, Greece
Designed by G Design Studio (Michalis Georgiou, Alexandros Gavrilakis), 2010

65. Kurakuen
Suburban district, Japan
Designed by Ken Miki & Associates, 1998
A monogram to promote a district of Nishinomiya City, overlooking Osaka Bay.

66. K College
Further and higher education college, UK
Designed by Rose, 2010
An identity for a new institution: K College was formed from the merger of West Kent College and South Kent College. Its monogram points in both directions.

67. Leo Houlding
Mountain climber, UK
Designed by Fivefootsix, 2008
Leo Houlding is a climbing prodigy who scales the world's most daunting rockfaces (such as El Capitan, a 600 m (1,970 ft) vertical cliff in Yosemite Valley) and crevasses.

68. Linden Centre for Contemporary Art
Art centre, Australia
Designed by Design By Pidgeon (David Pidgeon), 2009
A mark that reinforces Linden's claim to be a cornerstone for new art and artists in Victoria.

69. Layezee Beds
Bed manufacturer, UK
Designed by The Chase, 2003

70. Maruhon
Lumber trading company, Japan
Designed by Ken Miki & Associates, 1990
An 'M' inspired by diagonally cut timber.

71. m+associés
Marketing partnership, France
Designed by A2 Design, 2002
This 'm' doubles as a bridge, representing the unity between this partnership of small, successful French marketing firms.

72. Matta
Clothing and homewares retailer, USA
Designed by Mucca Design (Matteo Bologna, Christine Celic Strohl), 2004
Translating from the Italian as 'crazy woman', Matta was opened in New York's SoHo by designer Cristina Gitti, selling her urban-meets-East Indian fashions and fabrics. Its hand-drawn monogram captures the same texture and sophisticated feminine design.

73. The Malings
Family, Australia
Designed by Naughtyfish (Paul Garbett, Elise Santangelo), 2007
A modern family crest designed for Edith and Greyston Maling, playing on the sound of their name.

74. Melanie Grant
Jewellery broker, UK
Designed by Moot Design (Nitesh Mody), 2010
A monogram for a high-end jewellery broker that aims to recall the opulence of 1930s Paris.

63

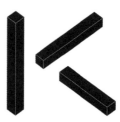

64

65

66

67

68

69

70

71

72

73

74

75. Manchester Literary Festival
Literary events, UK
Designed by Mark Studio, 2008
Originality in visual ideas tends not to flow from research and analysis of what already exists. Research can help to steer the creative mind in the right direction, but the ideas that make us sit up and take notice tend to bubble up out of a very human, unpredictable mixture of intuition, experience and random, inspirational events, such as an accidental collision of letterforms, the misreading of a word or image, a slip of the tongue or a shape seen in the things around us. The quietly iconic identity for the Manchester Literature Festival is an example of this.

The MLF was established in 2006 from the legacy of its highly successful predecessor, the Manchester Poetry Festival. The competition, both from other literary festivals around the UK and from Manchester's own crowded cultural scene, necessitated a strong, immediate identifier.

Mark Lester, founder of local design group Mark Studio, was staring vacantly at his bookshelves one day, possibly mulling over which volume might offer inspiration, when the solution presented itself sooner than he expected. 'I was fortunate that the letter "M" lends itself particularly well to a natural arrangement of books,' says Lester. Crafting the idea, he adds, took a good while longer.

Several years on, the reception to the logo continues to be very positive. Feedback suggests that its bold simplicity is a strong draw for corporate partners, funders and audiences.

76. Meyers Deli
Delicatessen, Denmark
Designed by Punktum Design (Søren Varming) and A2/SW/HK (Henrik Kubel), 2006
Part of a food group owned by Danish TV chef Claus Meyer. The theme of vertical bars, punctuated by the 'M' monogram, runs across packaging, stores and the group's other brands.

77. Mothercare
Retailer, UK
Designed by Pentagram (John Rushworth), 2004
Having dropped the maternal 'm' mark in the mid 1990s, Mothercare went to Pentagram's John Rushworth to redraw and revive it in 2004.

78. Museion
Contemporary art museum, Italy
Designed by Tomato (Michael Horsham), 2008
A spectacular, translucent cube, whose entrance is symbolized in this logo, Museion is a new landmark in Bolzano, northern Italy.

79. Mouttet
Food and pharmaceuticals company, Trinidad
Designed by Atelier Works (Quentin Newark), 2007
An abbreviation (from Victor Mouttet, long retired) that allows this holding company to 'hallmark' other companies as it adds them to its roster.

76

77

78

79

80. Mutants
Record label, UK
*Designed by Malone
Design (David Malone),
2010*

**81. Ilkka Marttiini
Finland**
Blacksmith, Finland
*Designed by Hahmo
(Jenni Kuokka,
Pekka Piippo, Antti
Raudaskoski), 2008*

82. M.Digest
Financial planning
newsletter, Hong Kong
*Designed by gardens&co
(Wilson Tang, Jeffrey
Tam), 2009*

83. Muzik
Music school, Israel
*Designed by Oded Ezer,
2005*
A confident, modern
mark for the first
independent music
school of its kind in the
Middle East, training
future artists and
producers in the creative
applications of music
technologies.

84. Marubiru
Mixed-use development,
Japan
*Designed by Chermayeff
& Geismar (Emanuela
Frigerio, Frank Dylla),
2002*
A 37-storey retail and
office tower at the exit
of Tokyo station whose
lower floors echo its
predecessor on the site:
an eight-storey building
completed in 1923, which
was, for a long time, the
tallest building in Asia
and a symbol of the
modern city.

85. The Mainstone Press
Art book publisher, UK
*Designed by Magpie
Studio (David Azurdia,
Ben Christie, Jamie Ellul),
2010*

**86. Museu d'Arquelogica
de Catalunya**
Archaeology museum,
Spain
*Designed by Summa
(Josep Maria Mir), 2000*

87. Merlin
Charity, UK
*Designed by Spencer du
Bois (Ben James), 2010*
Merlin specializes in
international health work,
sending medical experts
to major emergencies to
mobilize aid, shelter and
treatment.

88. Manbulloo
Mango farms, Australia
*Designed by Inkahoots,
2006*
An 'M' as voluptuous as
the Kensington Pride
mango, Manbulloo's
trademark fruit.

89. Nafsica
Singer-songwriter, USA
*Designed by G Design
Studio (Alexandros
Gavrilakis), 2010*

90. Northshore
Mixed-use development,
UK
*Designed by B&W Studio,
2008*
A solid-looking mark for
a proposed regeneration
project on the site of
Stockton-on-Tees'
former shipyards by
Urban Splash and Muse
Developments. The equal
length of the name's two
components allows the
square to be divided into
a balanced 'N' shape.

80

81

82

83

84

85

86

87

88

89

90

91. Pagliano Arredamenti
Furniture retailer, Italy
Designed by Giovanni Brunazzi, 1970
Occasionally, a symbol or logotype you've never seen before will stop you in your tracks. Out of nowhere – on a website for an obscure book publisher, for example, or over a hardware shop in a foreign town – a symbol or logotype will appear that is so arresting it seems to deserve a greater stage. The identity for Pagliano Arredamenti is just that kind.

Designed in 1970 for a furniture store close to the River Po in Casale Monferrato, a town in Piedmont, north-west Italy, it can be seen big, brilliant and proud on the company's white delivery vans. The company, established in 1933 by Giovanni Pagliano, specializes in planning and supplying modular furniture for kitchens, bedrooms and offices, such as shelving and storage systems.

In 1970, Pagliano's sons, Carlo and Emilio, asked Giovanni Brunazzi, a young, unknown graphic designer, to create a new symbol for the business. This logo is what he came up with: a 'P' made of two similar modular components fitting snugly together; bright red, too, as if part of a groovy new furniture system. A letter, a picture, a symbol made memorable with the minimum of elements.

The identity helped to establish both the designer and his client: Brunazzi went on to design identities for major clients such as Iveco, and founded Brunazzi & Associati, one of Italy's most successful branding consultancies; and Pagliano became one of the leading Italian suppliers of contemporary European furniture.

The mark did achieve wider recognition: it was selected by the celebrated French art critic Pierre Restany for the design section of *L'Enciclopedia dell'Arte.* But since then it hasn't been seen much outside Piedmont. It is published here to celebrate the logos that take you by surprise.

92. Nichols Consultancy
Headhunter, UK
Designed by Kimpton (David Kimpton, Katie Alger), 2010
A compass needle represents this headhunter's aim of pinpointing talent and guiding it to the right employers.

93. Pin Point Events
Event organizer, UK
Designed by Company, 2008

94. Paternoster Square
Mixed-use development, UK
Designed by CDT Design, 2003
The dome of St Paul's Cathedral marks the vicinity of this large retail and office scheme.

95. Popular
Music management agency, UK
Designed by Form (Paula Benson, Paul West, Matt Le Gallez), 2010
During a brainstorming session for this identity, a piece of A4 paper was folded at the corner to create the letter 'P', and the idea stuck.

92

93

94

95

96. Papatzanakis
Insurance brokerage, Greece
Designed by Designers United (Dimitris Koliadimas, Dimitris Papazoglou), 2010
A 'P'-shaped hermit crab shell suggests a sense of security and confidence.

97. Panthalassa
Super yacht, Italy
Designed by Powell Allen (Kerrie Powell, Chris Allen), 2009
A mark in the mould of a luxury brand for a luxury 56 m (184 ft) yacht with interiors by Foster + Partners. The monogram echoes the sweeping curves of the interiors and the contour lines of bathymetric charts.

98. Peak Performance
Sportswear label, Sweden
Designed by Stockholm Design Lab, 2008
A sharp-looking monogram for Scandinavia's largest functional sportswear label.

99. QVC
Broadcast retailer, USA
Designed by Mode (USA) (John Pietrafesa, Ian Varrassi, Maxim Vakhovskiy), 2007
A 'Q' that is also a cue to unwrap, and to start ordering gifts from QVC.

100. Raleigh International
Charity, UK
Designed by SEA (Bryan Edmondson), 2008
Raleigh runs life-changing volunteer expeditions in Borneo, India, Costa Rica and Nicaragua. Its stencil logotype and monogram evokes destination names painted on crates bound for far-away places.

101. Rock
Waterproofing systems provider, UK
Designed by Dowling Duncan (John Dowling, Rob Duncan), 2009

102. Ramblers
Charity, UK
Designed by Spencer du Bois (John Spencer, Amelia Costly, Alan Meeks), 2009
A tree trunk or a stem? A leaf or a pebble? Ramblers is the UK's walking charity, and its

monogram is whatever you find on your way.

103. Sansaw
Mixed-use organic estate, UK
Designed by SEA (Bryan Edmondson), 2007
Sansaw is a family-run rural estate and community in Shropshire that includes an organic farm, housing and offices for rent.

104. Roost
Homewares retailer, Australia
Designed by Sadgrove Design (Brian Sadgrove), 1995

105. Slurk
Café, Denmark
Designed by We Recommend, 2008
A tang of fruit peel in this identity for a Copenhagen juice and coffee shop.

106. Shift
Photographic exhibition, UK
Designed by Magpie Studio (David Azurdia, Ben Christie, Jamie Ellul), 2009
A shift in the digital camera's viewfinder makes a monogram for this exhibition about movement through London.

107. Sociotrendy
Sociological research body, Czech Republic
Designed by Toman Graphic Design (Jiri Toman), 2004

96

97

98

99

100

101

102

103

104

105

106

107

108. The Rogers Flooring Company
Flooring installation company, UK
Designed by Tom Rogers, 2009
Great visual ideas are hiding away, waiting to be discovered, in the names and occupations of people and businesses everywhere. But it takes a special kind of mind, and sometimes a special kind of client, for them to be sniffed out and put to work. Tom Rogers' client was special.

Phil Rogers has run his own small flooring business in rural Somerset, south-west England, since the early 1990s, specializing in carpeting, wooden flooring and restoration work for customers across the UK. His two eldest sons followed him into the business; Tom, their younger brother, went into graphic design.

After graduating from Somerset College of Arts & Technology in 2008, already with a D&AD New Blood Best Of Show Award under his belt, Tom went straight into a job with Brownjohn in London's West End. It was a dream start to his career, but he was still having problems explaining to his family what exactly it was he was doing as a 'graphic designer'. He decided to present them with an identity for the family business that would explain everything – a unique identity that reflected all that they did in a simple typographic mark.

He had set himself a tough brief, and inspiration was not forthcoming. 'I got stuck on the idea of the leg of an "R" (for "Rogers"), rolling up, representing a carpet, but I felt that that only represented one aspect of what they do, and could potentially make them look more like suppliers. After a few evenings spent working on it, I literally stumbled across it. By writing down lists of what they do, I came up with the fact that they "lay flooring", which resulted in that moment of realization; by lying a

lowercase "r" on its side, I could illustrate this in one succinct mark.'

The company – and family – gained an identity to be proud of; one that reflects the professionalism and quality of their work, and that positions them well for working alongside interior designers on projects. There is inspiration everywhere, but you have to look hard – sometimes, under the carpet – to find it.

109. Sterling Relocation
Relocation and removals service, UK
Designed by Spencer du Bois (John Spencer), 2009
Two arrows make an 'S' for this international home-moving business.

110. Taskers
Recruitment agency, The Netherlands
Designed by Boy Bastiaens/Stormhand, 2010

111. Taste Tideswell
Local enterprise campaign, UK
Designed by Peter and Paul (Peter Donohoe, Paul Reardon, Lee Davies), 2010
A campaign to promote Tideswell, a village in England's Peak District, as a food destination, put its trust in an edible 'T'.

112. Grupo Tragaluz
Restaurant group, Spain
Designed by Mario Eskenazi, 2008

109

110

111

GRUPO TRAGALUZ

112

113. Terrine
Restaurant, Germany
*Designed by SWSP
Design (Georg Schatz),
2006*

**114. National Training
Awards**
Employer awards, UK
*Designed by Purpose
(Stuart Youngs, Adam
Browne, Paul Felton,
Phil Skinner), 2010*

115. Ian Terry
Interior plants company,
UK
*Designed by Atelier
Works (John Powner,
Giovanni Rodolphi), 1999*
For a company that
takes the edge off office
interiors, a leafy 'T'.

116. Thompson Gallery
Fine art gallery, UK
Designed by GBH, 2001

117. Towner Gallery
Contemporary art
gallery, UK
*Designed by Together
Design, 2009*
A mark intended to
attract the widest
possible audience to this
award-winning municipal
gallery in Eastbourne,
and fashioned from a
single strip of paper to
reflect the sharp edges
and clean planes of its
new home, designed by
Rick Mather Architects.

118. Tinley Road
Fashion and footwear
label, UK
*Designed by Dowling
Duncan (Rob Duncan,
John Dowling, Lily
Piyathaisere), 2010*
A T-junction that is
used to create a repeat
pattern, like a street
grid, and to mark Tinley
Road as a destination
for the fashion-
conscious female.

119. Tom Devine
Property consultant, UK
*Designed by Elmwood
(Jon Stubley, Stephen
Woowat, Mark Howe),
2010*

120. U.Coffee
Coffee importer and
retailer, Japan
*Designed by Ken Miki &
Associates, 1989*
This brand of Ueshima
Coffee Foods has the
aroma of a coffee cup.

121. Unesta
Property services, UK
*Designed by Momin
Branding (Irfan Ahmed,
Daniel Matthews), 2009*
Based in London, Unesta
helps clients to invest in
property in India.

122. Unity Law
Legal practice, UK
*Designed by Peter and
Paul (Peter Donohoe,
Paul Reardon, Lee
Davies), 2010*
Unity Law specializes in
winning compensation
for employees who have
suffered accidents at
work, and its logo is
appropriately consumer-
facing.

123. Villalagos
Property development,
Uruguay
*Designed by Untitled
(David Hawkins, Glenn
Howard), 2007*

124. Vanity
Waxing salon, UK
*Designed by Studio
Paradise (Samuel Moffat,
Jade Abbott), 2010*
Vanity is a Brazilian
waxing salon; its logo
alludes delicately to the
area of concern.

113

114

115

116

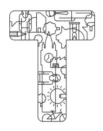

117

118

119

120

121

122

123

124

125. Verasis
Banking software, UK
Designed by A2 Design, 2005

126. Vitamed
Pharmaceutical company, Israel
Designed by Dan Reisinger, 1987

127. Viper Subsea
Offshore engineering provider, UK
Designed by Mytton Williams (Bob Mytton, Matt Michaluk), 2010
Named after the viperfish – not the snake – that inhabits the deep sea, Viper specializes in services and high-precision products for the offshore oil and gas industry.

128. Vivid
Home accessories retailer, Hong Kong
Designed by Hesign International (Jianping He, Jun Dai, Yawei Zhai), 2009

129. Verida Credit
Mortgage provider, Romania
Designed by Brandient (Iancu Barbarasa), 2008

130. The Waterfront
Residential development, Australia
Designed by SML (Vanessa Ryan, Troy Dagan), 2009

131. Whittingham
Furniture manufacturer, UK
Designed by Johnson Banks, 1994

132. Watermark
Women's leadership forum, USA
Designed by Moving Brands, 2010
This rippling mark for a San Francisco Bay Area women's networking forum (the Forum for Women Entrepreneurs & Executives) sprang from the notion of 'emanating influences'.

133. W'Law Weber Wicki Partners
Legal practice, Switzerland
Designed by Gottschalk + Ash International (Fritz Gottschalk, Sascha Lötscher, Irmi Wachendorff), 2009
A winking 'W' signals a more personal, direct contact with clients from this small, independent law firm.

134. Woolworths South Africa
Retail chain, South Africa
Designed by Vignelli Associates (Massimo Vignelli, Beatriz Cifuentes), 2009
The Woolworths brand in South Africa has no connection with its British/American namesake. More of a department store, specializing in food and clothing, it was modelled on Marks & Spencer in its early years. This typically unfussy mark from Vignelli Associates replaced a strangely Art Deco-style wordmark and 'W' in 2009.

135. YMCA of the USA
Charity, USA
Designed by Siegel & Gale, 2010
The YMCA's rebrand was prompted by inconsistency at local level and by a sense that its role in society – from championing civil rights to inventing volleyball – was not as well known as its gyms, swimming lessons and famous musical tributes. Its new identity adopts its widely used nickname – the Y – and softens the corners and colours of the previous logo to appeal to its modern, all-faith, all-ages, unisex audience.

136. Yritys 2.0
Research agency, Finland
Designed by Hahmo (Antti Raudaskoski), 2007
Yritys 2.0 ('Company 2.0') studies the impact of social media on businesses.

125

126

127

128

129

130

131

132

133

134

135

136

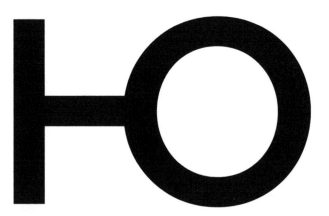

1. Hotel Olympia
Hotel, Greece
Designed by Designers United (Dimitris Koliadimas, Dimitris Papazoglou), 2006
It is often said that recessions and economic hardship stimulate greater levels of invention and creativity. It would seem on the surface that Greece's economic woes have had exactly that effect on the country's design community, prompting the emergence of a new, exciting generation of Greek graphic design studios.

There is little in the way of a graphic culture in Greece; the economy progressed from farming to tourism without first developing a manufacturing industry or the skills to brand and market companies and products to consumers. The country had no big brands or progressive businesses to champion design. Besides the striking 1960s travel posters of Freddie Carabott and Michalis Katzourakis, Greece has failed to win much in the way of international recognition for its design output.

Now, though, a new swell of design talent in the peninsula is making waves on the blogosphere, led by young, smart, English-speaking studios such as G Design Studio and Pi6 in Athens and Designers United in Thessaloniki. Their work is as visually sophisticated, rich in ideas and polished in its execution as anything else in Europe.

This identity for the newly refurbished Hotel Olympia in the centre of Thessaloniki is a good example, working on several levels with just a circle and two lines. First, it is a monogram of the name. Second, the reduction to these particular two letters (the same as in the molecular formula for water) offers a reference to the hotel's past life as a spa and a popular landmark of the city – a strong focus of the design brief. Third, the mark is an image

synonymous with hotels: a room key in a lock.

If Greek tourism, and its industry in general, could embrace the fresh thinking of its emerging design community, it would do the country's recovery no harm.

2. University of East Anglia
University, UK
Designed by Blast (Giff, Paul Tunnicliffe, Henry Sly, Martin Cox), 2008
Integrated initials convey the interdisciplinary nature of study at UEA, while highlighting an all-important creative spark.

3. Wood&Wood
Sign manufacturer, UK
Designed by Pentagram (Alan Fletcher), 1970
Designed by the late, great Alan Fletcher when Pentagram was still Crosby/Fletcher/Forbes, the Wood&Wood trademark capitalizes on what Fletcher called the 'logobility' – 'the capacity of a name to lend itself to typographic conversion' – of the double 'W'. More than 40 years later, the compact, engaging mark still makes the perfect sign for a sign company.

4. Victoria & Albert Museum
Museum, UK
Designed by Pentagram (Alan Fletcher), 1989
The strength, elegance and ingenuity of the V&A logotype, not to mention the three-dimensional quality that makes it so appropriate for a museum of beautiful objects, have made it a perennial favourite of graphic designers.

Alan Fletcher originally suggested that the museum apply the overlapping V&A logo that Michael Peters had created for V&A Enterprises, across the whole organization. The client insisted on something new. Fletcher's then-assistant Quentin Newark remembers wrestling with the Bodoni letterforms: 'I was pursuing a route trying to make the "waiter's hand" of the ampersand into the crossbar of the "A", but couldn't work out how to deal with the thin

downstroke. It looked awful. Alan scowled. The client was coming in for a progress meeting at 10am the next day.

'Alan came in at 9.30am – almost unheard of. He was very excited. He leaned over my ugly drawing and sliced off the downstroke of the "A". I just looked, trying to understand how he had known to do that, and I – who had struggled with the letters for two weeks – had not. We presented a photocopy at the meeting, and everyone knew that that cockled scrap of paper was something special.'

5. Nina Matos
Marketing consultancy, Singapore
Designed by B&B Studio (Shaun Bowen, George Hartley), 2009
Both an 'N' and an 'M', this minimalist mark expresses the collaboration of the two partners.

2

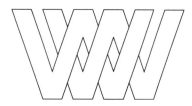

3

4

5

6. Warm Ground
Heating systems
specialist, UK
*Designed by Dowling
Duncan (John Dowling,
Rob Duncan, Eileen Lee),
2010*
Fashioning two initials
from a single element
warms up this identity
for an underfloor heating
specialist.

7. Yauatcha Atelier
Porcelain teaware
supplier, UK
Designed by North, 2009
An identity in the
ancient tradition of
makers' marks for the
fine china enterprise of
restaurateur Alan Yau.

8. *Your Wembley*
Magazine, UK
*Designed by Magpie
Studio (David Azurdia,
Ben Christie, Jamie Ellul,
Tim Fellowes), 2010*

**9. Zepter Museum of
Modern Arts**
Modern art museum,
Belgrade
*Designed by SVIDesign
(Sasha Vidakovic), 2009*
This museum was funded
by philanthropist Philip
Zepter, founder of the
Zepter International
conglomerate and one
of the world's richest
Serbs. Its identity
emulates an artist's
signature-scribble.

10. Philppe Guignard
Hospitality group,
Switzerland
*Designed by >moser,
2009*
This monogram reflects
the passion that pastry
chef Philippe Guignard
puts into his group of
restaurants and hotels.

**11. Nursing & Midwifery
Council**
Regulatory body, UK
*Designed by CDT Design,
2007*
Solid, conjoined
letterforms express
the trustworthiness
and solidarity of the
organization.

12. Mobilrabatten
Software developer,
Sweden
*Designed by
Lundgren+Lundqvist,
2010*
Mobilrabatten's app
tells smartphone users
about discounts and
special offers at shops
and restaurants in their
vicinity.

13. Red Felix
Events management
agency, UK
*Designed by Magpie
Studio (David Azurdia,
Ben Christie, Jamie Ellul),
2009*

**14. Neila Cohalan
Wyman**
Psychotherapist, USA
*Designed by Lance
Wyman, 1993*
Clarity, support and
flexibility in letter form.

**15. Mental Health
Foundation**
Charity, UK
*Designed by SEA (Bryan
Edmondson), 2010*

**16. Multimédia
Sorbonne**
Postgraduate faculty,
France
*Designed by Naji El Mir,
2006*
A Lebanese designer
resident in Paris, Naji El
Mir blends influences
from the visual cultures
of Europe and the Arab
world in his work. After
completing his Masters
in Interactive Multimedia
at Paris-Sorbonne
University, he was asked
to design a logotype for
the school.

17. Penrhyn Books
Publisher, UK
*Designed by FL@33
(Agathe Jacquillat, Tomi
Vollauschek), 2010*
After designing and
typesetting 'The Bitter
Sea', a series of books
on Roman Britain, by
historian and publisher
David Leedham, FL@33
developed this identity
for Leedham's imprint,
Penrhyn Books.

6

7

8

9

10

11

12

13

14

15

16

17

18. *The Obstetrician &*
Gynaecologist
Professional journal, UK
Designed by Atelier
Works (Ian Chilvers),
2008
Of course, it's not simply
the vision of the designer
that brings beautiful,
memorable corporate
marks into being. Without
client support, a great
idea will remain just that:
a great idea. A client
who is able to nurture
creative opportunities
can pave the way for
fresh, innovative design
in the unlikeliest places.
A learned medical journal,
for example.

The Obstetrician &
Gynaecologist (O&G)
is the peer-reviewed
quarterly journal for
continuing professional
development from the
UK's Royal College
of Obstetricians and
Gynaecologists. In
2008, Atelier Works
redesigned the journal
to bring structure, clarity
and ease of use to the
layouts. In the process,
editor-in-chief Professor
Neil McClure became
a champion of the
designer's cause.

'He seemed to believe
strongly in the project
and lobbied hard
to get the changes
through various internal
committees,' says Ian
Chilvers. 'Professor
McClure's manner
was very much like a
thoughtful and decisive
surgeon who was out
to fix a malady. Like any
good surgeon, he is used
to working with a team
of other specialists.
As a designer, I was
just another specialist
supporting him on a new
case.'

The reinterpretation of
the scientific shorthand
for 'female' as a pair of
letters – the journal's
initials – developed in
Chilvers' mind while
working on the layouts.
It created a symbiosis
that fitted the new
typographic front cover
style, and that *O&G's*
eminent editorial board
instantly warmed to.

McClure himself calls
the logo 'a stroke of
genius'. 'The journal has
gone from strength to
strength, and is now read

worldwide. Clearly the
quality of the content
has been vital to this but
the layout and the image
of the journal are what
make it identifiable and
accessible, and Ian's
scheme has given us
exactly the persona that
we wanted.'

19. The Women's
Organisation
Campaigning group, UK
Designed by Uniform
(Rachel Veniard), 2010
Formerly known as Train
2000, The Women's
Organisation encourages
entrepreneurialism with
training and advice for
women in business.
Its mark manages to
be both maternal and
professional.

20. The Armenian
Lexicon & Library
Project
Educational project, UK/
USA/Armenia
Designed by Studio
Special (David Lovelock),
2010
Armenian is an
endangered language,
which is why an
international group of
linguists is creating an
online bilingual lexicon
of Western Armenian. Its
logo combines a Western
'A' with the Armenian 'H'
character (for *Hayeren*,
the name of the Armenian
language) – which also,
fortuitously, resembles a
'Z', which means it can be
interpreted by everyone,
not just the linguists.

21. Kagawa Education
Institute of Nutrition
University, Japan
Designed by Ken Miki &
Associates, 2001
Aya Kagawa was a Tokyo
doctor who helped
to cure beriberi by
advocating the inclusion
of whole (unpolished)
rice in patients' diets. The
institute that bears her
name educates experts
in nutrition, food and
health; its logo, a stylized
'kn', aims to express 'the
rhythm of life'.

22. Hangar 10
Luxury jet hangar, USA
Designed by Design
Ranch (Ingrid Sidie,
Michelle Sonderegger,
Jeff Miller), 2010

19

20

21

22

23. 33RPM
Marketing company, UK
*Designed by B&W Studio
(Lee Bradley, Andy
Myers), 2009*
The initials of the
company's founder make
for a retro name. The
logo, though, is strictly
contemporary.

**24. Design Leadership
Award**
Professional award,
Hong Kong
*Designed by CoDesign
(Hung Lam), 2004*
A monogram that
celebrates the
'backbone' of the design
industry: corporate
leaders who apply design
strategically, and to
whom this award is given.

25. Martín Faixó
Winery, Spain
*Designed by Mario
Eskenazi, 2007*
For a winery named after
its husband-and-wife
owners, a logotype that
uses a stencil typeface
to unite their two initials,
in a similar manner to
the National Theatre's
former 'NT' mark by FHK
Henrion.

26. Lambeth First
Local partnership, UK
*Designed by Atelier
Works (Ian Chilvers),
2002*
Lambeth First is the Local
Strategic Partnership
for this south London
borough, giving
residents, businesses,
local services and
voluntary groups a say on
important local issues.

**27. Mondays At The
Foyer**
Musical events, Greece
*Designed by Designers
United (Dimitris
Koliadimas, Dimitris
Papazoglou), 2008*
To badge a series
of informal musical
interludes in the lobby
of Thessaloniki Concert
Hall, Designers United
fused drop capitals from
the Greek words for
'Monday' and 'foyer' (Δ
and Φ), to create a hybrid
symbol with resonances
of a treble clef.

28. John Digweed
DJ and producer, UK
*Designed by Malone
Design (David Malone),
2009*

**29. Shenkar College of
Engineering & Design**
Higher education college,
Israel
*Designed by Dan
Reisinger, 1982*
Dan Reisinger created
this mark for what, in
1982, was the Shenkar
College of Textile
Technology & Fashion
(known locally simply
as Shenkar), weaving
together an 'S' and the
Hebrew 'shin' (similar
in shape to a 'W'). The
mark was retained when
the name of the college
changed to reflect its
broader range of study.

30. Regatta Design
Cabinet door
manufacturer, Finland
*Designed by Hahmo
(Pekka Piippo,
Jenni Kuokka, Antti
Raudaskoski, Erik Bertell,
Hanna Hakala), 2008*

31. The British Larder
Restaurant, UK
*Designed by Peter and
Paul (Paul Reardon, Peter
Horridge), 2010*
An award-winning Suffolk
restaurant with its own
online 'recipe diary' and a
mark that uses an etching
style of shading to reflect
the artisan nature of the
establishment's food.

32. Lafayette Centre
Mixed-use development,
USA
*Designed by Lance
Wyman, 1984*
An intricate mark
intended to suggest
metalwork from the
period of the War of
Independence, in which
the Marquis de Lafayette
made his name.

33. CACT
Contemporary art
museum, Greece
*Designed by Designers
United (Dimitris
Koliadimas, Dimitris
Papazoglou), 2006*
A logotype for CACT –
the Thessaloniki Center
of Contemporary Art
– that fuses the capital
initials of the Greek
words for 'Art' and
'Center' (T and K), to
create a mnemonic of the
building's characteristic
wooden roof.

34. J Herwitt
Jeweller, USA
*Designed by Elixir Design
(Jennifer Jerde, Karin
Bryant, Nathan Durrant),
2005*
Jennifer Herwitt's
creations are all inspired
by insects.

23

D

24

25

1

26

27

28

29

30

31

32

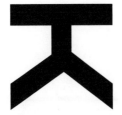

33

34

35. Deborah A Nilson
Legal practice, USA
*Designed by Area 17
(Audrey Templier), 2009*
All three initials in a
minimum of strokes make
an elegant monogram for
this attorney-at-law.

36. ArtWorks
Art education awards, UK
*Designed by Magpie
Studio (David Azurdia,
Ben Christie, Jamie Ellul,
Aimi Awang), 2008*

37. Cally Arts
Public art commissioner,
UK
*Designed by Practice
+ Theory (Andreas
Pohancenik), 2008*
A mark for a group that
works with King's Cross-
area artists in London to
create community-led
artworks and to get the
message out about the
social benefits of public
art projects.

38. Fothergill Wyatt
Property agency, UK
*Designed by Purpose
(Stuart Youngs, Faye
Greenwood, Adam
Browne), 2010*
In its understatement,
a distinctive move away
from the typical estate
agent's identity.

39. RBH Multimedia
Exhibition design
company, USA
*Designed by C&G
Partners (Steff
Geissbuhler), 2000*

40. Kingsland School
School, UK
*Designed by Atelier
Works (John Powner),
1996*
For a north London
school that was starting
afresh under a new
headteacher, an 'S' that
is also a celebratory
banner.

41. Good Co.
Coffee retailer, Australia
*Designed by Landor
Associates (Jason Little,
Joao Peres), 2009*

42. Faber & Faber
Book publisher, UK
*Designed by Pentagram
(John McConnell), 1981*
John McConnell
designed the famous
'ff' monogram and,
over a 15-year period,
established an instantly
identifiable look for
Faber & Faber's titles that
contributed hugely to the
publisher's growth.

43. Institute of Directors
Membership
organization, UK
*Designed by Pentagram
(Alan Fletcher), 1993*
Alan Fletcher's classical
logotype for the IoD
takes a more serious
and reflective tone than
most of his corporate
marks, in keeping with
the nature of the client.
It still plays a neat visual
trick, though, in sizing
each initial in accordance
with its importance.
The 'phi' symbol (Φ) he
created for art publisher
Phaidon (whom he joined
as art director, also in
1993) might also have
influenced his visual
thinking. Phi denotes the
golden ratio, an influence
on the work of artists
and architects since the
Renaissance.

44. Sion College
Membership
organization, UK
*Designed by Untitled
(Glenn Howard, David
Hawkins), 2007*
Founded in 1630, Sion
College is a body of
clergy that debates,
celebrates and supports
the activities of the
Anglican Church in
London. The spirit of
fellowship among the
members is intimated by
the linking of the initials.

45. Cardiff Waterside
Business community, UK
*Designed by Brownjohn
(James Beveridge, Tom
Rogers, Andy Mosley),
2008*
Cardiff Waterside is
the former Cardiff Bay
Partnership, now owned
by Aviva Investors. It is
a commercial zone in
Cardiff's former docks
area, once the world's
busiest port.

46. Art & Australia
Magazine, Australia
*Designed by Tomato
(John Warwicker), 2010*

35

36

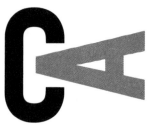

37

38

RBH

39

40

gc

41

42

IΦD

43

44

45

46

47. Gebrüder Heinemann
Distribution and retail group, Germany
Designed by Pentagram (Alan Fletcher), 1975
'Commercial marks are like people,' wrote Alan Fletcher in his inspirational cornucopia and swansong *The Art Of Looking Sideways.* 'Some are reasonably well put together but lack personality, others are dull or aggressive, or pompous, or unpleasant. Occasionally one encounters an interesting character.'

Fletcher spent his career making organizations look interesting. An avid recorder of optical puns, paradoxes, ephemera and phenomena, he took inexhaustible pleasure in putting ideas that made him smile to work for corporate clients, endowing them with the kind of visual punch and personality that communicated instantly with audiences.

Returning to London from the USA, having worked his way around the tutelage and influence of American design luminaries like Paul Rand, Saul Bass and Leo Lionni, he set up Fletcher/Forbes/Gill with Colin Forbes and Bob Gill, and helped to establish Design & Art Direction (D&AD). The first became the template for the modern British graphic design studio; the second had a major bearing on the uptake of design services within British industry. Fletcher/Forbes/Gill became Crosby/Fletcher/Forbes, which became Pentagram, which became one of the world's most enduring, admired and consistently commercially successful design groups.

Not much is on record about the mark Fletcher designed for Gebrüder Heinemann in the mid 1970s, apart from the fact that it bears the hallmarks of Fletcher's love of letterforms and the spaces in and around them. It is still proudly worn by the German consumer goods distribution group, and continues to identify its duty-free shops at busy international airports.

Not as familiar or celebrated as the logotypes he designed for the Victoria & Albert Museum, the Institute of Directors and Reuters, it nonetheless typifies the memorable simplicity, invention and wit that he brought to the corporate marks of dozens of lucky, interesting-looking organizations.

48. Covent Garden
Commercial district, UK
Designed by Bibliothèque, 2005

49. Lund Byggeri
Construction firm, Denmark
Designed by A2/SW/HK, 2010

50. All Change
Charity, UK
Designed by Magpie Studio (David Azurdia, Ben Christie, Jamie Ellul, Andy Hills), 2009
All Change is a north London charity specializing in arts projects in community settings. Its hybrid letterform reflects its combined arts approach.

51. Seawater Greenhouse
Sustainable irrigation systems provider, UK
Designed by Dowling Duncan (John Dowling, Rob Duncan), 2004
Seawater Greenhouse has developed a system of the same name that enables year-round crop production in the world's hottest, driest regions using seawater and sunlight, in a greenhouse.

48

49

50

51

52. College of Arts & Architecture
Art and design college, USA
Designed by Mode (USA) (John Pietrafesa, Maxim Vakhovskiy), 2010
Part of the University of North Carolina at Charlotte, the CoA&A strives for a close relationship between the arts, architecture and design, signalled by its logo of nested letterforms.

53. Eva Kecseti
Handbag designer, UK
Designed by Taxi Studio (Spencer Buck, Ryan Wills, Karl Wills), 2003

54. Store Build
Interior fit-out supplier, Japan
Designed by Nign (Kenichiro Ohara), 2009

55. Super OS
Artists' agent, Japan
Designed by Good Design Company, 2004

56. Embodied Media
New media arts practice, Australia
Designed by Inkahoots, 2007
A close relationship between the 'E' and 'M' symbolizes the collaborative, interdisciplinary nature of artist Keith Armstrong's work.

57. Living Architecture
Holiday rental company, UK
Designed by North, 2007
A social enterprise conceived by writer and philosopher Alain de Botton, Living Architecture commissions then rents out houses designed by leading architects as holiday lets.

58. Bevan Brittan
Legal practice, UK
Designed by CDT Design, 2004
A firm with a mixture of traditional values and innovative thinking finds expression in the interplay of a pair of Caslon 'b's.

59. TransFormal
IT consultancy, Germany
Designed by Thomas Manss & Company, 2001
TransFormal claims to provide the key to IT for its clients.

60. Independent Commission on Turkey
Political campaign, UK
Designed by Atelier Works (Quentin Newark), 2004
Designed for a grouping of prominent European politicians brought together to analyze aspects of Turkey's accession to the EU, inserting 'T' firmly into the centre of 'E'.

61. Scottish Opera
National opera company, UK
Designed by hat-trick (Gareth Howat, Jim Sutherland, Adam Giles), 2008
The big mouth strikes again: a singing 'O', and an 'S' coming out of it.

62. Unreserved
Campaigning alliance, USA
Designed by The O Group (Jason B Cohen), 2009
Unreserved is an alliance of entrepreneurs and business leaders aiming to foster the talents of American Indians interested in exploring careers in fashion and art.

63. Braincandy
Branding agency, Greece
Designed by G Design Studio (Michalis Georgiou, Alexandros Gavrilakis), 2009

52

53

54

55

56

57

58

59

E

60

61

62

63

64. BG Group
Oil and gas production,
UK
*Designed by Uffindell
(Gary Black), 1996*
Originally designed for
BG plc when British Gas
divested Centrica, this
monogram stuck when
the former reorganized in
1999 as BG Group plc.

65. Free & Equal
Campaigning group, UK
*Designed by Mark Studio,
2010*
Free & Equal works to
assert the rights of sexual
minorities discriminated
against in the global
south, with an identity
that makes its point in
most languages.

**66. Front Room
Recordings**
Record label, UK
*Designed by Malone
Design (David Malone),
2009.*

**67. Brand Design
Council of South Africa**
Professional association,
South Africa
*Designed by Mister
Walker, 2009*
Three characters in one
for the representative
body of graphic
designers and agencies
in South Africa.

68. Alwyne Estates
Property agency, UK
*Designed by 1977 Design
(Phil Dobson), 2005*

69. A Athletics
Sportswear company,
Belgium
*Designed by Coast
(David Nerinckx), 2009*
A monogram for
AAthletics, based in
Antwerp, intended to
stand for the company
and for the city, as a
centre of sport and
fashion.

70. Design Ventura
Manufacturing initiative,
UK
Designed by Rose, 2010
London's Design
Museum works with
aspiring young designers
and industry experts
to create new products
for sale in its shop. The
initiative, represented
by a pair of dovetailing
initials, is called Design
Ventura.

**71. Balthazar B and the
Beatitudes**
Rock band, UK
*Designed by &Smith,
2009*
Balthazar B at front of
stage with his Beatitudes
(which vary in number)
behind him.

72. Endpoint
Brand implementation
company, UK
Designed by North, 2010
Endpoint manages
the implementation of
branding programmes,
claiming to apply a
full-circle, start-to-finish
approach. Its mark
applies the same idea
to the 'e' and 'p' of the
company name.

73. Erritzøe
Legal practice, Denmark
*Designed by Punktum
Design (Søren Varming,
Abelone Varming, Henrik
Kubel), 2005*
Two of the initials of the
law firm's founder, Morten
Erritzøe Christensen,
also suggest a courtoom
in plan.

74. Hampstead Theatre
Theatre, UK
Designed by Rose, 2010
The grid units of the
building's 2003 facade
find an echo in this
logotype, which places
the theatre at the heart
of Hampstead.

75. Akerman Daly
Book publisher, UK
*Designed by Untitled
(David Hawkins, Glenn
Howard), 2010*
Jeremy Akerman and
Eileen Daly publish
writing by contemporary
artists.

64

65

66

67

68

69

70

71

72

73

74

75

9/11
MEMORIAL

1. 9/11 Memorial
Memorial, USA
Designed by Landor Associates (Rietje Gieskes), 2009
'I was on a bus in upstate New York when the towers were hit,' says Rietje Gieskes. 'The driver pulled over and everyone listened to the events unfold over the radio.'

Later that year, Gieskes moved to New York City and began her career at Landor on Park Avenue while the 9/11 site was still being cleared. 'Like most New Yorkers, I think of the event often. It is a part of daily life. People still look up when an airplane passes over the city. Creating an identity for a cause so close to our hearts was a challenge. Everyone wanted to rise to the occasion.'

The full legal name of the body responsible for the construction and operation of the 9/11 site – the National September 11 Memorial & Museum at the World Trade Center – was too long for most applications and most ordinary people, leading to a confusion of shortened versions. Landor's new name for the facility put an end to the perplexity.

Simplicity was the guiding principle behind the name and the logotype design. Tone was vital: the typeface, weight, colour and composition all had a part to play in making something that was direct and compelling, but also dignified and undateable.

'We reviewed a variety of different themes within our exploration, considering more literal visuals like the color of the sky that day, and more abstract ideas like the sense of hope, resilience, and national pride that people felt in the aftermath. The selected design is a balance of both, focusing on the simple, emotive power of the absent towers.'

2. Action Woking
Environmental initiative, UK
Designed by Buddy (David Jones, Mark Girvan), 2010
An initiative by combined heat and power (CHP) energy provider Thameswey to support Woking residents in reducing their carbon footprint.

3. ActionAid
Charity, UK
Designed by CDT Design, 2001; refreshed by CDT Design, 2006
The international development agency's identity gives a clear instruction.

4. Active Results
Schools analysis software, UK
Designed by Spencer du Bois (John Spencer), 2008

5. ADF Architects
Architectural practice, UK
Designed by Graphical House, 2007

2

Actio$_2$n Woking
THE LOW CARBON COMMUNITY

3

act:onaid

4

activeresults

5

6. Ágora
Cultural events, Portugal
Designed by Bürocratik (Adriano Esteves), 2006
This business is named after the large, open places of assembly in ancient Greece. The loop of the 'G' suggests a forum or auditorium.

7. Allude
Designer cashmere company, Germany
Designed by Bibliothèque, 2007
Classical, elegant Bodoni capitals are denuded of their serifs to make a more contemporary statement.

8. Almar
Concrete producer, Poland
Designed by logotypy. com (Wiktor Pawlik), 2000

9. Aquavia
Engineering consultancy, Portugal
Designed by Bürocratik (Adriano Esteves), 2006
For a firm specializing in road (*via* in Portuguese) and water (*aqua*) engineering, a ligature in which the two are united: the 'A' as the road, 'the 'V' as the river.

10. Bags
Bag manufacturer, Portugal
Designed by Bürocratik (Adriano Esteves), 2010

11. bijipub
Business book publisher, Japan
Designed by Nign (Kenichiro Ohara), 2009

12. Luis Albuquerque
Phoptographer, Canada
Designed by Hambly & Woolley (Bob Hambly, Emese Ungar-Walker), 2003
The two 'q's depict a camera lens – before and after the shot is taken.

13. Christian Constantin
Architectural practice, Switzerland
Designed by >moser, 2010

14. Blink
Vehicle charging stations, USA
Designed by Landor Associates (Paul Chock, May Hartono, Andy Baron, John Martinko), 2010
With a name that implies speed and effortlessness, Blink's combined 'i' and 'n', and unfussy font suggest efficiency and ease of use.

15. Boskke
Indoor plants, UK
Designed by Bibliothèque, 2010
Boskke makes the Sky Planter: a plant pot that hangs like a lamp from the ceiling. The leafy 'k's in the name imply such growth.

16. Waterman
Fountain pen manufacturer, France
Designed by Lippincott & Margulies, 1946
Industrial designer Gordon Lippincott and interior designer Walter Margulies were early advocates of a thoughtful, strategic, all-encompassing approach to the way companies identify themselves. But the Manhattan firm that went on to coin the term 'corporate identity' and design classic marks for General Mills, Betty Crocker, American Express, Chrysler and RCA, was more concerned with designing products, packaging and interiors for the first decade of its life. Its identity for Waterman (now based in Paris), with its signature flourish, or bow, was one of L&M's very first ventures into what would become its first line of business.

17. Connect Sheffield
Wayfinding system, UK
Designed by Atelier Works (John Powner, Natalie Turner), 2005
A double ligature connects this logotype with Sheffield's groundbreaking wayfinding system. The font, Sheffield Sans, based on typefaces created at the city's historic Stephenson Blake foundry, was designed for the project by Jeremy Tankard.

ágora

6

ALLUDE

7

ALMAR

8

AQUAVIA

9

BAGS

bijipub

10

11

12

13

blink

boskke

14

15

Waterman

Sheffield

16

17

18. Coop Himmelblau
Architectural practice, Austria
Designed by Made In Space, 2001
A logotype that makes one letter optional: with the 'L', *Himmelblau* translates as 'sky blue'; without it, *Himmelbau* means 'heaven construction'. Both could describe a practice whose buildings escape conventional categorization.

19. Coram Chambers
Barristers' chambers, UK
Designed by Spencer du Bois (John Spencer), 1999
The lower-case informality conveys an approachable image for this chambers specializing in family law and civil practice. The kerned characters represent the merger of the two chambers that formed Coram.

20. Cox
Furniture maker, UK
Designed by Honey, 2010
Handcrafted typography for a business creating traditional handcrafted furniture with a contemporary edge.

21. Exist
Design planning, Japan
Designed by Taste Inc (Toshiyasu Nanbu), 2007

22. D&AD Congress
Annual conference, UK
Designed by Rose, 2007
Appropriately for an association of designers and advertising creatives, three logotypes in one. The mark for D&AD's main members' conference contains Rose's logo for the organization, which places the monogram designed in 1962 by Fletcher/Forbes/Gill in a (pencil-esque) hexagon. The FFG mark was created by the pre-digital technique of placing the four characters in the visible sides of an open wooden cube and photographing the result.

23. David Higham
Literary agent, UK
Designed by Kimpton (David Kimpton, Katie Alger), 2009
The brackets formed by the letters (also the initials) at the centre of the logotype are used to frame lists of the famous authors on the agency's books, and highlight its association with them.

24. Curious Pictures
TV and film production company, USA
Designed by Pentagram (Paula Scher), 1993

25. Dialog
Architectural practice, Canada
Designed by Rethink, 2010
A firm that values the conversation between architect and client.

26. Exider
Industrial metal-working tools, Belarus
Designed by Denis Olenik Design Studio, 2007

27. Kettle of Fish
Digital production company, UK
Designed by Sam Dallyn, 2010

28. Halliwell Landau
Legal practice, UK
Designed by The Chase (Pete Richardson), 2000
More sly serif work to create brackets between names, this time to contain the firm's areas of expertise.

18

coram

19

20

EXIST

21

david higham
literary, film and tv agents

22

23

curiouspictures

24

25

26

halliwell landau

27

28

29. Exploratorium
Science museum, USA
*Designed by Landor
Associates (Margaret
Youngblood), 1998*
Founded in San
Francisco in 1969 by
physicist and educator
Dr Frank Oppenheimer,
Exploratorium nurtures
curiosity in science
and the environment
through multisensory
experiences.

30. Forart
Art foundation, Poland
*Designed by logotypy.
com (Wiktor Pawlik), 2009*

31. Foro
Winery, Portugal
*Designed by Bürocratik
(Adriano Esteves), 2006*

32. Fish + Chip Design
Design consultancy, UK
*Designed by Fish +
Chip Design (Christian
Holland), 2010*
A name and familiar
typeface (Neue
Helvetica) inspired by
owner Christian Holland's
desire for design to
be part of everyday
experience and thinking.

33. FMC Technologies
Oil and gas technologies
manufacturer, USA
*Designed by Lippincott
& Margulies, 1973*
FMC designs and
manufactures equipment
for the offshore oil and
gas industry, hinted at by
the notional pipeline in its
logotype.

34. Giff Gaff
Mobile phone network,
UK
*Designed by SomeOne
(Gary Holt, Laura Hussey),
2010*
Giff Gaff claims to keep
costs low for users
by allowing them to
participate in the brand
and business, and to
recruit new users by
creating their own SIM
order page. As the
network grows, more
variations on the basic
logotype are created for
users to draw on.

**35. Harvard
Maintenance**
Building maintenance,
USA
*Designed by Chermayeff
& Geismar, 2011*

36. First Graduate
Non-profit organization,
USA
*Designed by Landor
Associates (Nicholas
Aparicio, JJ Ha, Paul
Chock, May Hartono),
2007*
First Graduate helps
disadvantaged young
people in the San
Francisco Bay Area to
become the first in their
family to graduate from
college.

37. 50 Lessons
Business learning
service, UK
Designed by Rose, 2006
50 Lessons offers insight
and learning gleaned
from in-depth interviews
with influential business
leaders. For words
that are set in stone, a
classical typeface of
the kind found on stone
monuments.

38. Freedom
Travel agency, UK
*Designed by The Chase
(Lise Brian), 2009*

39. HealthScout
Online medical
information provider,
USA
*Designed by Onoma
(Roger van den Bergh),
2000*
The HealthScout site
is designed to help
consumers navigate their
way to answers to their
medical queries.

29

30

31

FISH+
CHIP

32

FMC

giffgaff

33

34

HARVARD MAINTENANCE

F¹RST GRADUATE

35

36

LES50NS

37

38

39

40. HeathWallace
Website design company, UK
Designed by Arthur-SteenHorneAdamson (ASHA: Emma Lucyn, Scott McGuffie, Marksteen Adamson), 2007

41. Howcast
Online instructional videos, USA
Designed by Pentagram (Paula Scher), 2009
For the site that has the how-to of everything, an 'H' that points the way to the next step.

42. Inmedias
Mediation service, Switzerland
Designed by Atelier Bundi (Stephan Bundi), 2009
A company that targets areas of disagreement.

43. Inpoc
Smartphone app retailer, Norway
Designed by Mission Design (Karl Martin Sætren), 2007
Inpoc is short for 'in pocket', to describe this company's range of mobile phone services and entertainment.

44. Integrity
Design management consultancy, UK
Designed by Atelier Works (Ian Chilvers), 1999
Standing between client and creative, managing the to and fro of the design process, is this company's business.

45. Javerdel
IT consultancy, Finland
Designed by Hahmo (Jenni Kuokka, Pekka Piippo, Antti Raudaskoski), 2008

46. Hive & Honey
Fashion label, USA
Designed by Dowling Duncan (John Dowling, Rob Duncan), 2010

47. ByAlex
Furniture design company, UK
Designed by Company, 2011
All of this design company's plywood furniture creations are based on an 'A'-shaped profile, such as the stool in the logotype.

48. Intuit
Financial software company, USA
Designed by Lippincott (Brendán Murphy, Christian Dierig, Peter Chun), 2008

49. Keikyu
Department store, Japan
Designed by Ken Miki & Associates, 1995

50. Klartext
Advertising media and logistics service, Germany
Designed by Lockstoff Design, 2008

heathwallace

40

Howcast

41

Inmedias

42

43

↑ntegr↓ty

JAVERDEL

44

45

HIVE&HONEY

ByALEX®

46

47

inTuiT

KEI KYU

48

49

klartext

50

51. Meiji Group
Dairy products and
confectionery group,
Japan
*Designed by Landor
Associates, 2009*
Soft, rounded, lower-
case letters provide
a friendly, human
connection to this major
foods group.

52. Kultohr
Sightseeing information
service, Germany
*Designed by Lockstoff
Design, 2010*
Call *Kultohr* ('culture ear')
on your mobile and listen
to information about
points of cultural interest
in the Rhein-Kreis Neuss
area of Germany.

53. Leontyna
Olive oil producer,
Australia
*Designed by Sadgrove
Design (Brian Sadgrove),
2004*
An olive grove and
artisan producer on the
Mornington Peninsula
near Melbourne named
after the founder's
mother who, aged 89,
helped to plant the first
trees in 2003.

54. Living
Furniture reseller, Greece
*Designed G Design
Studio (Michalis
Georgiou, Alexandros
Gavrilakis), 2010*

55. Marco
Contemporary art
museum, Mexico
*Designed by Lance
Wyman, 1990*
The acronym of
the Museo de Arte
Contemporeáneo
Monterrey is also the
Spanish word for 'frame'.
The square 'o' suggests
the museum's central
patio.

56. Korkers
Flyfishing footwear, USA
*Designed by Sandstrom
Partners (Jon Olsen,
Chris Gardiner), 2009*
A river runs through it;
the 'K', that is.

57. Luxury Trip
Premium taxi service,
Argentina
Designed by Ailoviu, 2007

58. Matthew Williamson
Fashion label, UK
*Designed by SEA (Bryan
Edmondson), 2011*

59. Mobil Corporation
Fuel and lubricants
company, USA
*Designed by Chermayeff
& Geismar, 1964*
The drive for Mobil's
adoption of Chermayeff
& Geismar's defiantly
modern visual identity
and Eliot Noyes' service
station architecture
came from a desire to
be welcomed in the
suburban communities
that were springing up
across America in the
early 1960s. It became
a beacon of the new,
clean, efficient aesthetic
that American industry
embraced at the start of
the race-to-the-moon
decade.

**60. Michael Popper
Associates**
Building services and
engineering consultancy,
UK
*Designed by Dowling
Duncan (John Dowling,
Rob Duncan), 2004*

61. Mobilise
Charity, UK
*Designed by Spencer
du Bois (John Spencer),
2007*
Thinner tyres than the
Mobil logotype but the
same metaphor. Mobilise
represents disabled
motorists in the UK and
campaigns for better
parking, refuelling and
access for disabled
people.

meiji

51

kultohr

52

LEONTYNA

53

Living

54

marco

Korkers™

55

56

MATTHEW
WILLIAMSON

57

58

Mobil

59

MichaePopper

mobilise

60

61

62. Moke
Rock band, The
Netherlands
Designed by The Stone
Twins (Declan and Garech
Stone), 2007
Not rock's first guitar-
related slash, but maybe
the first to be inspired by
the angle of the band's
guitar straps rather than
the instrument itself.

63. Moor
Housebuilder, Finland
Designed by Hahmo
(Pekka Piippo), 2007
A non-standard 'o'
for a business that
allows homebuyers to
customize the interiors
of their industrially
manufactured homes
using a Web-based
application.

64. Northern Ireland
Tourist Board
Tourist authority, UK
Designed by AV Browne,
2010

65. Nutrio
Wholesale bio-food
supplier, UK
Designed by GBH, 2000

66. PeliFilip
Legal practice, Romania
Designed by Brandient
(Cristian 'Kit' Paul), 2008

67. MRCPderm
Professional examination
revision website, UK
Designed by Graphical
House, 2010
The MRCPderm website
from St John's Institute
of Dermatology offers
support to those
qualifying through the
MRCP (UK) exam.

68. Moorhouse
Consulting
Project management
consultancy, UK
Designed by 300million
(Martin Lawless, Nigel
Davies, Natalie Bennett),
2010
The intimacy of the two
'o's – and suggestion
of an infinity symbol
– stems from the
rebranded company's
new organizing thought:
'Anything together'.

69. Petrolux
Energy broker, UK
Designed by Malone
Design (David Malone),
2009

70. Nobivac
Animal vaccine supplier,
UK
Designed by Uffindell
(Gary Black, Gary
Deardon), 2009
A transfusion of white
space represents the
administration of this
company's products.

71. Plan 8
Environmental
consultancy, Denmark
Designed by We
Recommend (Martin
Fredricson, Nikolaj Knop),
2006

72. Opet Petroleum
Oil and petroleum retailer,
Turkey
Designed by Chermayeff
& Geismar, 2004
Forty years after giving
Mobil its red wheel,
Chermayeff & Geismar
rebranded Turkish
fuel retail giant Opet
with a go-faster 'o' and
logotype.

73. Together
Footwear retail initiative,
Spain
Designed by Mario
Eskenazi (Mario Eskenazi,
Diego Feijóo), 2008
The Together project
by Spanish shoemaker
Camper brings together
international designers to
create one-off shoe lines
and shop interiors.

62

moor

63

northernireland

64

nutrio

65

PELIƒILIP

66

MRC⊕

67

Moorhouse

68

Petrolux

69

Nobivac

70

Plan8

71

⊟opet

72

to&ether

73

STVDIO

74. STVDIO
TV channel, Australia
Designed by Frost Design, 2010
Some designers have a way with words – a talent for spotting the graphic potential of conjunctions of letterforms to create immediate, eye-catching identities. Vince Frost is one of them. It is an ability that first drew attention in the mid 1990s when Frost was winning design plaudits for his work on *The Independent Magazine* on Saturday and *Big Magazine*. The latter's trademark was heavy, crunching headlines set in super-bold wooden type – a love of Frost's inherited from his father, a former printer – that would sometimes occupy the entire page. Words were fragmented, their syllables stacked, letters jammed in on their sides.

That love of re-composing language and letters to create new interpretations – to simplify while maintaining a point of difference – lent itself well to identity projects as Frost built his own studio, first in London, then in Sydney. It continues to serve the company well through logotypes such as this one for an arts channel launched in 2010.

The inspiration for this logotype pre-dates even Frost's beloved wood type and the invention of printing itself. The channel wanted an identity that represented both the channel's arts-driven content and the medium of its transmission. Frost explains, 'One of the names they suggested was "The Studio". I remembered from Latin lessons, there was no distinction between "V" and "U", which led me immediately to think of "STUDIO TV", and then of planting "TV" inside "STUDIO".' The Latinate substitution and use of a weighty slab serif establishes a connection with art history by association with the legacy of Ancient Rome and the Renaissance, while the vivid pink dispels any air of stuffiness.

75. The Preston and District Ex-Boxers Association
Sporting association, UK
Designed by The Chase (Mark Ross, Tommy O'Shaughnessy), 1986
Black 'I's – the stock in trade of these pugilistic alumni.

76. Trento DOC
Wine appellation, Italy
Designed by Minale Tattersfield (Marcello M Minale, Ian Delaney), 2008
Trento DOC is the appellation given to Italy's oldest Metodo Classico sparkling wine. The brand, shared by the 37 DOC producers in the Trentino region, positions their wine as the champagne of Italy, and refers to the remuage in which bottles are turned in pairs every day to encourage the production of bubbles.

77. UK Skills
Skills champion, UK
Designed by Purpose (Stuart Youngs, Adam Browne, Paul Felton, Phil Skinner), 2009
UK Skills champions high standards of training through events, awards and competitions.

78. Unique Models
Model agency, Denmark
Designed by Homework (Jack Dahl), 2008

75

TRENTODOC®

76

ukskills

77

UNIQUEMODELS

78

79. Purity
'Green' IT systems,
Norway
Designed by Heydays,
2009
Purity provides 'green'
storage and server
systems to large
corporations. The 'i' in its
name gives a clue to its
area of business.

80. QFort
Window systems brand,
Romania
Designed by Brandient
(Cristian 'Kit' Paul), 2007
The corner of a frame
alludes to this brand's
point of difference:
precision-engineered
window systems.

81. Qmunity
Lesbian, Gay, Bisexual
and Transgender (LGBT)
community centre,
Canada
Designed by Rethink,
2009
A speech bubble
indicates Qmunity's
aim of giving the LGBT
community in British
Columbia a voice as
well as resources and
services.

82. Unit
Post-production
company, UK
Designed by Company,
2006

83. Rippleffect Sound
Design
Sound design, Canada
Designed by Hambly &
Woolley (Bob Hambly,
Philip Mondor), 2005

84. Salvino
Italian delicatessen, UK
Designed by Atelier
Works (John Powner,
Henrietta Molinaro), 2006
Based on 1930s display
typefaces, this mark
makes well-judged use of
the olive oil bottle, as any
Italian deli would.

85. Pleasurealm
Restaurant group parent
company, UK
Designed by North, 2010

86. Poverty Over
Charity campaign, UK
Designed by Johnson
Banks and BMB Agency,
2009
A banner developed to
badge all of Christian
Aid's advertising and
communications,
focusing attention on the
charity's objective and
away from its name.

87. Rollasole
Footwear company, UK
Designed by Magpie
Studio (David Azurdia,
Ben Christie, Jamie Ellul),
2008
Rollasole sells rolled-up
ballet pumps from
nightclub vending
machines to give stiletto-
wearing clubbers a break
from footache.

88. World Policy
Institute
Internationalist policy
development, USA
Designed by Chermayeff
& Geismar, 1994

89. Weekend
TV channel, Israel
Designed by Oded Ezer,
2002

PURiTY

79

QFORT™

80

QMUNITY

81

UN1T

82

rippleffect
SOUND DESIGN

83

SALVINO

84

PLEASUREALM™

85

POVERTY

86

Rollasole

87

W●RLD POLICY

88

89

90. Samphire PR
Public relations company, UK
Designed by Dowling Duncan (John Dowling, Rob Duncan), 2007

91. Sendyne
Battery and semi-conductor technologies provider, USA
Designed by Onoma (Roger van den Bergh), 2011
Arrows allude to electron movement in a typical battery.

92. Smule
Smartphone application producer, USA
Designed by Six (John Kariolis), 2008
For some new logotypes, the key challenge is ensuring legibility and distinctiveness at the tiny size of a smartphone icon, just a few millimetres across. The logo for Smule, a Silicon Valley start-up creating music-making apps such as Ocarina for the iPhone, had to work at an even smaller scale, alongside the brand mark of each app.

93. Socialbox
Smartphone application, UK
Designed by Sam Dallyn, 2011
Socialbox allows users to watch TV 'with' friends in an online social environment through integration with Twitter, Facebook and 'audience visualizations'.

94. Sofami
Online furniture retailer, Poland
Designed by Elfen (Andrew Cavanagh, Guto Evans), 2010

95. St Pancras Renaissance Hotel
Hotel, UK
Designed by North, 2011
For the five-star establishment opening in the Victorian Gothic splendour of the former Midland Grand Hotel building, North created an identity that references the old hotel's connection with rail travel and St Pancras Station next door. The end product (based on Dalton Maag's Effra typeface) channels tradition and character without running into the buffers of reproduction, pastiche or hotel-chain nothingness.

96. Stereoscape
3-D film and TV production company, Finland
Designed by Hahmo (Erik Bertell, Ilona Törmikoski), 2009

97. Tea
Tea shop chain, UK
Designed by Mind Design, 2007

98. Switch
Lighting design consultancy, Singapore
Designed by &Larry (Larry Peh, Adora Tan), 2010
A representation of not just the designer's idea or brainwave (a light switch) but also of the design process: a semicolon symbolizes the pause for thought before proposing a solution.

99. The Armoury
Pub, UK
Designed by Purpose (Stuart Youngs, Paul Felton, Will Kinchin, Alice Reynolds), 2010
The wordmark for this pub in Wandsworth, south London, looks down the barrel of one of the cannons made by Henkel's Armoury nearby.

100. The Grow in Project
Ecumenical outreach venture, UK
Designed by Guild of Sage & Smith (Neil Tinson), 2006

90

91

92

93

sofami

94

ST PANCRAS

95

STEREOOSCAPE

96

97

SWITCH

98

THE ARMOURY

99

The Grow in Project

100

1. Accesspoint Technologies
IT solutions, UK
Designed by Ummocrono (Nina Wollner, Fredrik Jönsson), 2009
Accesspoint helps businesses transfer their data from in-house servers to cloud services – a move symbolized by the displaced dot.

2. Artica
Online art gallery, UK
Designed by 1977 Design (Paul Bailey, David Armstrong, Chloe Pillai), 2008
For an online gallery and shop, the dot of the 'i' becomes the coloured sticker placed next to a sold artwork.

3. Colmar Brunton
Market research firm, Australia
Designed by Elmwood (Sue Mould, Aja Shanahan), 2010
A market research firm that claims to get to the point – now that would be novel. The arrow signifies the client's 'journey to discovery'; the full stop represents the answers that await them.

4. Digit
Video conversion company, UK
Designed by Fivefootsix, 2009
Digit creates digital duplicates of video content for broadcast, tweaking each copy for its new file format. The differing dots echo the 'more than a duplicate' theme of the rebrand.

5. Synovia
Healthcare strategy consultancy, UK
Designed by Untitled (Glenn Howard, David Hawkins), 2004

6. iD Distribution
TV programme distributor, UK
Designed by The Chase (Harriet Devoy, Mark Atkinson), 2005
A redistribution of the dot from one 'i' to another makes the point.

7. Fillet Inc
Fashion label, Sweden
Designed by We Recommend (Martin Fredricson, Nikolaj Knop), 2009

The colour of the dots varies, depending on the piece of streetwear it appears on.

8. Grant Spencer
Legal practice, UK
Designed by A2 Design, 2009
A notional ® or ™ symbol marks this firm out as trademark attorneys.

9. Intuitive
Travel software, UK
Designed by Spencer du Bois (John Spencer), 2004
Dots with wanderlust for a company that makes web-based tour-operating systems.

10. John Lyall Architects
Architectural practice, UK
Designed by Mind Design, 2009

11. Howard
Kitchenware retailer, Norway
Designed by Mission Design (Karl Martin Sætren), 2006

Accesspoint˙

1

artica.

2

⋙→ colmar brunton.

3

digit

4

Synovia.

5

6

grant
spencer

7

8

intuitive

9

john.lyall.architects.

HOWARD.®

10

11

12. Jump Healthfoods
Healthfood retailer,
Australia
*Designed by Naughtyfish
(Danielle de Andrade),
2009*

13. KidStart
Loyalty scheme, UK
*Designed by 300million
(Martin Lawless, Nigel
Davies, Natalie Bennett,
Katie Morgan), 2005*
KidStart is a loyalty
scheme that allows
parents to save for their
child's future through
money-back offers
in shops.

**14. Kerry Phelan Design
Office**
Interior design studio,
Australia
*Designed by Fabio
Ongarato Design (Fabio
Ongarato, Meg Phillips),
2010*
A reserved, pre-
branding-era approach,
recalling design
atelier names of old,
to reflect the studio's
unpretentious qualities.

15. Lane
Financial marketing
company, UK
*Designed by &Smith,
2011*

16. Mediapulse
Market research
company, Switzerland
*Designed by Atelier Bundi
(Stephan Bundi), 2006*

17. Place Estate Agents
Property agency, UK
Designed by Hand, 2010
A dot that's a pin on a map
marking a destination for
house-hunters.

18. Eat
Cafe chain, UK
*Designed by Pentagram
(Angus Hyland), 2002*

**19. Montgomery Sisam
Architects**
Architectural practice,
Canada
*Designed by Hambly &
Woolley (Bob Hambly,
Dominic Ayre), 2004*
A terminal turned into a
dot links the names of the
firm's founders.

20. Nothotels.com
Online booking agency,
UK
Designed by GBH, 2000

21. Tonic
Post-production service,
Canada
*Designed by Rethink,
2004*

22. Verbatim
Foreign-language
printing service, UK
*Designed by hat-trick
(Gareth Howat, Jim
Sutherland), 2003*

jump.

12

•KidStart

13

K. P. D. O.

14

lane.

15

mediapulse

Place.

16

17

EAT.

18

MontgomerySisam

nothotelscom

19

20

tonic

verbatim.

21

22

1. text/gallery
Literary gallery, UK
Designed by Practice + Theory (Andreas Pohancenik), 2009
text/gallery puts the focus on art projects inspired by the written word, and the space between text and the visual arts. The forward slash emphasizes this departure from convention.

2. Postmedia Network
Newspaper and media group, Canada
Designed by Rethink, 2010
A forward slash that clearly signals where the National Post owner's future focus lies: in digital media.

3. Slash
Online city guide, France
Designed by Area 17 (Arnaud Mercier), 2010
Slash is an online guide to art events and venues in Paris.

4. Bambi/bylaura
Fashion label, UK/Spain
Designed by TwoPoints.Net, 2009
The identity for the label of designer Laura Figueras features a custom-made typeface (TpMartini, based on a 5x9 grid) and the ability to vary what follows the slash with the names of sub-brands and collections.

5. Derek Welsh Studio
Furniture design, UK
Designed by Graphical House, 2009
Bespoke type, an intricate 'W' and a unified forward slash echo the subtle details and craftsmanship of DWS's handmade designs.

6. SynsLaser
Laser eye surgery, Norway
Designed by Mission Design (Karl Martin Sætren), 2006
A slash that hints at the high-precision surgical instrument in question, without revealing any scary detail.

7. S4C
TV Channel, UK
Designed by Proud Creative, 2006
Branding that allows the UK's only Welsh-language public-service broadcaster to assert its identity, with a forward slash that is followed by messages and information in Welsh.

8. Geriljaworks
Industrial design company, Norway
Designed by Heydays, 2009
The placement of a forward slash in front of the name is meant to suggest this young, versatile design team's openness to partnerships and collaboration, allowing clients' names to precede its own.

9. Brook McIlroy
Architectural practice, Canada
Designed by Concrete (Cristian Oronez, Diti Katona, John Pylypczak), 2010

text/ gallery.

1

2

Slash/

3

bambi/bylaura

4

DW/S

5

SYNS/LASER®

6

S4/C

7

/GERILJAWORKS   BrookMcIlroy/

8   9

1. B&W Studio
Design consultancy, UK
Designed by B&W Studio (Steve Wills), 2005
The mark Lee Bradley and Steve Wills designed for their studio when it opened in 2005. The ampersand plays a big part in the company's materials and presentations.

2. Barnes & Noble
Bookseller, USA
Designed by Doyle Partners (Stephen Doyle, Tom Kluepfel), 2000
Here, the ampersand is a nod to the bookseller's heritage: Charles Barnes started printing books in 1873; his son William started selling them with G Clifford Noble in 1917.

3. Colin&Me
Bag and furnishing company, UK
Designed by Guild of Sage & Smith (Neil Tinson), 2009
A feline ampersand for a crafts business that uses reclaimed fabrics to make bags and home furnishings. Colin is the owner's cat.

4. DHKN
Accountancy practice, Ireland
Designed by Creative Inc (Mel O'Rourke, Sinead McAleer), 2009
Deasy Hannon and Kit Noone's company identity gained an ampersand as a device that could be repeated in branded materials.

5. Horse & Country TV
TV channel, UK
Designed by Method, Inc (Philip O'Dwyer), 2009

6. Marks & Clerk
Legal practice, UK
Designed by CDT Design, 2007
A name that has nothing to do with the company's area of business (trademark and patent attorneys), Marks & Clerk recalls its founders, a pair of Victorian engineer/inventors who moved rapidly into the boom area of intellectual property. It is now the largest IP firm in the UK.

7. ST&P
Branding and advertising firm, Australia
Designed by SML (Vanessa Ryan, Kelly Weber), 2010

A formal truncation of Samuelseon Talbot & Partners, the ST&P identity offers a focus on the firm's creative partnerships and, in print and online, a window on its projects and campaigns.

8. Keith Holland & Associates
Optometrist, UK
Designed by Arthur-SteenHorneAdamson (ASHA), 2009
A friendly, non-clinical central feature, visible to just about any potential customer.

9. Weeks & Cowling
Architectural design studio, UK
Designed by FL@33 (Agathe Jacquillat, Tomi Vollauschek), 2008

1

2

3

4

5

6

7

KEITH HOLLAND & ASSOCIATES

8

WEEKS & COWLING

9

1. Art Matters
Art foundation, USA
Designed by PS New York (Penny Hardy), 2007
A name and a point of view, underlined for emphasis, for a foundation that supports experimental artists making socially challenging work too radical for most grant-making authorities.

2. Heino
Food wholesaler, Finland
Designed by Hahmo (Pekka Piippo, Antti Raudaskoski), 2006

3. Surgical Aesthetics
Cosmetic surgery centre, UK
Designed by &Smith, 2010

4. Bonds
Clothing brand, Australia
Designed by Sadgrove Design (Brian Sadgrove), 1995
A brand held together by stitches.

5. Booz&Co.
Management consultancy, USA
Designed by Wolff Olins, 2008
Booz Allen Hamilton's separation of its USA government business from its commercial consulting business presented the opportunity to revive the original Booz brand, established by Edwin Booz in 1914. Calling the commercial arm Booz&Co. reassuringly suggested continuity; the logotype underlined a contemporary attitude.

6. Digital Links
Charity, UK
Designed by The Partners (Kevin Lan, Freya Defoe), 2009
The underscore, used in file names, email addresses and so on, connects the name of this charity with its mission: to provide access to digital technology for the economically or geographically excluded.

7. Ashdown-Ingram
Automotive components distributor, Australia
Designed by Sadgrove Design (Brian Sadgrove), 2005

8. Benito's Hat
Restaurant, UK
Designed by DesignStudio, 2009
The horizontal line features throughout the branding of this small Mexican restaurant chain in London.

9. The Architecture Foundation
Non-profit organization, UK
Designed by Peter and Paul (Paul Reardon, Peter Donohoe), 2009
A logotype that breathes gravitas without intimidation, stacked and underlined in architectural fashion to allow messages to be snapped on.

art matters

1

Heino

2

SURGICAL AESTHETICS

3

BONDS

4

booz&co.

5

DIGITAL_LINKS

ashdown ingram

6   7

BENITO'S HAT
MEXICAN KITCHEN

8

The Architecture Foundation

9

1. 1:1
Architecture and interior design company, Hong Kong
Designed by CoDesign (Eddy Yu, Hung Lam, Luke Lo), 2007
Less is more for this young design practice.

2. A la Feina Iguals
Equal rights agency, Spain
Designed by Summa (Tilman Solé, Patrizia Schopf), 2007
'Equality in employment,' says this wordmark for an agency of the Government of Catalonia, in different but equally effective quotation marks.

3. Alexander Hall
Financial advisor, UK
Designed by GBH, 2001

4. Arôme
Room fragrance company, Italy
Designed by Brunazzi & Associati (Andrea Brunazzi), 2004
Fragrant circumflexes take flight.

5. Böka
Restaurant, France
Designed by Area 17 (Audrey Templier), 2009
Functional type, intended to imply Scandinavian freshness and simplicity, adorned by a Häagen Dazs-style gratuitous umlaut, to conjure up an open mouth.

6. espai Maragall
Historic district, Spain
Designed by Summa (Tilman Solé, Lluís Serra), 2007
An identity for the 'Maragall area' of Gava, Catalonia, a civic centre for the performing arts. The sense of a space awaiting artistic expression is conveyed by the brackets, which are stencilled on to available surfaces.

7. Dia:Beacon
Art gallery, USA
Designed by Doyle Partners (Stephen Doyle), 2003
The addition of a colon to the Dia Art Foundation's identity allowed differentiation between its existing site in Chelsea, Manhattan and its new one in Beacon, NY.

8. Conservatoire de Lausanne
Music school, Switzerland
Designed by >moser, 2010
A logo in the key of music: a 'C' with overtones of a bass clef shows children and young adults where to start their musical learning.

9. Finish Creative Services
Packaging modelling service, UK
Designed by SVIDesign (Sasha Vidakovic), 2008
Finish produces highly finished packaging mock-ups for brand owners, design studios and ad agencies. The colon (with co-opted 'i's) intimates a long list of services.

1

2

3

4

böka

5

espai (Maragall)

6

Dia:Beacon

7

C:
conservatoire
de lausanne

8   9

10. NorrlandsOperan
Performing arts venue,
Sweden
*Designed by Stockholm
Design Lab, 2009*
An identity marking
NorrlandsOperan's
development from an
opera house to a centre
for the performing arts.

11. L-A-D-A
Film production
company, The
Netherlands
*Designed by Me Studio
(Martin Pyper), 2009*
Dashes like film punch
holes and a name
inspired by the Soviet
Russian car brand that
boomed in the 1970s lend
this identity an ironically
austere air.

12. Northern Icon
Online furniture retailer,
Estonia
*Designed by Northern
Icon (Paul Marin), 2008*
Not an asterisk or a
snowflake or a star
but a 'lobstick' – a trail
marker or monument,
first recorded in northern
Canada by Alexander
Mackenzie, and made
by stripping a tall,
conspicuous pine tree
of all but its uppermost
branches.

13. Libraries Alive
Library consultancy,
Australia
*Designed by Sadgrove
Design (Brian Sadgrove),
1997*

14. Música
Dance events, Australia
*Designed by Frost
Design, 2010*
A classic serif typeface
distinguishes this series
of high-end, large-scale
dance parties from its
more self-consciously
fashionable rivals. The
Portuguese word for
'music' was chosen as
the name as it contained
an accent on the 'u' – a
feature that reflected the
organizer's wish to create
a personal experience for
every guest.

**15. Love Language
London**
Language school, UK
*Designed by Studio
Paradise (Samuel Moffat,
Jade Abbott), 2010*
The type is Londonist –
Johnston Sans,
synonymous with the
London Underground –
and the accents are
taken from the three

languages available to
study: French, Spanish
and Portuguese.

16. Odin
Data network,
The Netherlands
*Designed by Lockstoff
Design, 2008*
Odin is the Online Data
Information Network:
a portal to databases
and documents
provided by the EU for
the European energy
research community.
The exclamation mark
puts the emphasis on
communication and,
by inverting the 'i',
information.

17. Lautstark
Speech therapy,
Germany
*Designed by Lockstoff
Design, 2010*

18. Pauffley
Design consultancy, UK
*Designed by Further
(David Shalam, Melanie
Edwards), 2008*
The pilcrow was devised
in the Middle Ages to
mark a new train of
thought in a passage of
writing, and adopted by
printers to designate
a new paragraph.
Pauffley's represents
the pause for thought
before inspiration
(hopefully) strikes.

10

11

12

13

músïca

14

LOVË
LÃNGÚAGÈ
LÒNDOÑ

odin!

15   16

[laʊtʃtark]

17

¶ Pauffley

18

19. Southern California Institute of Architecture
Architecture school, USA
Designed by Made In Space, 2010
A logotype designed to 'behave spatially', with its typography treated as a set of constantly shifting movable objects. In print, for example, the dash sits above the two word forms; in digital media, it becomes an underscore.

20. Pukstaavi
Book museum, Finland
Designed by Hahmo (Erik Bertell, Hanna Hakala, Jenni Kuokka, Antti Luostarinen, Mirva Mantere, Pekka Piippo, Antti Raudaskoski), 2010
Pukstaavi is old Finnish for 'letter'.

21. Secur
Security blinds company, UK
Designed by Grade Design (Peter Dawson, Tegan Danko), 2007
Some sturdy-looking square brackets and a bold sans serif conveys reassurance.

22. Westminster Employment
Employment service, UK
Designed by Playne Design (Clare Playne, Colin Goodhew), 2006
An asterisk that corresponds 'WE' (as in, 'WE* deliver…', 'WE* listen', etc.) to Westminster Employment, a free service that helps disabled Westminster residents get back into work.

23. Playgroup
Management training service, UK
Designed by Elmwood (Richard Scholey, Jon Stubley, Stephen Woowat, Natalie Woodhead), 2009
An assortment of characters for a service that offers training through changing role-play scenarios.

24. Classé
Audio components produer, Canada
Designed by Thomas Manss & Company, 2003
An acute accent on the 'E' doubles as part of the letter itself and provides a suitably integrated reminder of Classé's French-Canadian origins.

25. Masch Media
Public relations and marketing company, Germany
Designed by Claudius Design (Stefan Claudius), 2003
A mark that is intended to be recognizable with an 'M' in any typeface inside the brackets.

26. Austin-Smith:Lord
Architectural practice, UK
Designed by Zulver & Co, 2008

27. Grip
Team-building consultancy, Norway
Designed by Heydays, 2009
An identity for a cultural and creative workshop company based on the idea of positive change and movement (and of putting heads together in a common cause?).

19

20

21

22

?!á/g'*ue

23

CLASSÉ

24

Austin·Smith:Lord

25

26

Grip:

27

28. Adlib
Creative recruitment agency, UK
Designed by Taxi Studio (Spencer Buck, Ryan Wills), 2007

29. Art Tonic
Non-profit organization, Australia
Designed by Frost Design, 2010
Art Tonic provides hospital patients with a dose of contemporary art by curating installations that turn the sterile environment into a stimulating one. Its logotype unites the two worlds of art and medicine.

30. Connect a Million Minds
Educational initiative, USA
Designed by Doyle Partners (Stephen Doyle, Drew Heffron), 2009
A simple equation represents the mission of Time Warner Cable's philanthropic initiative: to arrest 'America's declining proficiency in science, technology, engineering and math' by inspiring young people.

31. FT100
Fair Trade index, The Netherlands
Designed by Tomato (Dylan Kendle), 2009
In contrast to the FTSE100, the FT100 is the index of monitored World Fair Trade Organization members, 100% committed to Fair Trade.

32. Foster + Partners
Architectural practice, UK
Designed by Thomas Manss & Company, 2006
The plus sign, beloved of architects, is married with Akzidenz Grotesk, beloved of graphic designers: both are cool, functional and understated. Foster's previous identity triggered a wholesale rush by architecture-related firms to Otl Aicher's Rotis typeface, whose attributes tend to divide typographers.

33. Frodo
Cosmetic surgery clinic, The Netherlands
Designed by Burobraak (Arjan Braaksma, Samuel Pernicha), 2010
Dr Frodo Gaymans,

botox and filler specialist, chose his first name to front his Amsterdam clinic. It is crowned by a device derived from the Golden Ratio, used by architects and artists since the Renaissance to determine aesthetically pleasing proportions.

34. Geozug Ingenieure
Engineering consultancy, Switzerland
Designed by Hotz & Hotz (Roman Imhof, Alexander Gächter), 2009
An alphanumeric logotype reminiscent of GPS code identifies this specialist in geographic information systems.

35. Holland & Knight
Legal practice, USA
Designed by Lippincott (Connie Birdsall, Rodney Abbott), 2008

36. infoMeteo
TV channel, Spain
Designed by Summa (Tilman Solé, Daniel Bembibre), 2010
A degree symbol highlights this weather channel's commitment to a data-led service made available through multiple platforms.

37. Jestico + Whiles
Architectural practice, UK
Designed by Jestico + Whiles (Aurelien Thomas, Ilka Sobels), 2009

28

29

30

31

Foster + Partners

32

FRODO

33

GEØZUG
1NGEN1EURE

Holland+Knight

34

35

infoMeteo°

jestico + whiles

36

37

38. Kolpa
Property agency,
The Netherlands
*Designed by Teldesign
(Rob de Bree), 2008*
Your next home, this way.

39. Karimi
Life coach, Germany
*Designed by SWSP
Design (Georg Schatz),
2010*

40. Matricia
Management software
service, Romania
*Designed by Brandient
(Cristian 'Kit' Paul), 2005*
A name and notation of
the matrix. No, not that
one; the mathematical
array of numbers or
symbols.

41. >moser
Branding consultancy,
Switzerland
*Designed by >moser,
2008*
An arrow employed as a
directional symbol, rather
than in its mathematical
'greater than' capacity.

42. NY Arts Program
Arts internship
programme, USA
*Designed by PS New York
(Penny Hardy), 2010*
NYAP places students
in leading creative and
arts organizations across
New York.

43. O+Co
Branding consultancy,
USA
*Designed by O+Co (Brent
Oppenheimer, John Kwo),
2008*

44. Westzone Publishing
Arts publisher, UK
Designed by Rose, 2004

45. Tahkokallio Design+
Design historian and
consultant, Finland
*Designed by Hahmo
(Hanna Hakala, Antti
Raudaskoski), 2009*
A wordmark for Päivi
Tahkokallio's one-woman
consultancy, specializing
in design effectiveness.

46. One Degree
Environmental initiative,
Australia
*Designed by Landor
Associates (Tim Warren,
Steve Clarke, Jason
Little), 2007*
In 2007, Rupert
Murdoch's News Limited
launched One Degree,
an initiative that made
the business carbon
neutral and continues
as a resource for others.

Its logo represents a
person with a thought
bubble – a motif repeated
with photography of
real employees in the
company's branded
material.

47. Workshop Events
Event design company,
Australia
*Designed by Naughtyfish
(Paul Garbett), 2010*
An apposite pronoun for
a company that organizes
social gatherings.

48. Wink
Watch brand, USA
*Designed by PS New York
(Penny Hardy, Shannon
Shelley), 2005*
Numerical letterforms
for a brand of timepieces
with kaleidoscope-style
dynamic watch faces,
from design group
Timefoundry.

38

39

40

>moser

41

NY+
ARTS=
PROGRAM
MANAGED BY OHIO WESLEYAN UNIVERSITY

42

O+CO

43

westzone°

44

tahkokallıo
design+

45

46

we°
workshop
events

47

48

Sometimes a logotype needs its own space: a frame or area in which to make its presence felt. The variables here are shape, proportion and the position of words and characters within the space. Geometric shapes allude loosely to badges and labels, but carriers and frames can take any form, from abstract to allegorical to literal.

Carriers & Corners

1. Artform Records
Record label, UK
Designed by Malone Design (David Malone), 2010

2. Autočechák
Used car dealership, Czech Republic
Designed by Toman Graphic Design (Jiri Toman), 2001

3. BPE
Legal practice, UK
Designed by Arthur-SteenHorneAdamson (ASHA: Scott McGuffie, Marksteen Adamson), 2007

4. Campaign to Protect Rural England
Campaign group, UK
Designed by Spencer du Bois (John Spencer), 2010
The CPRE champions the interests of the English countryside in policy development and on public platforms. Big, rustic letterforms, often with pictorial infills, capture its campaigning spirit.

5. Banc Sabadell
Bank, Spain
Designed by Mario Eskenazi, 1995
When Catalan Banc Sabadell decided to expand into southern Spain, it created a new company, called SolBank ('Sun Bank'). Mario Eskenazi designed this monogram in which a solid red circle stood for the sun. So successful was the brand that when Banc Sabadell went nationwide it adopted the SolBank identity for its own, changing only the colour from red to blue.

6. KPMG
Professional services firm, The Netherlands
Designed by Interbrand, 1987
KPMG's roots extend back to 1867, but the business itself was formed in 1987 with the merger of Peat Marwick International and Klynveld Main Goerdeler. Each initial represents a separate corporate strand, or name, from its history.
KPMG International's Trademarks are the sole property of KPMG International and their use here does not imply auditing by or endorsement of KPMG International or any of its member firms.

7. NoHo
Arts district, USA
Designed by Peloton (Todd Fedell, Tara Gordon), 2010
Lacking inspiration in the form of a recognizable landmark or a single, predominant arts culture (there are many), the identity for this North Hollywood Arts District echoes the letterforms and brightly coloured circular canopies of North Hollywood metro station.

8. WOSM
Vocational rehabilitation service, The Netherlands
Designed by Teldesign (Paul Vermijs), 2001
WOSM works with Dutch companies to reduce absence from work due to illness and injury. Putting people briefly in the spotlight to help them move on, is the message of its wordmark.

9. ZWN Group
Public transport group, The Netherlands
Designed by Onoma (Roger van den Bergh), 1994

10. The Healing Arts
Arts collective, UK
Designed by Lundgren+Lindqvist, 2010
A three-dimensional mark derived from the *Antahkarana*, an ancient Tibetan symbol for healing.

1

2

3

4

5

6

ARTS DISTRICT

7

8

9

10

1. BK Italia
Furniture manufacturer, Italy
Designed by Vignelli Associates (Massimo Vignelli, Beatriz Cifuentes), 2006
You could never accuse Vignelli Associates of over-complicating things. 'We are amazed at how afraid designers are of using simple shapes nowadays,' says Beatriz Cifuentes. 'In reality, they are the most memorable and therefore most appropriate for a long-lasting company image.'

For a project such as the rebranding of high-quality sofa-bed manufacturer BK Italia, visual simplicity was certainly going to be an advantage. Its branding programme had to encompass an expanse of brandable items from catalogues, price lists, stationery, booklets, brochures, posters and advertising to vehicles, clothing, architecture, trade-show stands and buttons for the sofas themselves.

A solid circle, in a similar warm red to the one BK Italia was already associated with, would reproduce consistently, easily at every size and in every medium. 'But the main reason [for the red circle],' says Cifuentes, 'was visual impact.' The simple shape and geometric, sans-serif lettering reflects BK's purist design aesthetic.

A total rebranding, from letterheads to lorries, for a client as passionate about design and quality as he is – it's no wonder that the project is one of Massimo Vignelli's favourites of recent years. He was even allowed to weed out 'less interesting' products from BK's range and replace them with on-brand models of his own design (Vignelli originally trained as an architect).

Simplicity and consistency have their rewards. Since the new identity was introduced, BK has experienced unprecedented growth in sales. At the time of writing, it was planning to expand into the American and Japanese markets. Whether a new dawn awaits BK's red disc in the land of the rising sun, only time will tell.

2. Design 360°
Magazine, China
Designed by milkxhake (Javin Mo), 2009

3. Cinereach
Non-profit film production foundation, USA
Designed by Method, Inc (Milena Sadée), 2009
An identity that built on its predecessor, a red 'stamped' circle, creating a prismatic effect to 'convey the notions of perspective and convergence', and confirm the foundation's increasing stature on the film scene.

4. Jelly Products
Product design company, UK
Designed by 1977 Design (Jonathan Beacher, Richard Stevens, Aimee Johnson), 2010
A name and mark that reflect the approachable, playful nature of Jelly's founder Sam Pearce and the company made in his mould.

5. ADM Promotions
Promotional products, UK
Designed by Arthur-SteenHorneAdamson (ASHA: Scott McGuffie, Marksteen Adamson, Leanne Thomas), 2009
A mark that acts as a stamp of endorsement, part of a repositioning to allow ADM to take a more strategic role in clients' branding programmes.

2

3

4

5

6. Mannerheim League for Child Welfare (Mannerheimin Lastensuojeluliitto)
Child welfare organization, Finland
Designed by Hahmo (Jenni Kuokka, Antti Raudaskoski), 2010

7. Leap
Web content management software service, Denmark
Designed by We Recommend (Martin Fredriscon, Nikolaj Knop), 2005

8. de sign de
Design museum, Japan
Designed by Ken Miki & Associates, 2010
Design with a smile for this riverside museum in Kita-ku, Osaka.

9. Detroit Institute of Arts
Art museum, USA
Designed by Pentagram (Abbott Miller), 2006
A mark to accompany the museum's $150-million renovation and reorganization, reflecting its art-historical collection and its position as a pillar of culture in the Motor City.

10. CFE
Employment and skills research consultancy, UK
Designed by Playne Design (Clare Playne, Sarah Williams, Cilena Rojas, Oliver Meikle), 2010
Bold drawn letterforms, focused by a circle, offer a stamp of integrity and seriousness.

11. La Ferme du Biéreau
Arts centre, Belgium
Designed by Coast (David Nerincx), 2008
A haystack reminds concert-goers of this music venue's former purpose.

12. My Italian Friends
Concept store, Belgium
Designed by Coast (Frederic Vanhorenbeke), 2009
Simple to use, easy to read, for this Italian food and wine store's signs, stickers, bags, tags, vans and price lists.

13. Helsinki-London Design Camp
Design promotion campaign, UK
Designed by Studio Emmi (Emmi Salonen), 2010

Helsinki is World Design Capital in 2012; this identity represents the Finnish Institute in London's programme for promoting Finnish design.

6

7

8

9

10

11

12

13

14. Dell
Personal computer brand, USA
Designed by Dell Global Brand Creative and Lippincott, 2009
Most major brands would say that it's not the design of an identity that's difficult; the real challenge is keeping it looking that way once the design company has left the scene. For businesses that grow quickly, the problem can become acute.

Dell was famously started in a college bedroom by Michael Dell in 1984, and 15 years later was the largest PC seller in the USA. In 1992, Siegel & Gale created the original Dell logotype, tilting the 'E' to reflect the founder's wish 'to turn the world on its ear' with his vision of tailored PCs. The mark became as familiar in the computer marketplace as IBM's or Apple's. But, by 2007, Dell's global expansion had spawned a motley crew of logo variants – a product of trying to control its application by some 800 creative agencies around the world. There were 3-D versions, logos inside grey button-like discs, logos inside black discs with a chrome gradient and more.

To remedy the situation, the company's global brand management team took the decision to start afresh and reclaim ownership of the brand with a new 'evolution' of the famous mark rather than try to enforce compliance with the existing one. The original mission of the company was revived and a new set of design principles drawn up for applying the brand, to be followed worldwide.

The tweaks to the logotype were subtle but significant. They revolved around the 'E', which was compressed slightly and tilted further to extend above and below the height and baseline of the other letters. This action drew the two 'L's to the left and made for a more compact, integrated mark, while the added ring is intended to forestall any

unauthorized attempts to mount it on grey or black discs or anything else.
©2012 Dell Inc. All Rights Reserved.

15. Baby Box
Nursery bedding company, Argentina
Designed by Ailoviu (Verónica Ridi, Marcos Zerene), 2010
A circle that's maternal and a baby B.

16. Abandon Normal Devices Festival
Cinema and new media festival, UK
Designed by Uniform (Marcus McCabe), 2009
An invitation to reject convention for an annual festival of new cinema and digital culture.

17. OneToBe
Furniture maker, Belgium
Designed by Coast (Frederic Vanhorenbeke), 2011

18. TLT Solicitors
Legal practice, UK
Designed by Uffindell (Nigel Hillier, Davon Pointer), 2006

15

16

17

18

19. Transportation Alternatives
Campaigning organization, USA
Designed by Onoma (Roger van den Bergh), 2008
Transportation Alternatives' mission is to encourage walking, cycling and public-transport use, and 'reclaim New York City's streets from the automobile'. Its traffic-sign-like logo shows the way.

20. Radiodada
Online broadcaster, Hong Kong
Designed by Tommy Li Design Workshop, 2008
An inquisitive elephant and a warren of letterforms represent this online station's exploration of arts and design issues in Hong Kong.

21. Pax
Campaigning organization, USA
Designed by Doyle Partners (Stephen Doyle, Martin Iselt), 2005
Pax works to prevent gun violence in the USA through overlapping programmes of activity.

22. Duck Duck Goose
Restaurant, Australia
Designed by gardens&co (Wilson Tang, Jeffrey Tam, Wong Kin Chung), 2010
A contemporary Chinese bar and restaurant in Melbourne's QV development, named after the traditional pre-school game in which a child (the goose) circles the others (ducks) until he picks one to chase him.

23. Mayne Health
Healthcare provider, Australia
Designed by Sadgrove Design (Brian Sadgrove), 2001

24. *Pose Magazine*
Fashion periodical, China
Designed by c+c workshop, 2009

25. Godzilla Sushi Bar
Restaurant, Greece
Designed by G Design Studio (Michalis Georgiou, Alexandros Gavrilakis), 2006

26. Showtime Networks
TV network, USA
Designed by Chermayeff & Geismar, 1997
The 'SHO' mark-within-a-mark is used in newspaper listings and as the channel's on-air identifier.

27. Librería Internacional Bilbao
Bookstore, Spain
Designed by Zorraquino (Miquel Zorraquino, Miren S Gaubeka), 2006

28. Helen Langridge Associates
Film production company, UK
Designed by Tomato (Simon Taylor), 2009

19

20

21

22

23

24

25

26

27

28

1. Brill
Cafe chain, Singapore
Designed by Couple, 2008
Brill is a food take-out business needing to convey care, attention and surprise in small, dense, urban retail settings.

2. World Outstanding Chinese Design Award
Design award, China
Designed by CoDesign (Hung Lam), 2004

3. Scandinavian Airlines
Airline, Sweden
Designed by Stockholm Design Lab, 1998
Uncomplicated, elegant, functional: an identity that conveys quintessentially Scandinavian qualities.

4. 14 oz.
Clothing retailer, Germany
Designed by Boy Bastiaens/Stormhand, 1999
The name of this German denim retailer is also the optimum per-yard weight for unwashed denim.

5. Goldman Sachs
Banking and securities company, USA
Designed by Lippincott & Margulies, 1970
Presence, authority, security: these are the qualities generated by setting the Goldman Sachs name in an elegant, high-contrast typeface and stacking it inside a square with luxurious breathing space. The original wordmark from 1970 was refined to breathe more 'air' (and composure) into it, but the vertical ligature between the first letters that cements the name together was kept. Since Goldman Sachs, New York Life and American Express all adopted blue-square marks in the 1960s and 1970s (all by Lippincott & Margulies), the motif has been seen as the go-to identity solution for safe establishment brands.

6. HOK
Architectural practice, USA
Designed by HOK (Gyo Obata), 1955; Toky Branding + Design (Eric Thoelke, Travis Brown), 2008
The red square mark designed by Gyo Obata when he founded HOK in 1955 (with George Hellmuth and George Kassabaum) was streamlined by Toky for new applications and redrawn with a modified Bodoni.

7. Hotel Arts Barcelona
Hotel, Spain
Designed by Thomas Manss & Company, 2003
Revising its own design for the luxury hotel after 10 years to signal a major refurbishment, Thomas Manss & Company added a twist to the arts theme by turning each letter into a minor artwork.

8. Zoo Concept Store
Retailer, United Arab Emirates
Designed by Hani Alireza, 2011

9. City University of New York
University, USA
Designed by Pentagram (Michael Bierut), 2004
Originally developed to badge an 'Invest in CUNY' fundraising campaign, the solid square with Trade Gothic Bold Condensed initials replaced a fussy, faintly paganistic-looking pentagon.

10. Conservatori Municipal de Música de Barcelona
Music conservatory, Spain
Designed by Serracatafau (Quim Serra), 2005

11. Indus Capital
Hedge fund, USA
Designed by Brownjohn (James Beveridge, Andy Mosley, Tom Rogers), 2008

12. Pravda
Bar/restaurant, USA
Designed by Mucca Design (Matteo Bologna), 1997
A Cyrillic-style, Eastern Bloc logo for the old-world Russian speakeasy and caviar bar that helped make its Lower Manhattan neighbourhood hip.

1

2

3

4

5

6

7

8

9

10

11

12

1. Acacia Avenue
Consumer research company, UK
Designed by Rose, 2001
Acacia Avenue: the stereotypical English residential street, where people take an avid interest in what other people say and do. Which is exactly what this company does.

2. AnnaLou of London
Jewellery brand, UK
Designed by Burobraak (Arjan Braaksma), 2008

3. Oikos
Interior paints and surface treatments company, Italy
Designed by SVIDesign (Sasha Vidakovic), 2007

4. CGA Bryson
Property development, Australia
Designed by Sadgrove Design (Brian Sadgrove), 1995

5. United Colors of Benetton
Clothing company, Italy
Designed by Massimo Vignelli, 1995
What started as an advertising slogan was adopted as the company's brand in 1991, during its notorious, taboo-breaking collaboration with photographer Oliviero Toscani. Vignelli moved the phrase from the centre of the green box to the upper left. This change of alignment asked that the text be read more as a statement than simply as a label name, a move that suited the serious, campaigning tone of many of its ads.

6. City of Westminster College
Further education college, UK
Designed by Atelier Works (Quentin Newark), 2011
An identity to mark the college's move to a new, purpose-built campus at Paddington Green, whose 'stepped' architecture the tilted rectangle represents.

7. Derbi
Motorcycle and scooter manufacturer, Spain
Designed by Summa (Tilman Solé), 2002

8. Facebook
Social network site, USA
Designed by Cuban Council and Test Pilot Collective (Joe Kral), 2005
Facebook's blue was a legacy from the identity Mark Zuckerberg created for the network when it was thefacebook.com – a colour he chose because of his red–blue colour blindness. Type designer Joe Kral crafted the logotype into shape.

9. Port Vell
Urban district, Spain
Designed by Summa (Josep Maria Mir), 1992
Port Vell, Barcelona's former port facility, was relaunched after the city's 1992 Olympic Games, as a regenerated urban district with its own distinctive identity.

10. Fatboy
Beanbag furniture, Finland
Designed by Hahmo (Pekka Piippo), 1998
The brand launched by Jukka Setala and Alex Bergman now sells beanbags, hammocks and lounge chairs across the world, all bearing the bright red Fatboy tag.

1

2

3

4

UNITED COLORS OF BENETTON.

5

CITY OF WESTMINSTER COLLEGE

6

DERBI

7

facebook

8

PORT VELL

9

fatboy

10

11. YouTube
Online video sharing, USA
Designed by Chad Hurley, 2005
Having a bona fide, qualified graphic designer in your ranks as a start-up business can have its benefits. Chad Hurley was a design graduate of Indiana University of Pennsylvania when he was taken on as the sole designer in a start-up encryption company in California, at the height of the dot-com boom.

The name the company later came up with for itself following a merger was PayPal, and Hurley designed a simple, outline logotype in a bold, italicized sans-serif typeface that served the company through phenomenal growth, until it was replaced in 2007.

At PayPal, Hurley hooked up with two computer scientitsts, Steve Chen and Jawed Karim, and hatched the concept of a video version of Flickr, developing a working site through 2005. 'The one thing we did worry about was branding,' Hurley said in an interview for the book *Designing Media*. 'You can have a great solution but beyond people relating to it, they have to remember the product they've used... We were trying to express this idea of personal television. We came up with the name of YouTube and wrapped that in a kind of simplified logo so that people could get a sense of what our site was about.'

The key, Hurley felt, to attracting its audience of young, web-savvy users was to design an identity (and a website) that felt as if it had 'been built by the community': playful, basic (in the same way as Google) and trustworthy because it didn't feel corporate and over-produced. In October 2006, Hurley and Chen sold YouTube to Google for $1.65 billion.

In 2011, the site was serving more than three billion video views a day, plus advertising, TV shows, movie rentals and music videos. The unfinished and edgy of yesterday can quickly become the slick and corporate of today.

12. Wildbore & Gibbons
Legal practice, UK
Designed by A2 Design, 2008
A modern mark for the UK's oldest independent firm of trademark attorneys.

13. Wright Brothers
Oyster farm and restaurant chain, UK
Designed by SomeOne (Gary Holt, Laura Hussey), 2010
A tiled effect suggests a logotype originally set into a fishmonger's wall.

14. Durex
Condom manufacturer, UK
Designed by Elmwood (Andy Lawrence, Simon Preece, Lyndsay Hales), 2007
'Durability, Reliability and Excellence,' three qualities admirable in a condom, was the phrase shortened by the London Rubber Company in 1929. The tweak by Elmwood involved softening the letterforms to reflect the shift of theme in the brand's marketing from safe sex to pleasure and sexual wellbeing.

15. The Swanswell Trust
Addict rehabilitation service, UK
Designed by Johnson Banks, 2008
One of a series of versions in which the slip of paper is transformed from crumpled to straightened-out, to represent the 'journey' of rehabilitated addicts.

12

13

14

15

16. House of Illustration
Gallery and events venue, London, UK
Designed by hat-trick (Gareth Howat, Jim Sutherland, Mark Wheatcroft, Alexandra Jurva), 2008
The vision of Quentin Blake for the House of Illustration – since he was Children's Laureate – is of the world's first centre dedicated to illustration in all its forms. Hat-trick's sketchbook page logo is able to incorporate any style of illustration, or can be left blank, to inspire others.

17. Velux
Roof windows company, Denmark
Designed by Stockholm Design Lab, 2004
The first Velux roof window was fitted in Denmark in 1942 by V Kann Rasmussen & Co, which later adopted the trademark as its corporate identity. The 2004 identity reduced the height of the slab-serif logotype to produce a more compact, legible mark.

18. Moving Images
Annual new-media conference, Denmark
Designed by We Recommend (Martin Fredricson, Nikolaj Knop), 2008

19. *Magazines Canada*
Periodical, Canada
Designed by Hambly & Woolley (Barb Woolley, Emese Ungar-Walker), 2009

20. Bibliothèque Régionale d'Aoste
Regional library, Italy
Designed by Brunazzi & Associati (Giovanni Brunazzi, Andrea Brunazzi), 1995

21. Paramount
Members' club, UK
Designed by Mind Design, 2009
An op-art-inspired identity for a club located on the top three floors of the Centre Point building in London, with several versions that each feature 33 rows of shapes found in the building's design (for its 33 floors).

22. John Howard Print Studios
Printmaking facility, UK
Designed by Two, 2007
An identity expressed mainly through stickers applied by hand to stationery, comprising the studio's name, set in the Akkurat typeface.

23. Shelta
Fashion retailer, Sweden
Designed by We Recommend (Martin Fredricson, Nikolaj Knop), 2010
A label for a street fashion store that, like the clothes, recalls hip hop and sneaker labels from 1980s New York.

24. Passion Foods
Organic food retailer, Australia
Designed by Sadgrove Design (Brian Sadgrove), 2002

25. Slice
TV network, Canada
Designed by Rethink, 2007
A slice of cake that appears in different colours – one for each 'guilty pleasure' – on a channel devoted to 'topics that matter to women'.

16

17

18

19

20

21

22

23

PASSION FOODS

24

25

1. ABF The Soldiers' Charity
Charity, UK
Designed by Dragon Rouge (David Beare, Gemma Walters, Mark Goldsmith), 2010
A change of name from The Army Benelovent Fund was accompanied by this visual identity, to capitalize on heightened awareness and respect among the British public for the armed forces.

2. Arrtco
Fashion retailer, China
Designed by Joyn:Viscom (Jiang Jian, Ronald Tau), 2005
A leaf/water droplet for a fashion brand with an environmental theme.

3. Arts Affaires
Art consultancy, France
Designed by FL@33 (Agathe Jacquillat, Tomi Vollauschek), 2007

4. Barcelona TV
TV channel, Spain
Designed by Summa (Tilman Solé, Rocío Martinavarro), 2005
Barcelona's own public TV station aims to give local citizens a voice.

5. The Customer Closeness Company
Consumer research, UK
Designed by Arthur-SteenHorneAdamson (ASHA: Chris Greenwood, Scott McGuffie, Marksteen Adamson), 2010
CCC draws its findings from conversations it establishes between brands and their customers.

6. The Faculty of Royal Designers for Industry
Honorary association, UK
Designed by Studio Dempsey (Mike Dempsey), 2005

7. Biblioteca Artur Martorell
Public library, Barcelona
Designed by Serracatafau (Quim Serra), 2007
A bookish icon that serves for this public library and as a pointer for Barcelona's network of school libraries.

8. Design for London
Civic design advisory group, UK
Designed by Tomato (Michael Horsham), 2009
Pushing the envelope?
Design For London supports 'good place shaping' across the city, on behalf of the Mayor of London.

9. L'Escalier
Contemporary art showroom, Singapore
Designed by &Larry (Larry Peh, Ter Yeow Yeong), 2006
The step cut into a triangle resembles a tangram puzzle piece or an element in the art of paper cutting. Enlarged as a silhouette, the logo doubles as a storecard and a swing tag.

10. Zendol B
Timber preservation producer, Romania
Designed by Brandient (Ciprian Badalan), 2009

11. Digital Cinema Media
Cinema advertising, UK
Designed by CDT Design, 2008
Projecting brands in cinemas all over the UK.

12. Evangelische Omroep
Public broadcaster, The Netherlands
Designed by Lava, 2009
One of a system of themed identifiers to launch the youth division of this Christian channel, Evangelical Broadcasting, part of The Netherlands Public Broadcasting system.

1

2

3

4

5

6

7

8

9

10

11

12

13. H.J. Heinz
Processed-food
manufacturer, USA
*Designed by H.J. Heinz,
1969*
While riding an elevated
train in New York City in
1896, Henry J Heinz was
impressed by a shoe
store's advertisement
for its 21 styles of shoe.
Although his company
was manufacturing more
than 60 products at the
time, Heinz thought 57
was a lucky number, and
started using the slogan
'57 Varieties' in all his
advertising.

In 1969, a century after
Heinz started bottling
horseradish that he had
grown in his garden,
a corporate identifier
that read 'HEINZ
57' was considered
unrepresentative of a
business that marketed
more than 1,250 varieties
in around 150 countries.

The '57' and all-upper-
case wordmark, set
in the famous Heinz
keystone – borrowed
from Pennsylvania,
the Keystone State,
the birthplace of
Heinz – continue to
appear on packaging.
The title-case version,
in a softer, shorter,
solid-red keystone, is
the corporate emblem
for a $10.7 billion global
business selling 650
million bottles of ketchup
a year and 1.5 million tins
of beans every day in the
UK alone.

14. Ice Cream Music
Production music library,
UK
*Designed by 1977 Design
(Paul Bailey, David
Armstrong, Chloe Pillai),
2010*
An online library of youth-
oriented production
music, with a lot of
flavours to choose from.

15. Fornetti
Italian cafe, USA
*Designed by Mucca
Design (Matteo Bologna,
Andrea Brown, Giona
Lodigiani), 2010*
An authentic Italian
artisan aesthetic for this
deli within the Foodparc
on Sixth Avenue,
Manhattan.

**16. Lakeside
Counselling**
Psychotherapy service,
UK

*Designed by Ark
(Jonathan Chubb), 2010*
An unintimidating identity
that conveys the essence
of the counselling
process to new clients.

17. Life Assay
Diagnostic device
manufacturer,
South Africa
*Designed by Mister
Walker (Garth Walker),
2010*

14

15

16

17

18. The New 42nd Street
Non-profit organization, USA
Designed by Chermayeff & Geismar (Steff Geissbuhler), 1996
A street sign signals the organization that oversaw the regeneration of the Times Square/42nd Street neighbourhood, and the rejuvenation of seven historic theatres.

19. Rambert Moves
Fundraising campaign, UK
Designed by hat-trick (Gareth Howat, Jim Sutherland, Adam Giles), 2010
For Rambert Dance Company's change of location to London's South Bank, this identity with shifting, choreographed planes was created to mobilize funds and support.

20. Malaparte
Private event space, Canada
Designed by Gottschalk + Ash International (Udo Schliemann), 2010
Malaparte is a sixth-floor private dining space in Toronto, with a rooftop terrace modelled on that of Villa Malaparte in Capri, which provided the breathtaking setting for Jean-Luc Godard's 1963 film *Le mépris* ('Contempt'), and is reached by a flight of reverse-pyramidal stairs.

21. Love From London
Film tourism resource, UK
Designed by KentLyons (Jon Cefai), 2010
Love from London is an online resource that maps major films and their locations across the capital.

22. Signature Theatre Company
Theatre company, USA
Designed by C&G Partners (Steff Geissbuhler, Alex Geissbuhler), 2007
Each season at the Signature Theatre Company in Manhattan is dedicated to the works of a single living American playwright. Its identity reverses the theatre's name out of a cloud of signatures of all its playwrights-in-residence.

23. MMM Festival
Music festival, Switzerland
Designed by FL@33 (Agathe Jacquillat, Tomi Vollauschek), 2010
The Festival de Musique des Montagnes du Monde is an eclectic mix of music from the world's mountain regions, and takes place at Anzère, 2,000 m (6,500 ft) up in the Swiss Alps.

24. Ling Lee
Health foods provider, Singapore
Designed by gardens&co (Wilson Tang, Jeffrey Tam), 2009

25. Skype
Internet communication software, Luxembourg
Designed by Skype, 2003
A name that started off as 'Sky peer-to-peer', which became 'Skyper', for which no domain names were available. Lopping off the 'r' created a name that led to a fluffy, friendly, cloud-like logotype and, like Hoover and Google, has become a verb as well as a brand.

26. Redfern
Regeneration zone, Australia
Designed by Frost Design, 2011
A smiling logotype that is part of a programme of redevelopment aimed at drawing visitors to Redfern-Waterloo, an inner-city suburb of Sydney and the heart of urban-Aboriginal Australia.

27. Laimar Films
Film production company, Spain
Designed by Zorraquino (Miguel Zorraquino, Miren S Gaubeka), 2010

18

19

20

21

22

23

24

25

26

27

1. 208 Duecento Otto
Restaurant, Hong Kong
*Designed by c+c
workshop, 2010*
Italian cuisine in a
restaurant channelling
Manhattan Meatpacking
District interior design,
at 208 Hollywood Road.

**2. Charlton Kings
Baptist Church**
Church, UK
*Designed by Arthur-
SteenHorneAdamson
(ASHA: Scott McGuffie,
Marksteen Adamson),
2010*
A church in Cheltenham,
keen to convey its
modern, approachable
identity and openness
to newcomers.

3. Arch Idea
Architectural practice,
Russia
*Designed by
Transformer Studio (Ivan
Danyshevsky, Nikita
Melnikov), 2009*
Dialogue: the way into
design.

4. ArkOpen
Architectural practice,
Finland
*Designed by Hahmo
(Paco Aguayo, Antti
Raudaskoski), 2006*
A name and an identity
that stem from the
firm's position as
Finland's leading
practitioner of 'open'
architecture, in which
buyers of prefabricated
apartments are free to
specify the plan and
materials of their new
home.

5. Land Securities
Property developer, UK
*Designed by hat-trick
(Gareth Howat, David
Kimpton, Jim Sutherland,
David Jones, Adam
Giles), 2007*
A mark for the UK's
largest commercial
property developer that
kept the type style of
the previous logotype
(including 'Land' in
bold), but turned its
lumpen accompanying
monogram into a pair of
corners/arrows that are
also used separately to
highlight information.

**6. Direction des Musées
de France**
Government museums
agency, France
*Designed by Studio
Apeloig, 2005*
A stamp of approval
from the French

Ministry of Culture for
museums that implement
recommended
conservation practice.

7. Globeride
Sports equipment group,
Japan
*Designed by Samurai
(Kashiwa Sato, Tomoatsu
Kasahara), 2009*

8. Emit
Sound design studio,
2010
*Designed by Graphical
House, 2010*
With echoes of
technological identities
of the 1970s, possibly of
obscure mid-Eurpoean
synth acts, this mark
incorporates corners
that refer to the studio's
acoustic panelling.

**9. American Museum
of Natural History**
Museum, USA
*Designed by Lance
Wyman, 1990*
An identity featuring
the museum's landmark
tower that, since new
buildings were added,
has been superceded but
which is still used in the
original building.

1

2

3

4

LandSecurities

5

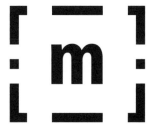

6

7

American
Museum of
Natural
History

8   9

10. Daydream Nation
Fashion label, Hong Kong
Designed by CoDesign (Eddy Yu, Hung Lam, Christy Chen), 2008
Possibly named after the Sonic Youth album, Daydream Nation designs fashion collections and features collaborations in music, theatre, dance and art in its flagship Hong Kong store: a brand that sees no restrictions on what it can do.

11. Moka
Coffee house, UK
Designed by Arthur-SteenHorneAdamson (ASHA: Leanne Thomas, Scott McGuffie, Marksteen Adamson), 2010
An aromatic surround (with hidden coffee beans) for a simple logotype creates a chic, richly flavoured mark.

12. Start Anywhere
Office space and facilities service, UK
Designed by Brownjohn (James Beveridge, Andy Mosley, Tom Rogers), 2008

13. Laline
Bathroom and beauty products brand, Israel
Designed by Dan Alexander & Co., 2005

14. Hans Appenzeller
Jewellery designer, The Netherlands
Designed by Onoma (Roger van den Bergh), 1989
An identity for designer Appenzeller and his store on Grimburgwal that's all about the art of creating perfect circles – necklaces, bracelets and rings.

15. HoHoJo
Online property search, Hong Kong
Designed by CoDesign (Eddy Yu, Hung Lam, Ray Cheung), 2010
In Cantonese, *hohojo* means 'very good for renting'.

16. Intersect
Not-for-profit Internet research service, Australia
Designed by Naughtyfish (Paul Garbett), 2008

17. Het Nationale Ballet
National ballet company, The Netherlands
Designed by Me Studio (Martin Pyper), 2003

Used as a 'window' on the world of ballet, the logo is usually applied on images of productions as a mini frame, reversed out in white. The range of position variants alludes to the movement of dancers on the stage.

18. Hard Turm Park
Mixed-use property development, Switzerland
Designed by Hotz & Hotz (Roman Imhof, Sidi Meier), 2008
While the open rectangle represents the three lower-level buildings of this development, each with its own courtyard, the stacked text creates a silhouette of the scheme's landmark tower.

10

11

12

13

14

15

16

17

18

19. Bryter Estates
Winery, USA
Designed by Hatch Design (Joel Templin, Katie Jain, Eszter T Clark), 2010
An old-world California crest for this Sonoma winemaker.

20. One Atlantic
Event space, USA
Designed by Mucca Design (Matteo Bologna, Christine Celic Strohl) and Darden Studio, 2010
With a primary audience of brides-to-be and event planners who might not be thinking of Atlantic City as the most sophisticated venue, the identity of this event space at the top of The Pier at Caesars in Atlantic City aims to convey light, airy elegance.

21. So... soap!
Community manufacturing scheme, Hong Kong
Designed by CoDesign (Eddy Yu, Hung Lam, Ray Cheung), 2010
So... soap! employs soap-makers in the community to package its organic products in recycled bottles. Its identity comprises an open square resembling the Chinese character for 'every district'.

22. The Naughton Gallery
Art gallery, UK
Designed by Studio Tonne (Paul Farrington), 2008
The long, L-shaped Naughton Gallery at Queen's University Belfast showcases paintings and sculpture from the university's own collection.

23. Town Hall Hotel
Hotel, UK
Designed by SomeOne (David Law, Therese Severinsen), 2010
Before the chic conversion of Neo-classical Bethnal Green Town Hall, SomeOne's designers, touring the empty building, discovered original oak filing cabinets, complete with brass windows for labels on their drawers. With the building's past playing a big part in the hotel's brand 'story', these clerical accoutrements offered a fitting frame for a logotype.

24. The Pew Center for Arts & Heritage
Arts centre, USA
Designed by Johnson Banks, 2009
A flexible identity whose variants reshuffle its component parts to highlight different initiatives and themes.

25. Holistic
PR and marketing, UK
Designed by Blast (Giff, Paul Tunnicliffe, Henry Sly), 2009

26. National Theatre Wales
Theatre company, UK
Designed by Elfen (Aaron Easterbrook, Guto Evans), 2009
An English-language theatre company with an identity that expresses its aim to create site-specific work and to have a dialogue with creators, participants and audiences.

27. Victor Russo's Osteria
Restaurant franchise, The Netherlands
Designed by Total Identity (Maarten Brandenburg), 2010
An Arcimboldo-style tableau of flavours and ingredients provides the backdrop for this Italian *osteria* franchise.

28. Émilie Bailey
Photographer, UK
Designed by &Smith, 2009

19

20

21

22

23

24

25

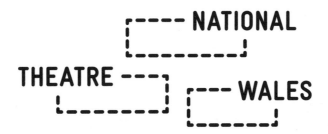

26

27

émilie
bailey

28

From Iran and Israel to China and
Hong Kong, typographic expression
is as rich and imaginative as it is
in the West. Each calligraphically
descended writing system offers
endless variation in the character
of its strokes, while bilingual
logotypes bring East and West
together through type.

E A S 東

מיכל מילר

oranjebloesem

原地建築

GULF GATEWAY

朝阳

1. *14 Blades*
Film, Hong Kong
*Designed by c+c
workshop, 2010*
For a kung-fu movie
focused on the elite
secret-service agents
(masters of the '14
Blades') of the Imperial
Court in the Ming
Dynasty, a Chinese
logotype based on the
royal seal of that period.

**2. Approach
Architecture Studio**
Architectural practice,
China
*Designed by
Joyn:Viscom (Jiang Jian),
2007*
Pixellation of the Chinese
characters creates an
industrious, under-
construction appearance
for this Beijing-based
architecture studio.

3. Honeymoon Dessert
Dessert house chain,
Hong Kong
*Designed by Tommy Li
Design Workshop, 2002*
A simple, classical
logotype reflects the
traditional, homemade
desserts on offer at a
chain that expanded
from one branch in Hong
Kong's Sai Kung district
to 100 branches across
the city state and China.

4. Origin Architect
Architectural practice,
China
*Designed by
Joyn:Viscom (Jiang Jian,
Jing Fing), 2011*
Representing this
new firm's back-to-
fundamentals approach,
this logotype resembles
bamboo scaffolding or a
child's matchstick puzzle.

5. Chuan Pictures
Film production
company, Singapore
*Designed by &Larry
(Larry Peh, Lee Weicong),
2009*
A production company
set up by Singaporean
film-maker Royston Tan,
Chuan Pictures takes its
name from the Chinese
for 'fountain'. The logo,
rendered in a custom-
made sans-serif face
inside a rising droplet,
aims to balance tradition
with modernity, stability
with dynamism.

6. NuZi
Lifestyle store, China
*Designed by CoDesign
(Eddy Yu, Hung Lam,
Sunny Wong), 2006*
NuZi is a multifunctioning
retail space in the
Taikang Lu art district of
Shanghai that promises
to bring Western design
and lifestyle products
to Chinese consumers.
Its goods come via
New Zealand – hence
the name – and its logo
symbolizes a bridge
between East and West.

7. Laidian Coffee Bar
Cafe, China
*Designed by Hesign
International (Jianping
He, Adger Yawei Zha),
2009*

8. Ying Kee Tea House
Tea brand, Hong Kong
*Designed by Tommy Li
Design Workshop, 2010*
Modern, contoured
characters set within
a traditional Chinese
window-frame
arrangement have helped
to rejuvenate this tea
brand, founded in 1881.

9. The Vietnam Woods
Restaurant, Hong Kong
*Designed by Tommy Li
Design Workshop, 2010*
A fusion of traditional
ink calligraphy and
contemporary minimal
characters reflects the
recent transformation
of this 30-year-old
Vietnamese restaurant
into a modern dining
room.

10. Taste Together
Restaurant chain, China
*Designed by Tommy Li
Design Workshop, 2010*
With a custom-made
typeface based on
its cow character
illustration, this
Vietnamese restaurant
chain signals its
speciality: beef pho.

**11. Zhejiang Daily Press
Group**
Media group, China
*Designed by MetaDesign
China (Martin Steinacker,
Linda Stannieder,
Sebastian Braun,
Katharina Lemke, Lu
Cheng, Sophia Lu), 2009*
A logotype whose
bold, angular lines
complement the
stronger, more circular
redrawing of the group's
former symbol.

1

2

3

4

5

6

7

英記茶莊

YING KEE TEA HOUSE

~1881~

THE VIETNAM WOODS

悦木

老趙

8

9

10

11

1. Darbiran Co
Security glass
manufacturer, Iran
*Designed by Iraj Mirza
Alikhani, 1990*
Nowhere in the Arab
world is logotype design
as vibrant and diverse as
it is in Iran. The country
possesses a proud
culture of calligraphy that
stretches back centuries.

Four hundred years ago,
Persia's writing system
diverged from that of
other Islamic cultures,
and with poetry and
literature dominating the
country's art, calligraphy
became a powerful
medium for lending
spectacularly original
visual expression to
these written works.

A number of calligraphic
styles developed: clean,
geometric Kufic styles
on one hand, and six
separate cursive script
styles on the other,
from the popular, highly
readable Naskh to the
energetic, monumental
Thuluth. It is upon this
rich calligraphic tradition
that Iran's modern
typography is based.

In poster and logotype
design, the tradition of
expressive calligraphy
has had an inspirational
effect, demonstrated
by many of the marks
here and on the next four
pages.

Iraj Mirza Alikhani started
designing in the mid
1980s and established
Ashna Advertising in
1991. 'Iranian calligraphy
offers a great variety to
logo designers,' says
Alikhani, 'and getting
familiar with the Seven
Calligraphic Styles is
a crucial priority for a
logotype designer.'

Alikhani's Naskh-style
mark for Darbiran,
a manufacturer of
toughened glass,
highlights the flexibility
available to Iranian
typographers in
fashioning figurative
references from written
script, or 'calligrams'.
'When designing a
logotype, I always try
to concentrate on the
subject itself. So I tried
to express the power,
potency and security
of Darbiran's products
through the use of a

compact composition of
characters, which, at the
same time, resembles a
clenched fist.'

**2. Al Jazeera Children's
Channel**
TV channel, Qatar
*Designed by Naji El Mir,
2005*
The droplet-like Al
Jazeera News logotype
was designed not by
a leading branding
agency but by a Qatari
man who heard about
the design competition
on his car radio and
sketched his entry in
20 minutes. It is now a
brand with considerable
equity: post 9/11, the
mark has identified
its footage on news
channels all over the
world. Its presence was
even made obligatory
in the identity for the
network's pan-Arab
children's channel. Naji
El Mir found a way for it to
cohabit with his simple,
rounded wordmark by
encompassing them both
within a circle.

3. *Art*
Magazine, Iran
*Designed by Mehdi
Saeedi, 2001*

4. DID Publications
Art and design publisher,
Iran
*Designed by Majid
Abbasi, 1999*
DID Publications is an
offshoot of DID Graphics,
one of Iran's leading
design studios, set up in
Tehran by Majid Abbasi
and Firouz Shafei. Its
logotype is a simple
Thuluth-style script.

5. Elahe Gallery
Art gallery, Iran
*Designed by Ebrahim
Haghighi, 1999*
Brushstrokes by one of
Iranian graphic design's
senior generation,
Ebrahim Haghighi, spell
the name of the Tehran
gallery and that of its
artist founder, Elahe
Djavaheri.

2

3

4

5

6. International News Network
TV channel, Iran
Designed by Mostafa Assadollahi, 1999

7. Ketab-e-Hafteh
Literary magazine, Iran
Designed by Behrooz Matinsefat, 1999
A masthead for a weekly periodical on books and writing.

8. Media Builder
Software service, Iran
Designed by Raad Design Studio (Iman Raad), 2008

9. Nahj al-Balagha Cultural Center
Museum, Iran
Designed by Mohammad Ehsai, 1982
This museum holds a collection of written works and speeches by Imam Ali, cousin and son-in-law of the Prophet Muhammad. Its logotype is written in a Thuluth calligraphic style.

10. Hamrah-e-Aval
Mobile phone network, Iran
Designed by Amrollah Farhadi, 2007
Hamrah-e-Aval ('First Operator') is Iran's primary mobile phone network. The rhythm in its logotype is intended to convey an approachable, dependable image to customers.

11. Grandmother Co
Health foods supplier, Iran
Designed by Mehdi Saeedi, 2001

12. Reza Abbasi Museum
Museum, Iran
Designed by Morteza Momayez, 1976
A logotype by the father figure of modern Iranian graphic design Morteza Momayez, for a museum of calligraphy in Tehran named after one of Ottoman-era Persia's greatest miniaturists.

13. Restaurant Mansour
Restaurant, Iran
Designed by Mehdi Saeedi, 2003

6

7

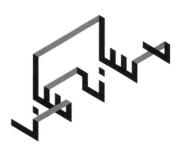

8

9

10

11

12

13

14. *Sher*
Poetry magazine, Iran
*Designed by Farzad
Adibi, 1998*

15. Tize Scissors
Rug-making equipment
provider, Iran
*Designed by Mehdi
Saeedi, 2004*

16. Noon Cultural Group
Art institute, Iran
*Designed by Damoon
Khanjanzadeh, 2002*

17. Mahnab Co
Imports and exports
company, Iran
*Designed by Mehdi
Saeedi, 2002*

18. Sahar Co
Food-processing
company, Iran
*Designed by Mehdi
Saeedi, 1999*

19. *Samarkand*
Literary magazine, Iran
*Designed by Majid
Abbasi, 2008*

20. Sematak Advertising
Advertising agency, Iran
*Designed by Mehdi
Saeedi, 2001*

21. *Shahr-e Hashtom*
Magazine, Iran
*Designed by
Mohammadreza Abdolali,
2007*
A highly geometric script
provides the masthead
for this journal on society
and culture.

14

15

16

17

18

سمرقند ٠٠٠

19

20

21

1. Globes
Business newspaper, Israel
Designed by Oded Ezer and Shimon Sandhaus, 1998
Oded Ezer is one of Israel's most exciting typographers, creating new Hebrew fonts and three-dimensional typographic artworks alongside his work for commercial clients. *Globes* is Israel's leading business daily, delivered each evening to 45,000 subscribers. Ezer's masthead is an update of the previous one, improving legibility with bold, geometric letterforms lightened by IBM-style striping.

2. Habimah National Theatre
National theatre, Israel
Designed by Dan Reisinger, 1968
Bold, modular characters include (reading right to left) an initial 'heh' letter and its reflected form as the last letter. These two characters became the building blocks of a menorah-like symbol. (A menorah is the candelabrum that is an emblem of Judaism and of Israel.)

3. Tel Aviv Museum of Art
Contemporary art museum, Israel
Designed by Dan Reisinger, 1977
Reisinger's monogram for Israel's leading museum of modern art features a 'mem' character (for 'museum') that echoes the plan of the building.

4. Lechem Eretz
Supermarket, Israel
Designed by Yotam Hadar, 2005
A logotype for *Lechem Eretz* ('Bread of the Land'), a modern yet ultra-orthodox kosher supermarket.

5. Lili
Artist, Israel
Designed by Oded Ezer, 2004
A minimal, rhythmic yet surprisingly readable logotype composed of characters from the very popular Frank-Rühl typeface with the lower part of each letter removed.

6. Michal Miller
Shoe designer–maker, Israel
Designed by Yotam Hadar, 2007
Yotam Hadar is a rising star of Hebrew typography, equally at home with designing commercial consumer-facing identities as with more research-based assignments, as shown by this minimalist logotype and his other work on these pages.

7. Signon
Magazine, Israel
Designed by Yotam Hadar, 2008
For the style supplement of a daily paper, paper folded into a stylish masthead.

8. Acca Festival of Alternative Theatre
Theatre festival, Israel
Designed by Yotam Hadar, 2005

9. Oded Ezer Typography
Typographer, Israel
Designed by Oded Ezer, 2003
An insect-like, biomorphic creation from Ezer for his own practice, in which the lower parts of the characters in the Frank-Rühl typeface are replaced by antenna-style extensions, reflecting the designer's interest in animated, or live, typography.

1

2

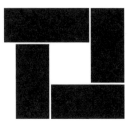

3

4

לילי

5

מיכל
מילר

6

7

8   9

1. 10 Architects
Book series, Iran
Designed by Kambiz Shafei, 2011
For this bilingual series of books and DVDs on contemporary Iranian architects, Shafei used '10' as the unifying element: one and zero are the only digits with the same shape in both Persian and Latin writing systems.

2. Bayn
Mobile phone network, Morocco
Designed by Lippincott (Brendán Murphy), 2006
The idea behind a thought bubble is to provide the flexibility to lead with either the Arabic or Latin name, and adapt the brand to regional or national audiences.

3. Berardi & Sagharchi Projects
Contemporary art agency, UK/Iran
Designed by Raad Design Studio (Iman Raad), 2008

4. Shanghai World Financial Center
Office development, China
Designed by Landor Associates, 2008
Shanghai World Financial Center is the city's tallest skyscraper, with an unusual, handle-like observatory on its upper floors. Its logo symbolizes 'current': a flow of information, finance, knowledge and potential through the building and between East and West. The Chinese character 'Shang' (from 'Shanghai'), meaning 'up' is embedded in the symbol.

5. Conflicts Forum
Political think tank, UK
Designed by Guild of Sage & Smith (Neil Tinson, Amin Fahs), 2010
Conflicts Forum aims to develop a new understanding between the Muslim world and the West.

6. *Art Tomorrow*
Magazine, Iran
Designed by Raad Design Studio (Iman Raad), 2010
English words and Thuluth-style Persian script intertwine in this masthead for a bilingual quarterly magazine.

7. Chaoyang 1919
Creative business park, China
Designed by Joyn:Viscom (Jiang Jian, Zheng Xiaochun), 2010
Chaoyang 1919 denotes the Beijing district and the year of construction of this former factory, now converted into a performance space and offices for TV and film production companies. The 'legs' of the '9's are cut at a 19-degree angle.

8. Tokyo Station City
Mixed-use property development, Japan
Designed by Landor Associates, 2010
A brand encompassing recent additions, including shops, restaurants and three skyscrapers, to Tokyo Station, with modern kanji characters fused to express 'Tokyo', complemented by the English wordmark.

1

2

3

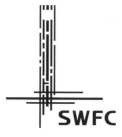

4

5

6

7

東

TOKYO STATION CITY

8

9. Carmelit
Subway system, Israel
Designed by Dan Reisinger, 1990
Graphic designers at work today in Israel and beyond owe a debt to Dan Reisinger. A citizen of the country from its foundation, he is responsible for the visual identity of numerous Israeli institutions, creating marks whose visual economy and dexterity in harmonizing Hebrew and Latin text set a benchmark for younger designers far and wide.

Reisinger was born in Yugoslavia. During the Nazi occupation of that country, his father, a craftsman and miniature painter, perished in Hungarian forced-labour units, along with many other members of his family. The boy was kept hidden by Serbian families until the Nazi withdrawal, and in 1949 emigrated with his mother to the newly formed state of Israel.

A training in art and design, a spell in the Israeli Air Force and a stamp design course with graphic designer Abram Games, plus periods in England at Central School of Art and designing for ICI, led Reisinger to open his own studio in Tel Aviv. His bilingual logotype for airline El Al, which combined the Latin and Hebrew wordmarks designed by Otto Treumann a decade earlier, brought Reisinger international attention, and the projects, honours and exhibitions flowed in abundance thereafter.

His identity for Carmelit, the underground funicular railway service that runs up and down Mount Carmel in Haifa, is a deceptively simple mark, apparently in the same mould as many other lean, dynamically oriented rail-related symbols. The interlocking arrows, though, contain a reference to the physical character of the Carmelit system, with its inclined tunnels, stepped platforms and slanted carriages, as well as representing both the Latin 'c' and Hebrew

'caf' initals of the name. A monogram, diagram and symbol all in one.

10. Gulf Gateway
Business club, UK
Designed by Momin Branding (Irfan Ahmed), 2009

11. Teva
Pharmaceutical company, Israel
Designed by Dan Reisinger, 1986
Brutalist treatment harmonizes Latin and Hebrew text.

12. Sendai Astronomical Observatory
Public observatory, Japan
Designed by Johnson Banks, 2008
This way to outer space. An arrow that makes light of the lengthy name in two languages is available in eight different versions, or directions, to point the way to information, exhibits and cosmological wonders.

13. Oranjebloesem
Catering company, The Netherlands
Designed by Burobraak (Arjan Braaksma), 2004
A Dutch/Arabic identity for a catering company specializing in combining Moroccan and Dutch food culture.

بوابة الخليج
GULF GATEWAY

10

11

SENDAI ASTRONOMICAL OBSERVATORY 仙台市天文台

12

اورنيابلوم
oranjebloesem

13

14. Michael Ku Gallery
Art gallery, Taiwan
*Designed by
Joyn:Viscom (Jiang Jian),
2008*

**15. MòChén Architects
& Engineers**
Architectural practice,
China
*Designed by Joyn:
Viscom (Jiang Jian), 2000*
A logotype based on
Ming furniture and
window-frame designs
conveys the philosophy
of this practice to root
its work in regional
cultural traditions. 'Mo'
is a traditional black
calligraphy ink; 'chen' is
the practice of bowing
one's head and bending
forwards to show
sincerity and respect.
The two combined can be
interpreted as 'devoted
to design'.

**16. Magic of Persia
Contemporary Art Prize**
Art award, UK
*Designed by Raad Design
Studio (Iman Raad), 2008*
A bilingual, tiled
wordmark for the annual
art prize of a non-profit
UK-based charity with
a mission to educate
young people on the
contribution of Persian
culture to society.

**17. Financeforce
Consulting**
Financial consultancy,
China
*Designed by Hesign
International (Jianping
He, Jun Dai, Yawei Zhai),
2009*

18. Life
Lifestyle store,
Saudi Arabia
*Designed by Hani Alireza,
2010*
Latin and Arabic
wordmarks both convey
the urban, experimental
spirit of this eclectic
lifestyle store.

19. Uniqlo
Clothes retailer, Japan
*Designed by Samurai
(Kashiwa Sato, Ko
Ishikawa), 2006*
Historically, Japan-based
businesses were at pains
to disguise their origins.
Kashiwa Sato's Uniqlo
logotype capitalized
on a burst of Western
interest in Japanese
pop culture, placing the
Katakana script on an
equal footing with the
Western wordmark.
Part of a rebranding

that transformed the
retailer's image and
fortunes, it retained the
flat, functional, graphic
qualities that Sato felt
were most associated
with Japanese design.

20. Matsuri Japan
Annual festival, UK
*Designed by Johnson
Banks, 2009*
The logotype for
London's annual *matsuri*
reads across for English
and down for Japanese.

21. Tambour
Paint and chemicals
company, Israel
*Designed by Dan
Reisinger, 1992*
Square counters inside
bold, stylized characters
create a unified
wordmark.

14

15

16

17

18

19

20

21

Not quite symbols, but not far off, these are wordmarks and monograms in which the verbal and visual start to diverge: where type becomes a vessel for or equal partner to pattern, emblem or image.

 brac

 smeg

 NYC

 Österreichische Nationalbibliothek

Hästens

Stir

 mace

GUY&MAX

 There is Sound.

BETWEEN BOOKS

bonair

 The Royal Mint

TROSSI

 SML

 COMSA EMTE

 Get London reading

Symbolic

 NATIONAL PARKS OF NEW YORK HARBOR

Grupo ⊕ Planeta

GERMAN MEBEL

 Peel's deli

ORANGE BOX

 OCEAN

C Charles Kendall

Fundación Sida y Sociedad

LD

 studio 2030

ə-clockwork talk

 Downtown ALLIANCE

 Obsidian

Clarity©

3rd Pillar of Health

 mace

 LA MODERNA

1. IamExpat
Online community
resource, The
Netherlands
*Designed by G Design
Studio (Alexandros
Gavrilakis), 2010*
IamExpat provides
information for
expatriates from
anywhere around the
world now living or
doing business in The
Netherlands.

2. London 2012
Olympic and Paralympic
Games, UK
*Designed by Wolff Olins,
2007*
Does typography matter
to the man or woman in
the street? The London
2012 Logo Affair would
indicate that it does.
'Bold', 'dissonant' and
'echoing London's
qualities of a modern,
edgy city', according
to Wolff Olins, the
logo intended to unite
succeeded in dividing
opinion in the UK like
no other corporate
emblem since, perhaps,
the BT 'piper' (also a
Wolff Olins creation). Its
performance as a vessel
for inclusive, uplifting
imagery that can 'engage
with a global audience
of four billion people' is
probably best judged
once the medals have
been pocketed and the
crowds have gone home.

3. Ide
IT outsourcing, Spain
*Designed by Zorraquino
(Miquel Zorraquino, Miren
S Gaubeka), 2010*

**4. Open Air Laboratories
Network**
Environmental initiative,
UK
*Designed by hat-trick
(Gareth Howat, Jim
Sutherland, Adam Giles),
2008*
Run by the Natural
History Museum
and the Biodiversity
Network, OPAL aims to
encourage people to
explore and enjoy their
local environment. A few
choice species appear in
the magnifying glass in
different applications.

5. City of Melbourne
City authority, Australia
*Designed by Landor
Associates (Jason Little,
Jefton Sungkar, Sam
Pemberton), 2009*
The centrepiece
of this 'city brand',

the monogram is
constructed from a
geometric framework
that allows endless visual
executions, intended to
convey the 'iconic and
multifaceted' nature of
the city and appeal to its
full range of audiences.

6. México
Tourism board brand,
Mexico
*Designed by Emblem
(Eduardo Calderón,
Claude Salzberger, Rubén
Pineda, Marco Gutiérrez),
2004*
Each letter contains
a decorative motif
representing a reason
for visiting Mexico,
from its pre-Columbian
archaeology ('M') to its
beaches ('O').

**7. Natural History
Museum**
Museum, UK
*Designed by hat-trick
(Gareth Howat, Jim
Sutherland, David
Kimpton, Ben Christie,
Jamie Ellul), 2004*
An identity intended to
convey the diversity of
the museum's exhibits,
research and scientific
credentials. The 'N' offers
a window on 35 different
images by leading wildlife
photographers, from
microscopic plankton to
planet Earth.

8. Crop
Hair salon, Canada
*Designed by Rethink,
2009*
Letterforms that look
scissor-cut, containing
pen illustrations of
different styles, for this
Red Deer, Alberta 'hair
boutique'.

1
_____

2
_____

ide.

3
_____

4
_____

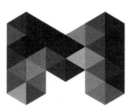
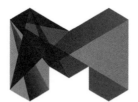
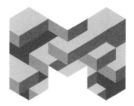

5

6

7

8

9. SLA Pharma
Pharmaceutical
company, Switzerland/UK
*Designed by Moot Design
(Nitesh Mody), 2010*
A logotype whose
pattern of nodes and
connectors allows the
plotting of any molecular
formula, emphasizing
the R&D basis of SLA's
specialisms.

10. SML
Graphic design
consultancy, Australia
*Designed by SML
(Vanessa Ryan), 2009*

11. Soup Broth Asia
Cafe, Singapore
*Designed by Couple,
2010*
Traditional patterns from
Japan, China, Burma,
Thailand and elsewhere
fill the bowls of this
wordmark, for a shop
that serves soups from
all over Asia.

12. Make Associates
Urban planning
consultancy, UK
*Designed by Funnel
Creative, 2007*
Different colours and
shades reflect the
diversity of place-making
approaches offered by
this consultancy.

13. Splitrock
Mineral water supplier,
Australia
*Designed by Sadgrove
Design (Brian Sadgrove),
1989*

14. NYC
City tourism organization,
USA
*Designed by Wolff Olins,
2008*
For New York City &
Company, the official
marketing and tourism
body, super-bold, rugged
letterforms with the
capacity to reflect the
'infinite complexity' of
NYC's five boroughs and
190 neighbourhoods
through changing
textures and imagery.

15. The Rumpus Room
Multimedia brand
communications agency,
UK
*Designed by
Bibliothèque, 2010*
The Rumpus Room
works with brands,
advertising agencies and
broadcasters to develop
digital communications.
Its ligatured monogram
is enlivened by an array
of visual expressions,

from solid colours to
photography and full-
motion video.

**16. The Turner
Collective**
Experimental furniture
practice, Australia
*Designed by Mark
Gowing Design, 2009*
A series of rectangles
whose areas are in the
Golden Ratio form a
'T' that can be 'made'
from a range of the
materials found in the
practice's work.

9

10

11

12

SPLITROCK

13

14

15

16

1. Limapuluh
Cafe, Japan
*Designed by Nign
(Kenichiro Ohara), 2001*
Limapuluh is Malay
for '50' and the name
of this Malaysian cafe
in Aoyama, where the
logotype models a cup,
saucer and plate.

2. Akta
Cable network, Romania
*Designed by Brandient
(Alin Tamasan), 2008*
A brand mark lit up by
the kind of control lights
found on DVD players,
modems and home-
cinema equipment.

3. Amanda Patton
Garden designer, UK
*Designed by Neon Design
(Dana Robertson), 2008*

4. Antaar
Interiors and lifestyle
retailer group, Estonia
*Designed by Loovvool
(Hannes Unt, Kadri-Maria
Mitt), 2009*
The logo of this home-
oriented shops group
depicts human habitation
of a different age.

5. Bonair
Tennis tournament,
Australia
*Designed by Design By
Pidgeon (David Pidgeon,
Josh Tatarynowicz), 2009*

6. Downtown Alliance
Business improvement
district, USA
*Designed by Chermayeff
& Geismar, 1999*
The Alliance for
Downtown New York
works to enhance the
quality of life in Lower
Manhattan for workers,
residents and visitors.
The twin towers that
formed the logotype's
two 'I's were redrawn
post 9/11.

7. Fig Food Co.
Soup producer, USA
*Designed by Sandstrom
Partners (Jon Olsen,
Chris Gardiner, Kelly
Bohls), 2010*
A taste of Arcimboldo
for a producer of
100%-plant-based,
organic, kosher soups.

8. Graham Gill Carpets
Carpet retailer, UK
*Designed by Fivefootsix,
2005*

9. La Moderna
Pasta maker, Mexico
*Designed by Lance
Wyman, 1970*

1

2

3

4

bonair

5

6

7

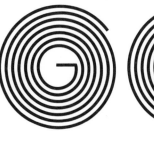

8

9

10. Melinda
Apple-growers'
collective, Italy
*Designed by Minale
Tattersfield (Marcello
Minale Snr, Marcello M
Minale), 1990*
An exercise by Trentino's
16 apple-growing
cooperatives to
distinguish and market
their produce has since
become a major food
brand with a wide range
of food products.

**11. National Parks of
New York Harbor**
Park service, USA
*Designed by Chermayeff
& Geismar (Steff
Geissbuhler), 2005*
To raise awareness
of New York City's
surprising number
of parks and public
spaces, an identity
programme with 23
separate wordmarks
was developed, one for
each destination, using
a changing alphabet to
display the features of
each place.

12. 90 Hairdressing
Hair salon, UK
*Designed by Mark Studio,
2010*
A memorable design
solution in the palm of
the client's hand.

13. Orange Box
Young people's centre,
UK
*Designed by B&W Studio
(Steve Wills, Alex
Broadhurst), 2010*
For a purpose-built
youth space in Halifax, a
purpose-built typeface.
The logotype showcases
some of the custom-
made characters, of
which there are three for
each letter.

14. Lisa Desforges
Copywriter, UK
*Designed by Fivefootsix,
2008*
A typographic depiction
of the copywriter's
role, to create unique
personalities with words.

15. Dub Hooligan
Record label, UK
*Designed by Studio
Paradise (Samuel Moffat,
Jade Abbott), 2010*
Mixing records, visually
speaking.

**16. Very Important
Announcements**
Event communications
agency, UK
*Designed by Powell
Allen (Chris Allen, Kerrie
Powell, Alexis Abraham),
2011*
A suite of logos to
represent this company's
range of web-to-print
communications for
births, weddings,
funerals and other life-
stage events.

17. Peel's Deli
Cafe, UK
*Designed by Elmwood
(Martyn Hayes), 2009*

**18. Peel District
School Board**
Regional education
authority, Canada
*Designed by Hambly &
Woolley (Barb Woolley,
Bob Hambly, Frances
Chen), 2005*

10

11

12

13

14

DUB
H⊚⊚LIGAN

15

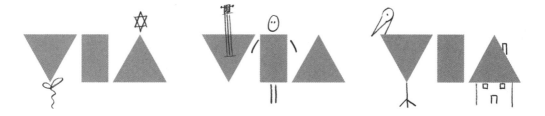

16

Peel's deli

⚫peel

17   18

1. AOL
Internet services and
media, USA
Designed by Wolff Olins,
2009
Having started the
book with unadorned,
concrete typography, we
end it in territory where
the logotype is almost
disappearing from view.
There is a logotype in this
identity, but it is quiet,
unassuming, almost
apologetic: a functional
sans-serif acronym,
set not in conventional,
shouty upper case but in
more retiring title case,
followed by a full stop.
A group of letters made
to look like a word, but
which is not. While it is
fashionably self-effacing,
it does beg the question
of how the 'word' should
be pronounced.

All of the action, however,
happens in the ever-
changing objects and
graphic effects behind
the logotype. Without
them, the white logotype
becomes invisible. The
'Aol.' name is revealed
by the pictorial content,
which ranges from
ink-blots and abstract
swirls, to a goldfish (a
nod to Michael Wolff's
famous 1971 identity for
construction firm Bovis),
cartoon creatures, birds,
flowers and falling leaves.
In video applications,
the slow-mo reveals
include leaping cats,
skateboarders and
falling paint.

This identity could
seem to imply that AOL
(which is synonymous
with Internet access)
is defined by content
generated by others: that
it is a presence noticed
only when someone
else is doing something
interesting. In actual fact,
AOL's strategy, following
its departure from Time
Warner, is the reverse:
to lose its reputation for
user-unfriendly Internet
services and become 'a
media company for the
21st century', working
with journalists, artists
and musicians to create
'extraordinary content
experiences'.

How that washes with
American Internet users
remains to be seen. The
AOL name is not one that
they cherish: the number
of AOL subscribers fell

from 27 million in 2001 to
six million in 2009. With
the name apparently
non-negotiable, though,
the 'non-logo' approach
and visual fireworks do
a good job of deflecting
attention away from it.

The identity achieved its
first objective: to cause a
furore among journalists,
bloggers amd 'opinion
formers'. The brand must
now live up to its promise.
What Paul Rand said is
true of every logotype
in this book: 'A logo is
less important than the
product it signifies; what
it represents is more
important than what it
looks like.'

2. Alzheimer's
Association
Non-profit health
organization, USA
Designed by Studio/lab
(Jill Hoffheimer, Kelly
Bjork, Jody Work), 2004
An accompanying
symbol representing the
human head and the lab
flask – this is both a care
network and the world's
largest, private, non-
profit funder of dementia
research.

3. ArtFund
Funding and fundraising
organization, UK
Designed by Johnson
Banks, 2010
A change in management
led to a change of name
(dropping the 'The') and
the desire for a less
attention-grabbing mark
than Johnson Banks'
previous one for the
organization, which
fused a painting frame
with a heart.

4. Bad Huis Theater
Arts centre,
The Netherlands
Designed by Burobraak
(Arjan Braaksma, Roy
Oosrebeek), 2010
The architecture of
this converted 1920s
bathhouse, with its
circular floor plan, is
complemented by
Gill-style lettering.

5. Between Books
Art and design book
publisher, UK
Designed by Magpie
Studio (David Azurdia,
Ben Christie and Jamie
Ellul), 2010
Something between a
book and a monogram.

alzheimer's ℚ association

2

3

4

5

6. Bluebird
Coffee vending equipment manufacturer, Australia
Designed by Naughtyfish (Paul Garbett), 2007

7. BRAC
Non-governmental organization, Bangladesh
Designed by CDT Design, 2010
What started life in 1972 as the Bangladesh Rehabilitation Assistance Committee is now the world's largest NGO, working across the globe to alleviate poverty, illiteracy, disease and social injustice.

8. Breakfast Briefings
Networking club, UK
Designed by Further (James Beveridge, Ben Jeffery, Rob Day), 2009
A mark for a breakfast network event to debate issues in branding and communications, in-between the croissants.

9. BullGuard
Digital data security producer, UK
Designed byPurpose (Stuart Youngs, Nathan Webb, Lars Teglbjærg), 2010

10. Charles Kendall
Supply chain management company, UK
Designed by Brownjohn (James Beveridge), 2009
A lion salient – with both hind legs on the ground – is a rare posture in heraldry; more of a leap than the fighting lion rampant. For a company that frequently delivers development aid at short notice, and whose second initial the lion seems to suggest, it's a good fit.

11. Clarity
Diamond consultancy, UK
Designed by Blast (Giff, Paul Tunnicliffe, Dan Bown), 2010
A multifaceted copyright symbol refers to this firm's individual and impartial take on the economics of the diamond industry.

12. Österreichische Nationalbibliothek
National library, Austria
Designed by Bohatsch and Partner (Walter Bohatsch, Andreas Niederer), 2001
An open book and a comma's pause, to contemplate, perhaps, the national library's collections of maps, music manuscripts, rare books and papyri.

13. Clockwork Talk
Presentation skills training company, Canada
Designed by Hambly & Woolley (Bob Hambly, Jen Clark), 2004
Training for speeches and presentations that engage, inspire and run to plan is this company's stock-in-trade.

14. Comsa Emte
Construction company, Spain
Designed by Summa (Tilman Solé, Marga Oller), 2009
A merger of two of Spain's largest infrastructure and engineering companies brings together their respective simplified symbols.

15. *Dose*
Entertainment magazine, Canada
Designed by Rethink, 2010
A daily *Dose* of entertainment news from this magazine-style paper and website is delivered with an accompanying, possibly pain-numbing, capsule.

6

7

Breakfast Briefings

8

BullGuard™

9

 Charles Kendall

 Clarity

10

11

 Österreichische Nationalbibliothek

12

clockwork talk

 COMSA EMTE

13

14

 dose™

15

16. E. Tautz
Menswear brand, UK
*Designed by Moving
Brands, 2008*
Successfully channelling
dapper, upper-class
English doolalliness
with a logo-monogram-
illustration lock-up that
could have been devised
by a madcap 1930s
printer, E. Tautz has
recycled its heritage of
keeping the nation's toffs
in breeches, sports suits
and coats, to clothe a
new generation of gents.

**17. European Farming
& Food Partnerships**
Agricultural and food
consultancy, UK
*Designed by Purpose
(Stuart Youngs, Rob
Howsam, Adam Browne,
Paul Felton), 2009*

18. Exmouth Market
Urban neighbourhood, UK
*Designed by Atelier
Works (Quentin Newark),
2008*
Part of a campaign
designed to show
landlords the Debenham
Trust's commitment
to London's laid-back,
fashionable Exmouth
Market, this smiling
logotype recalls one of
the street's most famous
former residents: King
of the Clowns, Joseph
Grimaldi.

19. Film North
Film festival, Canada
*Designed by Concrete
(Diti Katona, John
Pylypczak, Jordam
Poirier), 2010*

20. Free2go
Roadside assistance
service, Australia
*Designed by Mark
Gowing Design, 2005*
An authoritative but
youthful air marks this
out as a service for the
younger generation:
16–20-year-olds, to
be specific.

21. German Mebel
Furniture distributor,
Germany
*Designed by SWSP
Design (Georg Schatz),
2009*

22. Corpgroup
Conglomorate, Chile
*Designed by Vignelli
Associates (Massimo
Vignelli, Beatriz
Cifuentes), 2007*

23. Get London Reading
Literature campaign, UK
*Designed by KentLyons
(Mark Diggins), 2008*

24. Grupo Planeta
Publishing and media
group, Spain
*Designed by Summa
(Wladimir Marnich), 1999*

25. Oyster Marine
Yacht building and
brokerage company, UK
*Designed by SVI Design
(Sasha Vidakovic), 2010*

16

17

18

19

20

21

CORPGROUP

22

23

24

25

26. Helen Bamber Foundation
Human rights organization, UK
Designed by Studio Dempsey (Mike Dempsey), 2006

27. Home
Furniture retailer, UK
Designed by The Chase (Steve Conchie), 2010
Merseystride, a Liverpool-based social enterprise helping homeless and long-term unemployed people, established this retail operation to offer jobs and training opportunities to those without a home. The identity draws on the graphic style of the flat-pack furniture delivered to the store.

28. Kikkoman
Food product manufacturer, Japan
Designed by Landor Associates, 2008
A switch to lower-case letters softens the logotype of the soy-sauce and seasonings manufacturer; the hexagon 'stamp' suggests a respect for traditional techniques.

29. Mace Group
Construction management and consultancy, UK
Designed by Home, 2008
The symbol refers to the group's range of services and to the skylines it is instrumental in changing.

30. Monastic Productions
Scriptwriting service, UK
Designed by Taxi Studio (Spencer Buck, Ryan Wills, Marie Jones), 2010
Praying for inspiration? The founders of Monastic, responsible for the BBC's *Life on Mars* and *Ashes to Ashes*, need look no further than the nib of their pen.

31. New British Design
Furniture brand, UK
Designed by Together Design, 2010
NBD hand-picks young British designers to work with on prototyping, manufacturing and promoting their works.

32. Obsidian
Property developer and investor, UK
Designed by Untitled (David Hawkins, Glenn Howard), 2007
A black disc, etched with contour lines, suggests not only the volcanic glass of the brand name but also the scale of its property developments.

33. Ocean Consulting Group
Business continuity and crisis management group, Australia
Designed by Mark Gowing Design, 2010
A typographic style typically suited to a luxury brand is intended to convey a sense of calm and well-being for companies planning for crises and emergencies.

34. Refresh Beauty Spa
Urban spa, UK
Designed by Playne Design (Claire Playne, Sarah Williams, Cilena Rojas), 2008

35. Royal Opera House
Opera house, UK
Designed by SomeOne (Therese Severinsen, Gary Holt, Christopher Wormell), 2010
The Royal Opera House in Covent Garden is home to both the Royal Opera and the Royal Ballet. In the previous identity, the Royal Coat of Arms dominated the wordmark, which ran on a single line and at small sizes was almost unreadable. This design achieves a better balance by stacking the words, which are set in the Gotham typeface, a huge hit with audiences of all kinds since it featured in Barack Obama's successful Presidential campaign. Positive and negative woodcuts of the crest ensure that it works on both light and dark backgrounds.

26

27

28

29

NEW
BRITISH
DESIGN

30

31

Obsidian

OCEAN

32

33

REFRESH
BEAUTY SPA

ROYAL
OPERA
HOUSE

34

35

36. Opta
New business incubator, UK
Designed by GBH, 2001

37. Parker Marketing
Marketing consultancy, USA
Designed by Cue (Alan Colvin, Kate Gabriel), 2009
Icons put the company's key values – purpose, connection and vigilance – at the forefront of its identity.

38. Pedlars
Online housewares retailer, UK
Designed by Pedlars, 2004
The Pedlars pooch is a regular on the pages of the online shop.

39. Peppersmith
Chewing gum brand, UK
Designed by B&B Studio (Shaun Bowen), 2010
The peppermint-leaf moustache evokes a kind of English Edwardian authenticity for this natural gum brand, recalling an era before chemically based chew-sticks.

40. Hästens
Bed manufacturer, Sweden
Designed by Stockholm Design Lab, 2001
Hästens opened for business as a saddle-maker in 1852 but soon found a sideline, handcrafting beds and filling mattresses with the same horsehair used for its primary business. Hästens (*häst* is Swedish for 'horse') beds are still made by hand using only natural fillings.

41. South Street Seaport Museum
Museum, USA
Designed by Lance Wyman, 2000
Wood type from the museum's collection, combined with images representing New York's maritime history.

42. Fundación Sida y Sociedad
Non-profit foundation, Spain
Designed by Mario Eskenazi and Diego Feijóo, 2007
This foundation devotes itself to the control and prevention of HIV/AIDS in developing countries, where the stencil logo can be easily and cheaply applied to crates and supplies.

43. Smeg
Domestic appliance brand, Italy
Designed by Franco Maria Ricci, 1977
Established by the Bertazzoni family in the 1940s, Smalterie Metallurgiche Emiliane Guastalla set new standards for the engineering and style of its products. Long before kitchen appliances were considered style statements, Smeg commissioned designs from the likes of Mario Bellini and Renzo Piano. And a logotype from Franco Maria Ricci, designer, aesthete, Bodoni devotee and publisher of the lavish art journal, *FMR*. Ricci also devised the even more durable logotype for luxury kitchen brand SCIC. Who said all lowercase logotypes were new?

44. Stir
Yogurt bar chain, USA
Designed by Elixir Design (Jennifer Jerde, Nathan Durrant), 2009

45. Studio 2030
Architectural practice, USA
Designed by Cue (Alan Colvin, Paul Sieka), 2007
A forward-looking firm with an emphasis on sustainability and lightening the burden that buildings place on the planet.

@opta™

36

37

PEDLARS 🐕

38

PEPPERSMITH™

39

Hästens

40

41

Fundación
Sida
y Sociedad

42

43

44

45

46. Third Pillar of Health
Fatigue management
company, UK
*Designed by Playne
Design (Clare PLayne,
Sarah Williams,
Oliver Meikle, Kieran
Fairnington), 2010*
Sleep, after cardio-
vascular fitness and
nutrition, is the third pillar
of health. This company
offers assessment and
training programmes to
help businesses reduce
fatigue and improve the
energy levels of their
employees.

47. There Is Sound
Record label, UK
*Designed by Studio
Paradise (Samuel Moffat,
Jade Abbott), 2010*

**48. The Health
Foundation**
Charity, UK
*Designed by Together
Design, 2010*
A virtuous circle –
identification, innovation,
demonstration and
encouragement
– visualizes the
healthcare improvement
programmes of this
charity.

49. The Royal Mint
National mint, UK
Designed by North, 2007
The Royal Mint's
rebranding sought to
steer its identity away
from commemorative
coins and figurines in
Sunday supplement
ads, and to restore the
polish and prestige
that its history merited.
A redrawn Royal Coat
of Arms was set in an
abstract design derived
from the Tudor Rose
on England's first gold
sovereign in 1489, and
the dial plates used in
coin production. North
developed a custom-
made typeface, Nexus
Serif, for the mint and
crafted a logotype with a
unique ligature between
the 'y' and 'i'.

50. Supermarket
Fashion retailer, Denmark
*Designed by
We Recommend
(Martin Fredricson,
Nikolaj Knop), 2008*
A minimarket-style
sticker for an ironically
downmarket brand
selling a mix of labels
from streetwear to
high fashion.

51. Weldon
Hardwood flooring
manufacturer, UK
*Designed by Purpose
(Giles Redmayne, Lee
Manning), 2010*

52. Syntecor
Ticketing database
software company, UK
Designed by GBH, 2009
'1 + 1 = 3' alludes to this
company's promise of
combining data sets
to create a powerful
resource.

53. Trossi
Lifeboat institution,
Finland
*Designed by Hahmo
(Jenni Kuokka), 2005*

46

47

48

49

supernarket

50

By Appointment to
H.M. The Queen
Suppliers of Hardwood Flooring
Weldon, Norton Disney

By Appointment to
H.R.H. The Prince of Wales
Suppliers of Hardwood Flooring
Weldon, Norton Disney

WELDON

51

(■ + ■ = ◆) syntecor™

52

TROSSI

53

Client Index
Page numbers refer
to text

A

A la Feina Iguals 240
à point books 64
aarrkk 30
AAthletics 208
AAYA 128
Abandon Normal Devices
  Festival 259
ABB Group 60
Abbott Laboratories 167
ABF The Soldiers' Charity
  270
Acacia Avenue 264
Acca Festival of
  Alternative Theatre 292
Accesspoint
  Technologies 230
Acocsa 167
Acqua Design 55
Acting Company, The 69
Action Woking 211
ActionAid 211
Active Results 211
Ad Kinetsu 124
ADF Architects 211
Adlib 246
ADM Promotions 255
Afrique Contemporaine
  64
Ágora 212
Åhléns 167
Ai Fiori 174
AJM Productions 102
Akerman Daly 208
Akta 306
Albuquerque, Luis 212
Alexander Hall 240
Al Jazeera Children's
  Channel 287
All Change 205
Allude 212
Almar 212
Alpenmilch Zentrale 77
Alphabetee 167
Altitude Music 94
Altitude Volvo 168
Alwyne Estates 208
Alzheimer's Association
  311
Amanda Patton 306
Amanda Wakeley 108
Amazee 56
American Airlines 17
American Cinema Editors
  142
American Museum of
  Natural History 276

Amlin 40
Ancillotto 142
Ancoats Urban Village
  168
Angels Motel 74
Anglesea Sports &
  Recreation Club 167
Anida 102
AnnaLou of London 264
Annie 108
Anorak 118
Antaar 306
Anthony Nolan 108
AOL 311
Appenzeller, Hans 278
Appleton & Domingos
  132
Approach Architecture
  Studio 284
Aquavia 212
Arboretum Kalmthout 40
Arc Biennial 86
Arch Idea 276
architectsAlliance 40
Architecture Centre
  Devon & Cornwall 162
Architecture Foundation,
  The 238
ArkOpen 276
Armenian Lexicon &
  Library Project, The 199
Armoury, The 228
Arôme 240
Arrtco 270
Ars 162
Art 287
Art & Australia 202
Art Tomorrow 294
Art Tonic 246
Arteria 156
Artform Records 252
ArtFund 311
Artica 230
ArtMatters 238
Arts Affaires 270
Arts for Health Cornwall
  and Isles of Scilly 142
ArtWorks 202
Arup 36
AsBuilt 86
Ash St Cellar 80
Ashburton 118
Ashdown Ingram 238
Asia Pacific Interior
  Design Awards 97
Asociación Profesional
  de Diseñadores de
  Iluminación 142
Asprey 18
Assin 64
Association of Art
  Historians 44
Association of
  Photographers, The 110
Asylum 56
At What Cost 122
Atelier LaDurance 32
Atelier Pedro Falcão 124
Atelier 210 60
Austin Smith:Lord 244
Australian Centre for
  Contemporary Art 52
aut.architektur und tirol
  52
Autočechák 252
Avid Reader 46
Avvio 60

B

Baby Box 259
Bad Huis Theater 311
Bags 212
Bailey, Émilie 280
Balthazar B and the
  Beatitudes 208
Bambi/bylaura 234
Banc Sabadell 252
Bankside Mix 137
B&W Studio 236
Barcelona pel Medi
  Ambient 168
Barcelona TV 270
Barnes & Noble 236
Barneys New York 142
Bayn 294
Beacon 142
Beautiful Books 168
Bendis Financial 168
Benito's Hat 238
Berardi & Sagharchi
  Projects 294
Bespoke Careers 48
Bettys 88
Between Books 311
Bevan Brittan 206
bFelix 98
BG Group 208
Biblioteca Artur Martorell
  270
Bibliothèque Régionale
  d'Aosta 268
Bidfreight Port
  Operations 42
Big Science Read 154
Big Talk 64
bijipub 212
Biketreks 66
Bite 118
BK Italia 255
Black Panda 62
Black Sun 80
Blanc Kara 86
Blink 212
Bloc 168
Blokk Architects 64
Blonde + Co 110
Blue Gallery 80
Bluebird 312
Blurrr 92
Böka 240
Bolefloor 168
Bonair 306
Bonds 238
Boniface, Kevin 110
Booket 138
Bookfactory 113
Booz&Co. 238
Boskke 212
Boyd Baker House 94
BPE 252
BRAC 312
BrainagencyMedia 114
Braincandy 206
Brand & Value 64
Brand New Alliance 86
Brand Design Council of
  South Africa 208
Breakfast Briefings 312
Breakthrough Breast
  Cancer 138
Bree Collection 51
Briffa Phillips 97
Brill 262
Brit Awards, The 168
British Academy of

Songwriters,
  Composers & Authors
  168
British Larder, The 200
British Library 134
Broadgate 168
Brook McIlroy 234
Brooklyn Academy of
  Music 113
Bruised 60
Brussels Electronic
  Music Festival 62
Bryter Estates 280
BullGuard 312
Bullionstream 168
BurdaStyle 18
Burgiss Group, The 138
ByAlex 218

C

CACT 200
Calderdale Council 140
Cally Arts 202
Campaign to Protect
  Rural England 252
Campbell Soup Company
  73
Canon 32
Canterbury School of
  Architecture 128
Capital Partners 124
Caponata 168
Cardiff Waterside 202
Carmelit 297
Casa Lever 142
Castleton 170
Cath Kidston 70
Caviar Productions 170
Central, The 170
Central School of Speech
  & Drama 88
Ceri Hand Gallery 62
Certio 160
CFE 256
Cha Cha Moon 48
Channel 9 TV 51
Chaoyang 1919 294
Charles Kendall 312
Charlton Kings Baptist
  Church 276
Chartered Society of
  Physiotherapy 128
Chelsea, The 77
Chilvers, Ian 176
Christian Constantin 212
Christopher Lee 77
Chuan Pictures 284
Chuck Choi 144
Cinema Nova 114
Cinereach 255
Circa 126
Circus 55
City of Melbourne 302
City of Westminster
  College 264
City University of New
  York 262
Clarity 312
Classé 244
Claudine Colin
  Communication 144
Clockwork Talk 312
Colin&Me 236
Collectors Gallery 148
College of Arts &
  Architecture 206

College of Built
  Environments 134
Colmar Brunton 230
Colourhouse, The 150
Columba 144
Columbus 170
Come Enjoy 59
Company Books, The 152
Comsa Emte 312
Conception Marketing
  170
Conflicts Forum 294
Connect Sheffield 212
Connect a Million Minds
  246
Conservatoire de
  Lausanne 240
Conservatori Municipal
  de Música de Barcelona
  262
Consortium for Street
  Children 170
Conspiracy Group, The
  170
Constitutional Court of
  South Africa 40
Coolera, wind & drinks 92
Coop Himmelblau 214
Coram Chambers 214
Corlion Violins 102
Corpgroup 314
Corridor 170
Couple 156
Covent Garden 205
Covert Music 144
Cox 214
c+c workshop 52
Crate & Barrel 21
Creas Foundation 170
Creative Group, The 77
Creative Industries
  Development Unit 110
Crisis 60
Crisp Media 170
Cristina Guerra
  Contemporary Art 17
Criterion Collection, The
  170
Crop 302
Crown Metropol 88
Croydon Food Group 170
Cubus 18
Cuneó, Ollivier Philippe
  78
Cupcake 48
Curious Pictures 214
Customer Closeness
  Company, The 270
Cwmni Da 124

D

Dab Hand Media 132
DACS 124
Daiwa 66
Dalton Maag 48
Danfoss 70
Danish Fashion Institute
  Academy 44
Dansmakers Amsterdam
  144
Darbiran Co. 287
Davies, Sarah 154
Davis Evolution 118
Daydream Nation 278
de sign de 256
Deborah A. Nilson 202

Dell 259
Della Valle Bernheimer 62
de.MO Books 148
Dendy Cinemas 114
Depken & Partner 172
Derbi 264
Derek Welsh Studio 234
Design Academy
  Eindhoven 80
Design Leadership Award
  200
Design Ranch 172
Design 360° 255
Design Ventural 208
DeTodo 148
Detroit Institute of Arts
  256
Dew Tour 172
De Webfabriek 64
DHKN 236
Dia:Beacon 240
Dialog 214
Dialog In The Dark 122
Diathlasis Architectural
  Lighting 172
Dickens 2012 107
DID Publications 287
Diderot 162
Digit 230
Digital Cinema Media 270
Digital Illusions Creative
  Entertainment 126
Digital Links 238
Digweed, John 200
Direction des Musées de
  France 276
Directory 118
Dorchester Collection,
  The 156
Dose 312
Double Good Windows
  92
Douglas Entertainment
  18
Downtown Alliance 306
dropyx 59
Dub Hooligan 308
Duck Duck Goose 260
Duecento Otto 276
Duke 80
Durex 267

E

East End Arts Club 172
Eat 212
Eaton 114
Eden Island 118
Edinburgh International
  Festival 172
Edison, The 98
El Japonés 148
Elahe Gallery 287
ElAstiC 74
Electric Works 78
Ellis Miller 144
Embodied Media 206
Emit 276
Endpoint 208
Engage 114
English National Opera
  147
Engraved Stationery
  Manufacturers
  Association 172
Epromotores 172
Erco 23
Erritzøe 208

Erskine 80
ESADE 44
espai Maragall 240
Essence Pictures 162
Estudio 108
European Farming &
  Food Partnerships 314
Eva Kecseti 206
Evangelische Omroep
  270
Evo 30
Exider 214
Exist 214
Exmouth Market 314
Expert Digital 172
Exploratorium 216
Eye Develop 162
Eye Place 156

F

Fabbrica 39
Faber & Faber 202
Façade 64
Face 122
Facebook 264
Factset Research
  Systems 66
Faculty of Royal
  Designers for Industry,
  The 270
Faixó, Martín 200
Fashion Fringe 110
Fashion Human Rights 78
Fashion World Talent
  Awards 78
Fatboy 264
FaulknerBrowns
  Architects 126
FCE 138
FedEx 117
Feesability 172
Fenwick 74
Ferguson Whyte 160
Ferme du Biéreau, La 256
Ferrer Grupo 162
Ferrovial 30
Festland 80
50 Lessons 216
Fig Food Co. 306
Fillet Inc 230
Film North 314
Financeforce Consulting
  298
Finish Creative Services
  240
Finovino 118
Firescape 102
FireWater 88
First Booking 114
First Graduate 216
FirstCut Studio 90
Fischer Spooner 147
Fish + Chip Design 216
Flow 102
Flow Life Coaching 104
Fluid 70
Fluid Nail Design 174
FMC Technologies 216
Folksam 32
Fonds Podium Kunsten
  147
Foodily.com 24
Foodparc 39
For 117
Forart 216
Forge, The 174
Fornetti 273

Foro 216
Foster + Partners 246
Fothergill Wyatt 202
14 Blades 284
14 oz. 262
FramePage 126
Free & Equal 208
Free2go 314
Freed, Peter 97
Freedom 216
Fresh Co. 44
Freymadl, Hans 126
Friday 174
Fridcorp 70
Friends of the Simon
  Stevin Institute for
  Geometry 174
Friendship Works 40
Frodo 246
From Scratch 124
Front Room Recordings
  208
FT100 246
Fundación Sida y
  Sociedad 318
Further 174
Future Designs 94
Futures Company, The
  113

G

G Design Studio 174
Gallery Litvak 118
Gebrüder Heinemann
  205
Geozug Ingenieure 246
Geriljaworks 234
German Mebel 314
Gertrude Contemporary
  52
Get London Reading 314
GF Smith 120
Gibson Guitar
  Corporation 78
Giff Gaff 216
Giles, Allie 102
Globeride 276
Globes 292
GMW 110
Godzilla Sushi Bar 260
Goldlog 32
Goldman Sachs 262
Golla 30
Good 23
Good Co. 202
Good Measures 162
Google 35
Gorbals, The 104
Gott's Roadside 98
Graduates Yorkshire 160
Graham Gill Carpets 306
Grandmother Co 288
Grant Spencer 230
Gravitas 24
Gr(eat) 46
Green Park 40
Greenpeace 83
Grip 244
Grow in Project, The 228
Grupo Planeta 314
Grupo Tragaluz 189
GSA Venture Partners 36
Guggenheim Partners 24
Guinness Partnership,
  The 174
Gulf Gateway 297

H

Habimah National
  Theatre 292
Hahmo Design 24
Hakoltov 174
Halcón Vineyards 70
Halcyon Hotel, The 176
Halliwell Landau 174
Hampstead Theatre 208
Hamrah e Aval 288
Hand 174
Hand me Down 74
Hangar 10 199
Hans Sipma Photography
  52
Hanzehof 117
Haptic 90
Hard Turm Park 278
Harrods 70
Harrow View 176
Harvard Maintenance
  216
Hästens 318
Healing Arts, The 252
Heal's 24
Health Foundation, The
  320
HealthScout 216
Hearst Corporation 24
HeathWallace 218
Hecker Phelan & Guthrie
  102
Heino 238
Heinrup 176
Heinz, H. J. 273
Helen Bember
  Foundation 316
Helen Brown Massage
  174
Helen Langridge
  Associates 260
Heller 18
Helsinki -London Design
  Camp 256
Hemtex 88
HEMU 42
Henderson Leyland 126
Hepworth Wakefield, The
  29
Hermes Mass Transit 176
Herrenabig 147
Hertz 18
Herwitt, J. 200
Higham, David 214
Highly Solar Energy 176
Hiscox 160
Historic House Trust 44
Hive & Honey 218
Hodgson, Deborah 102
HoHoJo 278
HOK 262
Holistic 280
Holland & Knight 246
Holmes Mackillop 162
Home 316
Home 3 Assistance 134
Honeymoon Dessert 284
Hopscotch Films 74
Hoptimist 70
Horse & Country TV 236
Horse Feathers Home
  104
Hostage 176
Hotel Arts Barcelona 262
Hotel Olympia 195
Hotel Omm 110
Houlding, Leo 178
Hourigan International

176
House of Illustration 268
House of Propellers 94
Howard 230
Howcast 218
Howe Baugeschäft 176
Hulton Archive 46
Human Genome
  Sciences 144
Hurrell, Tess 114

I

IamExpat 302
Ian Terry 190
Ice Cream Music 273
iD 40
iD Distribution 230
Ide 302
IDTV 52
ILIVETOMORROW 108
Ilkka Marttiini Finland182
Independent
  Commission on Turkey
  206
Independent State 104
Indie 12
Inditex 24
Indus Capital 262
Infinite Sum 94
infoMeteo 246
Inmedias 218
Inpoc 218
INREV 120
Institute of Directors 202
Integrity 218
Intermédiations 137
International Center for
  Journalists 24
International Council of
  Museums UK 152
International Creative
  Union Center 44
International News
  Network 288
Intersect 278
inter view 110
Intro Garde 137
Intuit 218
Intuitive 230
io 74
I/Object 39
Ivan Hair Salon 120
Ivy 74
iwa 74

J

Jade Jagger for yoo 176
Jamie Oliver 144
Janelle 176
Japan Design Society
  126
Japlab 66
Jarman Award, The 56
Javerdel 218
JBPR 48
JCL Records 156
Jeep 18
Jelly Products 255
Jerde 98
Jerwood Gallery 26
Jestico + Whiles 246
Joe and co. 98
John Howard Print
  Studios 268

John Jones 160
John Lyall Architects 230
Joly Beauty 44
Joyce and Jonathan Hui
  156
Jump Healthfoods 232
Just Moved 80
JW Trading 24

K

K College 178
Kagawa Education
  Institute of Nutrition 199
Kaiser Sound Studios
  104
Kajimoto Music Office
  126
Karimi 248
Kaspar 32
Katz PR 176
Kaya 86
Keith Holland &
  Associates 236
Kelkyu 218
Kemistry Gallery 32
Kerik 56
Kerry Phelan Design
  Office 232
Ketab-e-Hafteh 288
Kettle of Fish 214
KidStart 232
Kikkoman 316
Kilver Dance Studio 178
Kilvil 40
King's Cross Social Club
  102
Kingsland School 202
Kino Cinema 46
Klar! 92
Klartext 218
Knabenchor Gütersloh
  148
Knickelkopp 80
Knoll 21
Kolpa 248
Komono 124
Kondyli Publishing 178
Kopiosto 39
Korkers 220
KPMG 252
Kress (Samuel H)
  Foundation 26
Kristin Morris Jewelry
  160
Krrb 74
Kubota Corporation 120
Kultohr 220
Kurakuen 178
Kwaku Alston
  Photography 86
Kx, The 94

L

Lab, The 69
L-A-D-A 242
Lafayette Centre 200
Laidian Coffee Bar 284
Laidlaw Foundation 138
Laimar Films 274
Lakeside Counselling
  273
Laline 278
Lambeth First 200
La Moderna 306

Land Securities 276
Lane 232
L'Anima 102
Lankabaari 78
Lara Gut 80
La Strada 70
Lautstark 242
Layezee Beds 178
LazyLazy.com 18
Lea Singers 73
Lean Alliance 124
Leap 256
Lechem Eretz 292
Leong Ka Tai
  Photography 156
Leontyna 220
L'Escalier 270
Le Vieux Manoir 147
Libraries Alive 242
Librería Internacional
  Bilbao 260
Lichthaus Arnsberg 23
Life 298
Life + Times 62
Life Assay 273
Lili 292
Lilium 104
Lill Rechtsanwälte 138
Limapuluh 306
Linden Centre for
  Contemporary Art 178
Ling Lee 274
Lisa Desforges 308
Lisson Gallery 26
litl 73
Living 220
Living Architecture 206
Living Beauty 48
Loft Investments 30
Lokalt Företagsklimat
  138
London Chamber
  Orchestra (LCO) 132
London 2012 302
Longwalk 92
Love From London 274
Love Language London
  242
Low Income Investment
  Fund 42
Luna Design 148
Lund Byggeri 205
Lusben 73
Luxury Trip 220
Lyons 56

M

Mace Group 316
McGarry & Eadie 117
McNay Art Museum, The
  32
Mad Cow 84
Magazines Canada 268
Magic of Persia
  Contemporary Art Prize
  298
Magnusson Fine Wine
  156
Mahnab Co 290
Mainstone Press, The
  182
Maison de Photo, La 126
MAK Center 92
Make Associates 304
Malaparte 274
Malings, The 178
Manbulloo 182

Manchester Literature
  Festival 181
Mannerheim League for
  Child Welfare 256
Marawa the Amazing 48
Marco 220
Margarets, The 90
Mark Warner 90
Marks & Clerk 236
Marmalade Toast 148
Martha Stewart
  Omnimedia 140
Martin Prosperity
  Institute 46
Marubiru 182
Maruhon 178
Masch Media 244
Mass LBP 26
Massif 56
Matricia 248
Matsuri Japan 298
Matta 178
Matthew Williamson 220
Mattura 148
Mayne Health 260
MC Partners 36
M.Digest 182
MEA Accountants 52
Media Builder 288
MediaCom 26
Mediapulse 232
Meiji Group 220
Melanie Grant 178
Mellow Mushroom 83
Mental Health
  Foundation 196
Merlin 182
Metropolitan Wharf 134
México 302
Meyers Deli 181
MICA 108
Michael Ku Gallery 298
Michael Popper
  Associates 220
Michal Miller 292
Midi 64
Millennium Models 156
Milton Agency, The 117
Mini McGhee 108
Mini Museum Mürren 42
Mint Furniture 98
Miquelrius 104
Miso 159
MMM Festival 274
Mobil Corporation 220
Mobilise 220
Mobilrabatten 196
MòChén Architects &
  Engineers 298
Mode Zonen 120
Moderna Museet 84
Moka 278
Moke 222
Molton Brown 36
Monastic Productions
  316
Mondays At The Foyer
  200
Montgomery Sisam
  Architects 232
MONU 94
Moor 222
Moorhouse Consulting
  222
Mordisco 118
MoreySmith 48
>moser 248
Motherboard 62
Mothercare 181

Motor Neurone Disease
  Assocation 120
Moulinex 78
Mount Anvil 150
Mouse Awards 113
Mouttet 181
Moving Images 268
m+associés 178
MRCPderm 222
m/studios 108
M2b 104
Multilingua 83
Multimédia Sorbonne
  196
Muscular Dystrophy
  Campaign 46
Museion 181
Museo Italiano Cultural
  Centre 56
Museu d'Arqueologica de
  Catalunya 182
Museum Links 134
Museum of American
  Finance 150
Museum voor
  Communicatie 83
Museums & Galleries
  NSW 144
Música 242
Mutants 182
Muzik 182
My Italian Friends 256

N

Nafsica 182
Nahj al Balagha Cultural
  Center 288
Nailxpress 18
National Library of Ireland
  132
National Parks of New
  York Harbor 308
National Theatre Wales
  280
National Training Awards
  190
National Youth Choirs of
  Great Britain 152
Nationale Ballet, Het 278
Natural History Museum
  302
Naturopathica 98
Nau Capital 138
Naughton Gallery, The
  280
NBS 126
NCM Interiors 62
Nederlandse Staatsloterij
  30
Negro Rojo 110
Nest.co.uk 144
New British Design 316
New 42nd Street, The 274
New Museum 152
New York 104
New York Palace, The 36
Nichols Consultancy 185
Nimmin 51
Nina Matos 195
9/11 Memorial 211
Nine Point Nine 126
90 Hairdressing 308
NL Ruhr 98
NOBA 60
Nobivac 222
NoHo 252
Noon Cultural Group 290

NorrlandsOperan 242
Northern Icon 242
Northern Ireland Tourist
  Board 222
Northsea Capital 36
Northshore 182
North/South/East/West
  48
Norton & Sons 36
Norton Motorcycles 107
Nothotels.com 232
Nowhere Resorts 73
Nursing & Midwifery
  Council 196
Museum of Modern Art,
  The 137
Nutrio 222
NuZi 284
NY Arts Program 248
NYC 304

O

Obsidian 316
*Obstetrician &
  Gynaecologist, The* 199
Ocean Consulting Group
  316
Octink 134
Oded Ezer Typography
  292
Odin 242
Ogee74 52
Oikos 264
oki ni 40
Okinaka 24
Ole Lund 104
Oliver & Bonacini
  Restaurants 46
Olmo Reverter
  Photography 124
On Pedder 98
One Atlantic 280
One Degree 248
OneToBe 259
1:1 240
Only 62
Open Air Laboratories
  Network 302
Open Museum, The 84
Openfield 21
Opera North 66
Opet Petroleum 222
O+Co 248
Opta 318
OQO 52
Orange Box 308
Oranjebloesem 297
Origin Architect 284
Orso 124
Ossie Clark 152
Österreichische
  Nationalbibliothek 312
Oyster Marine 314
Oyuna Cashmere 120

P

Pacific Place 86
Pagliano Arredamenti
  185
Palau Foundation 66
Panthalassa 186
Papatzanakis 186
Paramount 268
Parc Central del

Poblenou 51
Parfumerie Leni 90
Park Lane 98
Parker Marketing 318
Parrotta Contemporary
  Art 152
Passion Foods 268
Paternoster Square 185
Patrick Heide
  Contemporary Art 148
Pauffley 242
Pax 260
Peak Performance 186
Pearson Lyle 32
Pedlars 318
Peel District School
  Board 308
Peel's Deli 308
PeliFilip 222
Penoyre & Prasad 132
Penrhyn Books 196
People Tree 32
Peppersmith 318
Perplex 114
Peter Ellis New Cities 55
Peter Taylor Associates
  Limited 128
Petrolux 222
Pew Center for Arts &
  Heritage, The 280
Peyton and Byrne 152
Philippe Guignard 196
pHuel 84
Pilobolus Dance
  Company 150
Pin Point Events 185
Pizza Nova 107
Place Estate Agents 232
Plan 8 222
Playgroup 244
Pleasant Studio 102
Pleasurealm 226
Plywood 66
Popular 185
Popular Front 56
Port Vell 264
Pose Magazine 260
Postmedia Network 234
Poverty Over 226
Pravda 262
Press, The 88
Preston and District Ex
  Boxers Association, The
  225
Preston Kelly 128
Pueblo Chico 42
Pukstaavi 244
Puntari 40
Purity 226

Q

QFort 226
Qmunity 226
Quintessentially 29
QVC 186

R

Radiodada 260
RadLyn 108
Rainy City Stories 152
Raleigh International 186
Rambert Moves 274
Ramblers 186
Randstad Uitzendbureau

159
Raw Space 120
RBH Multimedia 202
Red Felix 196
Red Ladder Theatre
  Company 152
Redfern 274
Refresh Beauty Spa 316
Regatta Design 200
Regional Acting Studio
  90
Republic 29
Resilica 66
Restaurant at the Royal
  Academy of Arts, The
  150
Restaurant Mansour 288
Rethink 132
Reuter & Kucher
  Steuerberater 128
Reza Abbasi Museum 288
RIBA Bookshops 148
Ricoh 26
Rigby & Peller 36
Rippleffect Sound Design
  226
Roam Digital 122
Rock 186
Rogers Flooring
  Company, The 189
Rollasole 226
Rondo Media 120
Roost 186
RooX 78
Rothfield 88
RoTq Architects 97
Rotterdam Academie van
  Bouwkunst 128
Royal Mint, The 320
Royal Opera House 316
RTVE 42
Rumpus Room, The 304
Ruth Tomlinson 23

S

Saba 159
Sadie Coles HQ 17
Sahar Co 290
St Mary le Bow Church
  150
St Pancras Renaissance
  Hotel 272
Saks Fifth Avenue 107
Salvino 226
Samarkand 290
Samphire PR 228
Sanderson, Rupert 35
Sansaw 186
Santarelli and CO 69
Saratoga Associates 120
Satoko Furukawa 107
Saunders, Ben 142
Saveurs Nobles 70
Savoy, The 26
Savviva Lifestyle
  Management 56
Scandinavian Airlines
  262
Schalwijk, Bob 140
Science Museum 150
Scotland + Venice 35
Scottish Opera 206
Seawater Greenhouse
  205
Secur 244
Self Publish, Be Happy
  152

Sematak Advertising 290
Sendai Astronomical
  Observatory 297
Sendyne 228
Seven 138
Seven Film Gallery 128
750mph 142
seymourpowell 30
S4C 234
Shahr-e Hashtom 290
Shanghai World Financial
  Center 294
Shelta 268
Shenkar College of
  Engineering & Design
  200
Sher 290
Shift 186
Show And Tell 52
Showtime Networks 260
Sigmond, Ragne 32
Signature Theatre
  Company 274
Signon 292
Silver Plate 122
Sion College 202
Sirca 30
Six Wines Eight 48
64 Knightsbridge 98
Skype 274
SLA Pharma 304
Slash 234
Slice 268
Slowly 60
Slurk 186
Smeg 318
Smith Partners 55
SML 304
SMP Partners 92
Smule 228
So...soap! 280
Social Traders 56
Socialbox 228
Sociotrendy 186
Soda Reklamebyrå 35
Sofami 228
Softbox 69
Solo Mobile 69
SOM 42
Sonic Editions 160
Sony Corporation 39
Sorg Architects 94
SoundCircus Kees Kroot
  42
Sounds Like Brisbane 90
Soup Broth Asia 304
South Street Seaport
  Museum 318
Southern California
  Institute of Architecture
  244
Speirs + Major 48
Spiritualized 18
Splitrock 304
ST Holdings 17
Stadium 56
Standard 8 140
ST&P 236
Stara Piekarnia 150
Start Anywhere 278
StartSkuddet 148
Statik Dancin' 150
Steam 122
Stedelijk Museum 29
Stereoscape 228
Sterling Relocation 189
Sternen, Restaurant 118
Stir 318
Store Build 206
Strange Beast 104

Streethearts *see*
  thestreethearts.com
Streetlab 17
Strum 92
Studio Daminato 108
Studio RBA 59
Studio Sam 128
Studio 2930 318
STVDIO 225
SugarSin 35
Super OS 206
Supermarket 320
Surgical Aesthetics 238
Surus 88
Suttergut 56
Swanswell Trust, The 267
Sweet Little Things 84
Switch 228
Syfy 21
Synovia 230
SynsLaser 234
Syntecor 320

T

Tahkokallio Design+ 248
Takano, Aya 142
Take Ten 46
Tama Art University 113
Tambour 298
Tampereen
  Ammattikorkeakoulu
  (TAMK) 78
Tank Stream Bar 78
Taryn Rose International
  36
Taskers 189
Taste Tideswell 189
Taste Together 284
Tate 92
Tautz, E. 314
Tea 228
Teach First 21
Tel Aviv Museum of Art
  292
10 Architects 294
Teplitzky's 70
Teppanyaki 84
Terrine 190
Terry Moore Design 26
TESS Management 59
Teva 297
text/gallery 234
There Is Sound 320
thestreethearts.com 83
Third Light 159
Third Pillar of Health 320
Thirst 55
33RPM 200
Thompson Gallery 190
3DW 124
Tickety Boo 97
Tiffany & Co. 36
Tilt Design 138
Tim Wood Furniture 159
Tinley Road 190
Title 128
Tize Scissors 290
TLT Solicitors 259
Together 222
TOJO 44
Tokyo Station City 294
Tom Devine 190
Tomorrow 32
Tonic 232
Toohey, Louise 132
Top Drawer 154
Toronto Life 154

Toronto Magazine 154
Tossed 140
Town Hall Hotel 280
Towner Gallery 190
TransFormal 206
Transportation
  Alternatives 260
Trento DOC 225
Tricolette Yarns 90
Trinity Laban
  Conservatoire of Music
  and Dance 94
Trommpo 140
Trossi 320
Tschine, Restauraunt 29
Tubestation 60
Tuke & Bloom 140
Tukes 86
Turnaround for Children
  156
Turner Collective, The
  304
Tuveri 122
Typopassage 59

U

Über Gallery 92
UCLA Architecture &
  Urban Design 128
U.Coffee 190
UIP 86
UK Skills 225
Unesta 190
Uniqlo 298
Unique Models 225
Unit 226
Unit Architects 52
United Colors of
  Benetton 264
Unity Law 190
Univerità IUAV di Venezia
  148
University of East Anglia
  195
University of
  Westminster 154
Unreserved 206
Upplevelseindustrin 60
Urban Splash 30
Urban Strategies 110
Usual Suspects 154

V

Valkekz 160
Vanity (waxing salon) 190
Vanity (women's clothing)
  51
Velux 268
Verasis 192
Verbatim 232
Verida Credit 192
Vertical Garden Design
  132
Vertigo 140
Very Important
  Announcements 308
Via Snella 36
Viavai 156
Victor Russo's Osteria
  280
Victoria & Albert Museum
  195
Victoria Beckham 122
Vietnam Woods, The 284

Viewpoint Photography
  94
Villalagos 190
Vincenzo 90
Vinifiti 98
Viper Subsea 192
Virgin Galactic 40
Vision Pablishing 110
Visual Intelligence
  Agency 128
Vitamed 192
Vitsœ 26
Vivid 192
Vivid Research 88
Von Rotz 60
Vumi 124

W

Walktall.com 154
Wapping Project
  Bankside, The 150
Warm Ground 196
Water By Design 92
Waterfront, The 192
Waterman 212
Watermark 192
We Jane 74
Weekend 226
Weeks & Cowling 236
Weldon 320
Wellicious 78
Werner Sobek
  Engineering & Design 84
Western Union 108
Westminster
  Employment 244
Westzone Publishing 248
Whitney Museum of
  American Art 52
Whittingham 192
Wildbore & Gibbons 267
Wilhelm 138
Willem and Anne 156
Wink 248
W'Law Weber Wicki
  Partners 192
Women's Organisation,
  The 199
Wood&Wood 195
Woolworths South Africa
  192
Workshop Events 248
World Outstanding
  Chinese Design Award
  262
World Policy Institute 226
WOSM 252
Wright Brothers 267
Wyman, Nella Cohalan
  196

X

Xococava 137

Y

Yauatcha Atelier 196
Yde & Toklum 84
Ying Kee Tea House 284
YMCA of the USA 192
Yoo Mee 84
Your Wembley 196
YouTube 267

Yritys 2.0 192
Yrkeshögskolan
  Göteborg 108

Z

Zendol B 270
Zepter Museum of
  Modern Arts 196
Zhejiang Daily Press
  Group 284
Zildjian 77
Znips 90
Zoo Concept Store 262
ZWN Group 252

Designer Index
Page numbers refer
to text

A

Abbasi, Majid 287, 290
Abbott, Jade see Studio
  Paradise
Abbott, Rodney
  (Lippincott) 246
Abdolali, Mohammadreza
  290
Abraham, Alexis (Powell
  Allen) 308
Adair, Ryan (The
  Partners) 104
Adamson, Marksteen see
  ArthurSteenHorne-
  Adamson (ASHA)
Adger Yawei Zha (Hesign
  International) 284
Adibi, Farzad 290
Aguayo, Paco (Hahmo)
  276
Ahmed, Irfan (Momin
  Branding) 190, 297
Aicher, Otl 23
Ailoviu 220
Alexander, Dan see Dan
  Alexander & Co.
Alger, Katie (Kimpton) 26,
  185, 214
Alikhani, Iraj Mirza 287
Alireza, Hani 262, 298
Allen, Chris (Powell Allen)
  186, 308
Alloviu 148, 259
Alós, Adriana
  (Serracatafau) 51
&Larry
– Chuan Pictures 284
– Eye Place 156
– L'Escalier 270
– Marmalade Toast 148
– MONU 94
– Studio Daminato 108
– Switch 238
Andrade, Danielle de
  (Naughtyfish) 232
Andrew, Shanin
  (Sandstrom Partners)
  56
&Smith
– AJM Productions 102
– Altitude Music 94
– Émile Bailey 280
– Balthazar B and the
  Beatitudes 208
– The Conspiracy Group
  170
– 45 Park Lane 98

– Lane 232
– The New York Palace 36
– SugarSin 35
– Surgical Aesthetics
  238
Aparicio, Nicholas
  (Landor Associates)
  216
Apeloig, Philippe see
  Studio Apeloig
A Practice for Everyday
  Life (APFEL) 29
Arabatzis, Diamantis
  (G Design Studio) 124
Arbenz, Kim (Hotz & Hotz)
  147
Area 17
– Asylum 56
– Böka 240
– BurdaStyle 18
– Deborah A Nilson 202
– Dew Tour 172
– GSA Venture Partners
  36
– Krrb 74
– Life + Times 62
– Motherboard 62
– Slash 234
– Vertical Garden Design
  132
Ark 273
Armstrong, David (1977
  Design) 230, 273
Arquin, Ingrid (Coast) 60,
  64, 86, 124
ArthurSteenHorne-
  Adamson (ASHA) 218,
  236, 252, 255, 270, 276,
  278
Assadollahi, Mostafa 288
Atelier Bundi (Stephan
  Bundi) 42, 51, 137, 218,
  232
Atelier Pedro Falcão 17,
  124, 132, 138
Atelier Works
– Blue Gallery 80
– Caponata 168
– Ian Chilvers 176
– City of Westminster
  College 264
– The Company Books
  152
– Connect Sheffield 212
– Double Good Windows
  92
– Exmouth Market 314
– The Forge 174
– Ian Terry 190
– Independent
  Commission on Turkey
  206
– Integrity 218
– Kingsland School 202
– Lambeth First 200
– Mouttet 181
– The Obstetrician &
  Gynaecologist 199
– Salvino 226
Atkinson, Mark (The
  Chase) 230
A2 Design
– Castleton 170
– Croydon Food Group
  170
– Grant Spencer 230
– m+associés 178
– Verasis 192
– Wildbore & Gibbons
  267

A2/SW/HK 26, 104, 126,
  154, 205
Awang, Aimi (Magpie
  Studio) 202
Ayre, Dominic (Hambly &
  Woolley) 104, 232
Azurdia, David see
  Magpie Studio

B

Badalan, Ciprian
  (Brandient) 270
Bailey, Paul (1977 Design)
  48, 94, 102, 144, 230,
  273
Baker, Eric (The O Group)
  174
Balius, Andreu (Summa)
  30
B&B Studio 195, 318
B&W Studio
– Biketreks 66
– B&W Studio 236
– Calderdale Council 140
– Green Park 40
– Miso 159
– Northshore 182
– Orange Box 308
– Republic 29
– Seven 138
– 33RPM 200
Baravalle, Giorgio (de.
  MO) 78, 86, 122, 148
Barbarasa, Iancu
  (Brandient) 192
Barmettler, Thomas (Hotz
  & Hotz) 56
Baron, Andy (Landor
  Associates) 212
Bateson, John see
  Bateson/Studio
Bateson/Studio 126
Bather, Zoë (Studio8) 52,
  88, 142
Bauer, Erwin K. see bauer
  konzept &
  gestaltungbauer
  konzept & gestaltung
  59, 77
Beacher, Jonathan (1977
  Design) 255
Beare, David (Dragon
  Rouge) 270
Bembibre, Daniel
  (Summa) 30, 42, 246
Bennett, David (OPX) 40
Bennett, Natalie
  (300million) 60, 78, 222,
  232
Benson, Paula (Form) 185
Bereuter, Zita (Bohatsch
  und Partner) 52
Bergh, Roger van den
  (The Chase) 216
Bergh, Roger van den
  (Onoma) 176, 228, 252,
  260, 278
Berks, Sara (Area 17) 36
Bertell, Erik (Hahmo) 40,
  78, 86, 126, 200, 228,
  244
Beveridge, James
– (Brownjohn) 30, 162,
  176, 202, 262, 278, 312
– (Further) 174, 312
Bibliothèque
– Allude 212

– Boskke 212
– Covent Garden 205
– Engage 114
– The Rumpus Room 304
– Speirs + Major 48
Bickerstaff, Bill (OPX) 40
Bierut, Michael
  (Pentagram) 107, 113,
  262
Birdsall, Connie
  (Lippincott) 246
Bjork, Kelly (Studio/lab)
  311
Black, Gary (Uffindell)
  208, 222
Blackburn, Garry (Rose)
  29
Blackburn, Kevin (The
  Chase) 152
Blast 92, 195, 280, 312
Balius, Andreu (Summa)
  30
BMB Agency 226
Bob Design 90, 113
Bohatsch, Walter see
  Bohatsch and Partner
Bohatsch and Partner 52,
  312
Bohls, Kelly (Sandstrom
  Partners) 306
Bologna, Matteo see
  Mucca Design
Bonafede, Enrico
  (Homework) 147
Bos, Ben (Total Design)
  159
Bowen, Shaun (B&B
  Studio) 195, 318
Bown, Dan (Blast) 312
Boy Bastiaens/
  Storm-hand 32, 174,
  189, 262
Braaksma, Arjan see
  Burobraak
Bradley, Lee (B&W Studio)
  29, 40, 66, 138, 140,
  200
Brandenburg, Maarten
  (Total Identity) 280
Brandient 172, 192, 222,
  226, 248, 270, 306
Braun, Sebastian
  (MetaDesign China)
  284
Brechbühl, Erich see
  Mixer
Bree, Rob de (Teldesign)
  248
Brian, Lise (The Chase)
  216
Brin, Sergey 35
Broadhurst, Alex (B&W
  Studio) 66, 140, 308
Brown, Andrea (Mucca
  Design) 39, 88, 273
Brown Travis (Toky
  Branding + Design) 262
Browne, Adam (Purpose)
  190, 202, 225, 314
Browne, AV 222
Brownjohn 30, 162, 176,
  202, 262, 278, 312
Browns 140, 150, 160
Brunazzi & Associati 80,
  122, 240, 268
Brunazzi, Andrea
  (Brunazzi & Associati)
  80, 240, 268
Brunazzi, Giovanni 185,
  268
– (Brunazzi & Associati)
  268

Bryant, Karin (Elixir
  Design) 200
Buck, Spencer see Taxi
  Studio
Buddy 70, 140, 159, 211
Bull, Dan (Six) 168
Bundi, Stephan see
  Atelier Bundi
Burgess, Alexis (Bob
  Design) 113
Burkhardt, Mireille (Bob
  Design) 90, 113
Büro Uebele Visuelle
  Kommunikation 51, 84,
  128, 152, 156
Burobraak 46, 246, 264,
  297, 311
Bürocratik
– Ágora 212
– Aquavia 212
– Bags 212
– Foro 216

C

Calderón, Eduardo
  (Emblem) 302
Campbell's 73
C&G Partners
– American Cinema
  Editors 142
– Chuck Choi 144
– Low Income
  Investment Fund 42
– The McNay Art
  Museum 32
– Museum of American
  Finance 150
– Peter Freed 97
– RBH Multimedia 202
– Samuel H Kress
  Foundation 26
– Signature Theatre
  Company 274
Canon 32
Carter, Matthew 137
Carter, Phil 107
Carter Wong Design 107,
  144
Cartlidge Levene 48, 144
Casey, Ben (The Chase)
  110, 170
Cavanagh, Andrew (Elfen)
  228
CDT Design
– ActionAid 211
– Bevan Brittan 206
– BRAC 312
– Broadgate 168
– Digital Cinema Media
  270
– English National Opera
  147
– GMW 110
– Home 3 Assistance 134
– London Chamber
  Orchestra 132
– Marks & Clerk 236
– Nursing & Midwifery
  Council 196
– Paternoster Square
  185
– Vision Publishing 110
Cefai, John (KentLyons)
  56, 107, 274
Challinor, Chris (The
  Chase) 110
Chandler, Ross (Hambly &

Woolley 154
Chase, The
– Conception Marketing
  170
– Creative Industries
  Development Unit 110
– Freedom 216
– Halliwell Landau 214
– Home 316
– Hostage 176
– iD Distribution 230
– Layezee Beds 178
– The Preston and
  District Ex Boxers
  Association 225
– Red Ladder Theatre
  Company 152
Chen, Christy (CoDesign)
  278
Chen, Frances (Hambly &
  Woolley) 24, 46, 104,
  308
Chermayeff & Geismar
– Barneys New York 142
– Downtown Alliance 306
– Engraved Stationery
  Manufacturers
  Association 172
– Factset Research
  Systems 66
– Guggenheim Partners
  24
– Harvard Maintenance
  216
– Hearst Corporation 24
– Kaya 86
– Marubiru 182
– Mobil Corporation 220
– The Museum of Modern
  Art 137
– National Parks of New
  York Harbor 308
– The New 42nd Street
  274
– Opet Petroleum 222
– Pilobolus Dance
  Company 150
– Saratoga Associates
  120
– Showtime Networks
  260
– World Policy Institute
  226
Cheung, Jan (milkxshake)
  108
Cheung, Ray (CoDesign)
  156, 278, 280
Chilvers, Ian (Atelier
  Works) 80, 176, 199,
  200, 218
Chock, Paul (Landor
  Associates) 212, 216
Christie, Ben see Magpie
  Studio
Chubb, Jonathan (Ark)
  273
Chun, Peter (Lippincott)
  218
Cifuentes, Beatriz
  (Vignelli Associates)
  192, 255, 314
Clark, Eszter T (Hatch
  Design) 77, 280
Clark, Jen (Hambly &
  Woolley) 312
Clarke, Richie (Mode (UK))
  86
Clarke, Steve (Landor
  Associates) 248
Claudius, Stefan see

Claudius Design
Claudius Design
– Festland 80
– Firescape 102
– Howe Baugeschäft 176
– Knickelkopp 80
– Masch Media 244
Coast
– AAthletics 208
– AsBuilt 86
– Atelier 210 60
– Blanc Kara 86
– Brussels Electronic
Music Festival 62
– Collectors Gallery 148
– Friday 174
– From Scratch 124
– I/Object 39
– Komono 124
– La Ferme du Bléreau
256
– Midi 64
– My Italian Friends 256
– Okinaha 24
– OneToBe 259
– Statik Dancin' 150
CoDesign
– Daydream Nation 278
– Design Leadership
Award 200
– FCE 138
– HoHoJo 278
– Joyce and Jonathan
Hui 156
– Leong Ka Tai
Photography 156
– NuZi 284
– 1:1 240
– So...soap! 280
– World Outstanding
Chinese Design Award
262
Coenen, Susanne
(Lockstoff Design) 102
Cohen, Jason B (The O
Group) 174, 206
Colvin, Alan (Cue) 56, 108,
128, 318(2)
Company 185, 218, 226
Conchie, Steve (The
Chase) 316
Concrete
– architectsAlliance 40
– Bite 118
– Brook McIlroy 234
– Fabbrica 39
– Film North 314
– Mass LMP 26
– Pizza Nova 107
– Xococava 137
Cornwell Design
– Ash St Cellar 80
– Davis Evolution 118
– Fridcorp 70
– Hecker Phelan &
Guthrie 102
– Ivy 74
– Lyons 56
– Mad Cow 84
– Rothfield 88
– Tank Stream Bar 78
– Teppanyaki 84
Cortada, Eduardo
(Summa) 40, 44
Costin, Phil (Mode (UK))
48, 86, 98, 102
Costly, Amelia (Spencer
du Bois) 186
Couchman, Ryan
(Concrete) 118

Couple 154, 156, 262, 304
Cox, Martin (Blast) 195
c+c workshop 52, 59,
108, 260, 276, 284
Creative Inc 60, 132, 159,
236
Crouwel, Wim (Total
Design) 29
Cuban Council and Test
Pilot Collective 264
Cue
– Parker Marketing 318
– Popular Front 56
– Preston Kelly 128
– RadLyn 108
– Studio 2030 318

D

Dagan, Troy (SML) 182
Dahl, Jack see Homework
Dallyn, Sam 214, 228
Dan Alexander & Co 64,
92, 102, 278
Danfoss 70
Danko, Tegan (Grade
Design) 244
Danyshevsky, Ivan
(Transformer Studio)
276
Darden Studio 280
Davies, Justin (Purpose)
21
Davies, Lee (Peter and
Paul) 189, 190
Davies, Nigel (300million)
60, 78, 124, 222, 232
Dawson, Peter (Grade
Design) 152, 156, 244
Day, Rob (Further) 312
Deardon, Gary (Uffindell)
92, 222
Defoe, Freya (The
Partners) 238
Delaney, Ian (Minale
Tattersfield) 225
Dell Global Brand
Creative 259
de.MO 78, 86, 122, 148
Dempsey, Mike (CDT
Design) 132, 147 see
also Studio Dempsey
Denis Olenik Design
Studio 56, 214
Design By Pidgeon
– Altitude Volvo 168
– Anglesea Sports &
Recreation Club 167
– Bonair 306
– Boyd Baker House 94
– Linden Centre for
Contemporary Art 178
– Museo Italiano Cultural
Centre 56
– Studio Sam 128
– Tilt Design 138
Design Ranch 172, 199
Designbolaget 92, 114
Designers United
– CACT 200
– Diathiasis Architectural
Lighting 172
– Hotel Olympia 195
– Mondays At The Foyer
200
– Papatzanakis 186
– Seven Film Gallery 128
DesignStudio 124, 176,

238
Devoy, Harriet (The
Chase) 230
Diedrich, Ellen (Summa)
66
Dierig, Christian
(Lippincott) 218
Diggins, Mark
(KentLyons) 314
Dios, Sandra (Summa)
102
Dobson, Phil (1977
Design) 208
Donaldson, Tim
(hat-trick) 138
Donohoe, Peter (Peter
and Paul) 78, 189, 190,
238
Dowling, John see
Dowling Duncan
Dowling Duncan
– Future Designs 94
– Hive & Honey 218
– Michael Popper
Associates 220
– Museum Links 134
– NCM Interiors 62
– Pearson Lyle 32
– Rock 186
– Samphire PR 228
– Seawater Greenhouse
205
– Tinley Road 190
– Warm Ground 196
Doyle, Stephen see Doyle
Partners
Doyle Partners 44, 140,
236, 240, 246, 260
Dragon Rouge 270
Droog, Andrew (B&W
Studio) 29, 40, 138
Duncan, Rob see Dowling
Duncan
Durrant, Nathan (Nathan
Durrant Design) 70 see
also Elixir Design
Dylla, Frank (Chermayeff
& Geismar) 182

E

Easterbrook, Aaron
(Elfen) 120, 124, 280
Ecob, Alex (Studio8) 52
Edmondson, Bryan see
SEA
Edwards, Matt (Fabio
Ongarato Design) 88
Edwards, Melanie
(Further) 242
Egli, Simon 59
Ehsai, Mohammad 288
Elder, Simone (Fabio
Ongarato Design) 64
Elfen 120, 124, 228, 280
Elixir Design
– Gott's Roadside 98
– J Herwitt 200
– Jerde 98
– Naturopathica 98
– Stir 318
– Taryn Rose
International 36
Ellery, Jonathan (Browns)
150, 160
Ellul, Jamie see Magpie
Studio
El Mir, Naji 196, 287

Elmwood 97, 190, 230,
244, 267, 308
Emblem 302
Emmen, Jaco (Teldesign)
30
Erdpohl, Karen (Creative
Inc) 132
Ervin, Don (George
Nelson Associates) 167
Eskenazi, Mario
– Ars 162
– Asociación Profesional
de Diseñadores de
Iluminación 142
– Banc Sabadell 252
– Barcelona pel Medi
Ambient 168
– El Japonés 148
– Fundación Sida y
Sociedad 318
– Grupo Tragaluz 189
– Hotel Omm 110
– Martín Faixó 200
– Mordisco 118
– Negro Rojo 110
– Together 222
Esteves, Adriano
(Bürocratik) 212(3), 216
Estudio Diego Feijóo 92,
148, 167, 170
Evans, Adam (Seven) 138
Evans, Guto (Elfen) 120,
124, 228, 280
Ezer, Oded
– Globes 292
– Lili 292
– Muzik 182
– Oded Ezer Typography
292
– Weekend 226

F

Fabio Ongarato Design
– Assin 64
– Australian Centre for
Contemporary Art 52
– Crown Metropol 88
– Gertrude
Contemporary 52
– Kerry Phelan Design
232
– On Pedder 98
– Social Traders 56
– Über Gallery 92
Façade Design 160
Fahs, Amin (Guild of Sage
& Smith) 294
Fairnington, Kieran
(Playne Design) 320
Farhadi, Amrollah 288
Farrington, Paul (Studio
Tonne) 280
Farrow 17, 18, 36, 150, 152
Fausti, Tania (SML) 86
Fedell, Todd (Peloton)
252
Feijóo, Diego 168, 222,
318
see also Estudio Diego
Feijóo
Fellowes, Tim (Magpie
Studio) 117, 196
Felt Branding 23, 134
Felton, Paul (Purpose)
190, 225, 228, 314
Fenn, Steve (Studio8) 52,
142

Firth, Darren (Six) 59
Fish + Chip Design 216
Fivefootsix 178, 230, 306,
308
FL@33 196, 236, 270, 274
Fletcher, Alan
(Pentagram) 60, 195(2),
202, 205
Forbes, Colin
(Pentagram) 120
Form 80, 108, 185
Foushee, Anneka (Nathan
Durrant Design) 70
Fredricson, Martin see
We Recommend
Freitas, Juliane (Landor
Associates) 18
Frigerio, Emanuela
– (C&G Partners) 32, 144,
150
– (Chermayeff & Geismar)
120, 182
Frost Design 78, 225, 242,
246, 274
Funnel Creative 80, 104,
304
Further 174, 242, 312

G

G Design Studio
– Braincandy 206
– G Design Studio 174
– Godzilla Sushi Bar 260
– IamExpat 302
– Ivan Hair Salon 120
– Kondyli Publishing 178
– Living 220
– Nafsica 182
– Orso 124
Gabriel, Kate (Cue) 318
Gächter, Alexander (Hotz
& Hotz) 246
Ganouchi, Samir (Hotz &
Hotz) 70
Garbett, Paul see
Naughtyfish
gardens&co 77, 98, 176,
182, 260, 274
Gardiner, Chris
(Sandstrom Partners)
220, 306
Gatt, Elizabeth (1977
Design) 102
Gaubeka, Miren S see
Zorraquino
Gavrilakis, Alexandros
(G Design Studio) 120,
174,178, 182, 206, 220,
260, 302
GBH
– Alexander Hall 240
– Bankside Mix 137
– Nothotels.com 232
– Nutrio 222
– Opta 318
– seymourpowell 30
– 64 Knightsbridge 98
– Syntecor 320
– Thompson Gallery 190
– Virgin Galactic 40
Geismar, Tom
(Chermayeff & Geismar)
142
Geissbuhler, Alex (C&G
Partners) 274
Geissbuhler, Steff
– (C&G Partners) 42, 97,

142, 202, 274
– (Chermayeff & Geismar)
142, 172, 274, 308
Geller, Hillary (Studio/lab)
134
Geoff Halpin Design 107
George Nelson
Associates 167
Georgiou, Michalis
(G Design Studio) 120,
124, 174, 178, 206, 220,
260
Gericke, Michael
(Pentagram) 124, 170
Gibbons, Darrell (Mode
(UK)) 86, 98, 102
Gibson 78
Gieskes, Rietje (Landor
Associates) 211
Giff see Blast
Giles, Adam (hat-trick)
206, 274, 276, 302
Girvan, Mark see Buddy
Give Up Art
– Big Talk 64
– Bloc 168
– Crisp Media 170
– FireWater 88
– North/South/East/
West 48
– ST Holdings 17
– Surus 88
Goldsmith, Mark (Dragon
Rouge) 270
Good Design Company
40, 73, 107
– Dialog In The Dark 122
– Super OS 206
– Tama Art University 113
Goodall, Simon 126
Goodhew, Colin (Playne
Design) 244
Gordon, Tara (Peloton)
252
Gottschalk + Ash
International 46, 192,
274
Gottschalk, Fritz
(Gottschalk + Ash
International) 192
Gowing, Mark see Mark
Gowing Design
Grade Design 152, 156,
244
Graphical House
– ADF Architects 211
– Canterbury School of
Architecture 128
– Derek Welsh Studio
234
– Emit 276
– Ferguson Whyte 160
– Holmes Mackillop 162
– Mini McGhee 108
– MRCPderm 22
– Scotland + Venice 35
– TOJO 44
Gray, Jordan (Design
Ranch) 172
Green, Tom (Bob Design)
90
Greenwood, Chris
(ArthurSteenHorne-
Adamson (ASHA)) 270
Greenwood, Faye
(Purpose) 202
Guild of Sage & Smith
102, 228, 236, 294
Gundersen, Britt (OPX)
148

Gunn Associates 77
Gutiérrez, Marco (Emblem) 302

H

Ha, J J (Landor Associates) 216
Hadar, Yotam
– Acca Festival of Alternative Theatre 292
– Flow 102
– Hakoltov 174
– Lechem Eretz 292
– Michael Miller 292
– *Signon* 292
Haghighi, Ebrahim 287
Hahmo
– ArkOpen 276
– Columbus 170
– Fatboy 264
– FramePage 126
– Golla 30
– Hahmo Design 24
– Heino 238
– Ilkka Marttini 182
– Javerdel 218
– Koplosto 39
– Mannerheim League for Child Welfare 256
– Moor 222
– Pukstaavi 244
– Puntari 40
– Regatta Design 200
– Stereoscape 228
– Tahkokallio Design+ 248
– Tampereen Ammatti-korkeakoulu (TAMK) 78
– Trossi 320
– Tukes 86
– Yritys 2.0 192
Hakala, Hanna (Hahmo) 40, 200, 244, 248
Hales, Lyndsay (Elmwood) 267
Hambly, Bob *see* Hambly & Woolley
Hambly & Woolley
– Clockwork Talk 312
– Gravitas 24
– Horse Feathers Home 104
– Laidlaw Foundation 138
– Lilium 104
– Luis Albuquerque 212
– *Magazines Canada* 268
– Martin Prosperity Institute 46
– Montgomery Sisam Architects 232
– Peel District School Board 308
– Rippleffect Sound Design 226
– *Toronto Magazine* 154
– Urban Strategies 110
Hammersley, Stuart *see* Give Up Art
Hancox, Keith (Mytton Williams) 176
Hand 97, 102, 118, 174, 232
Hardy, Penny (PS New York) 238, 248(2)
Hartley, George (B&B

Studio) 195
Hartono, May (Landor Associates) 212, 216
hat-trick
– Breakthrough Breast Cancer 138
– Edinburgh International Festival 172
– Friendship Works 40
– House of Illustration 268
– Land Securities 276
– Natural History Museum 302
– Open Air Laboratories Network 302
– Rambert Moves 274
– Scottish Opera 206
– Strum 92
– University of Westminster 154
– Verbatim 232
Hatch Design 77, 280
Havas, Nick (Façade Design) 160
Hawkins, David (Untitled) 108, 132, 150, 152, 190, 202, 208, 230, 316
Hayes, Martin (Elmwood) 308
Hayman, Luke (Pentagram) 104
Heffner, August (Doyle Partners) 44, 140
Heffron, Drew (Doyle Partners) 246
Heinz, H. J. 273
Heitman Ford, Erica (Mucca Design) 88
Henrik Nygren Design 84
Herzog, Michael (bauer konzept & gestaltung) 59
Hesign International
– Financeforce Consulting 298
– Highly Solar Energy 176
– International Creative Union Center 44
– Joly Beauty 44
– Laidian Coffee Bar 284
– Lichthaus Arnsberg 23
– Vivid 192
Hesselink, Scott (Elixir Design) 120
Heydays 83, 118, 226, 234, 244
Hillier, Nigel (Uffindell) 92, 259
Hillman, David (Pentagram) 36
Hills, Andy (Magpie Studio) 205
Hinz, Nate (Cue) 56
Hoffheimer, Jill (Studio/lab) 311
Hoffmann, Julia (MoMA) 137
Hoffmann, Julia (Pentagram) 170
HOK 262
Holland, Christian (Fish + Chip Design) 216
Holt, Gary (SomeOne) 90, 216, 267, 316
Home 316
Homework
– Aya Takano 142
– Danish Fashion Intitute Academy 44

– Fischer Spooner 147
– Gr(eat) 46
– The Lab 69
– Mode Zonen 120
– Unique Models 225
– Yde & Toklum 84
Honey 160, 214
Horridge, Peter (Peter and Paul) 78, 84, 200
Horsham, Michael (Tomato) 181, 270
Hotz & Hotz
– Geozug Ingenieure 246
– Hard Turm Park 278
– Herrenabig 147
– Kaspar 32
– Le Vieux Manoir 147
– Restaurant Sternen 118
– Restaurant Tschine 29
– Saveurs Nobles 70
– Softbox 69
– Suttergut 56
– Vincenzo 90
– Von Rotz 47
Howard, Glenn (Untitled) 108, 132, 150, 190, 202, 208, 230, 316
Howat, Gareth *see* hat-trick
Howe, Mark (Elmwood) 190
Howsam, Rob (Purpose) 21, 170, 314
Hung Lam *see* CoDesign
Hurley, Chad 267
Hussey, Laura (SomeOne) 104, 176, 216, 267
Hyland, Angus (Pentagram) 18, 46, 232
Hyperkit 48, 94, 98, 156

I

Imhof, Roman (Hotz & Hotz) 29, 32, 56, 60, 69, 70, 118, 147, 246, 278
Inkahoots
– Arc Biennial 86
– Avid Reader 46
– Embodied Media 206
– McGarry & Eadie 117
– Manbulloo 182
– Raw Space 190
– Regional Acting Studio 90
– Sounds Like Brisbane 90
– Steam 122
– Vumi 124
– Water By Design 92
Interbrand 134, 252
Iselt, Martin (Doyle Partners) 260
Ishikawa, Ko (Samurai) 298

J

Jackson, Frances (OPX) 126, 148
Jacobs, Holger (Mind Design) 48(2), 55, 59
Jacquillat, Agathe (FL@33) 196, 236, 270, 274
Jain, Katie (Hatch Design)

77, 280
James, Ben (Spencer du Bois) 182
Jeffery, Ben (Further) 174, 312
Jenkins, Matt (Give Up Art) 88
Jerde, Jennifer *see* Elixir Design
Jestico + Whiles 246
Jiang Jian *see* Joyn:Viscom
Jianping He (Hesign International) 44(2), 176, 192, 284, 298
Jing Fing (Joyn:Viscom) 284
Jockisch, Steve (Mucca Design) 70, 77, 142
Jõeleht, Robi (Loovvool) 162
Johnson, Adam (OPX) 40
Johnson, Aimee (1977 Design) 255
Johnson Banks
– Anthony Nolan 108
– ArtFund 311
– Matsuri Japan 298
– Mouse Awards 113
– The Pew Center for Arts & Heritage 280
– Poverty Over 226
– Rupert Sanderson 35
– Science Museum 150
– Sendai Astronomical Observatory 297
– The Swanswell Trust 267
– Trinity Laban Conservatoire of Music and Dance 94
– Unit Architects 52
– Whittingham 192
Jones, David
– (Buddy) 70, 140, 159, 211
– (hat-trick) 276
Jones, Marie (Taxi Studio) 316
Jones, Nick (Browns) 140
Jong, René de (Teldesign) 30
Jönsson, Fredrik (Ummocrono) 172, 230
Joyn:Viscom
– Approach Architecture Studio 284
– Arrtco 270
– Chaoyang 1919 294
– Michael Ku Gallery 298
– MòChén Architects & Engineers 298
– Origin Architect 284
Jun Dai (Hesign International) 44, 192, 298
Jurva, Alexandra (hat-trick) 268

K

KalleGraphics
– Angels Motel 74
– Goldlog 32
– The Margarets 90
– NOBA 60
– Plywood 66
– Ragne Sigmond 32

– Silver Plate 122
– StartSkuddet 148
Kamber, Nadine 137
Kapprell, Beate (Büro Uebele Visuelle Kommunikation) 128, 152, 156
Kariolis, John (Six) 24, 228
Kasahara, Tomoatsu (Samurai) 66, 276
Katholm, Mads (Me!Me!Me!) 62, 70
Katona, Diti *see* Concrete
Kedar, Ruth 35
Kedgley, Jason (Tomato) 122
Ken Miki & Associates
– Ad Kinetsu 124
– de sign de 256
– Japan Design Society 126
– Kagawa Education Institute of Nutrition 199
– Keikyu 218
– Kurakuen 178
– Maruhon 178
– U.Coffee 190
– UIP 86
Kendle, Dylan (Tomato) 132, 246
KentLyons
– Dickens 2012 107
– Get London Reading 314
– The Jarman Award 56
– Love From London 274
– Tomorrow 32
– Top Drawer 154
– Tricolette Yarns 90
Khanjanzadeh, Damoon 290
Kidston, Cath 70
Kijmedee, Bina (Landor Associates) 18
Kimpton 26, 185, 214
Kimpton, David (hat-trick) 276, 302 *see also* Kimpton
Kinchin, Will (Purpose) 170, 228
Kirlew, Michael (Gottschalk + Ash International) 46
Kluepfel, Tom (Doyle Partners) 236
Knapp, Judith (Hotz & Hotz) 60
Knop, Nikolaj *see* We Recommend
Koliadimas, Dimitris *see* Designers United
Koll, Michael (Dan Alexander & Co) 64
Komlosy, Piers (Purpose) 170
Koukodimos, Tom (Concrete) 107
Kral, Joe (Test Pilot Collective) 264
Kubel, Henrik (Punktum Design) 208
Kuokka, Jenni (Hahmo) 78, 86, 126, 182, 200, 218, 244, 256, 320
Kuroki, Yasuo 39
Kwo, John (O+Co) 248

L

Lai, Maurice (Fabio Ongarato Design) 56
Lamothe, David (Area 17) 56, 62
Lan, Kevin (The Partners) 238
Landor Associates
– Blink 212
– City of Melbourne 302
– Exploratorium 216
– FedEx 117
– First Graduate 216
– Good Co. 202
– Hertz 18
– Human Genome Sciences 144
– Kikkoman 316
– Meiji Group 220
– 9/11 Memorial 211
– One Degree 248
– Ricoh 26
– Shanghai World Financial Center 294
– Tokyo Station City 294
Lang, Andy (Mind Design) 55
Laurie, Yarra (Fabio Ongarato Design) 52
Lava 52, 83, 98, 144, 147, 270
Law, David (SomeOne) 104, 176, 280
Lawless, Martin (The Partners) 110
see also 300million
Lawrence, Andy (Elmwood) 267
Leader, Lindon (Landor Associates) 117
Lee, Beca (Landor Associates) 144
Lee, Eileen (Dowling Duncan) 196
Le Gallez, Matt (Form) 185
Lemke, Katharina (MetaDesign China) 284
Lidgett, Arran (Form) 80
Lin, James (Fabio Ongarato Design) 52, 92
Lin Yu (Hesign International) 44
Lippa, Domenic (Pentagram) 24
Lippincott 108, 218, 246, 259, 294
Lippincott & Margulies 73, 114, 212, 216, 262
Little, Jason (Landor Associates) 202, 248, 302
Lizotte, Dave (Gunn Associates) 77
Llopis, Olga (Summa) 160
Lo, Luke (CoDesign) 240
Lockstoff Design
– Corilon Violins 102
– Klartext 218
– Kultohr 220
– Lautstark 242
– Odin 242
Lodigiani, Giona 273
logotypy.com 150, 212, 216
Loovvool
– Antaar 306
– Bendis Financial 168

– Bolefloor 168
– Caviar Productions 170
– Essence Pictures 162
– JW Trading 24
– MInt Furniture 98
Lötscher, Sascha
(Gottschalk + Ash
International) 192
LoveBranding 140
Lovelock, David (Studio
Special) 88, 114, 199
Loxley, Adam (Purpose)
170
Lu Cheng (MetaDesign
China) 284
Lu, Sophia (MetaDesign
China) 284
Lucyn, Emma
(ArthurSteenHorne-
Adamson (ASHA)) 218
Lundgren+Lindquist 30,
108, 196, 252
Luostarinen, Antti
(Hahmo) 244

M

McAleer, Sinead (Creative
Inc) 236
McCabe, Marcus
(Uniform) 62, 259
McConnell, John
(Pentagram) 202
McGilvray, Stephen
(Browns) 140
McGuffie, Scott
(ArthurSteenHorne-
Adamson (ASHA)) 218,
252, 255, 270, 276, 278
Made in Space 92, 97,
214, 244
Magpie Studio
– All Change 205
– ArtWorks 202
– Between Books 311
– Harrow View 176
– Helen Brown Massage
174
– The Mainstone Press
182
– The Milton Agency 117
– Red Felix 196
– Rollasole 226
– Shift 186
– Your Wembley 196
Malone, David see
Malone Design
Malone Design 182, 200,
208, 222, 252
Manchipp, Simon
(SomeOne) 176
Manning, Lee (Purpose)
320
Manning, Luke (Taxi
Studio) 94
Manning, Scott (Felt
Branding) 23, 134
Mantere, Mirva (Hahmo)
244
Marin, Paul (Northern
Icon) 242
Mark Gowing Design
– Bruised 60
– Circa 126
– FirstCut Studio 90
– Free2go 314
– Hopscotch Films 74
– MEA Accountants 52

– Museums & Galleries
NSW 144
– Ocean Consulting
Group 316
– Roam Digital 122
– Show And Tell 52
– Title 128
– The Turner Collective
304
Mark Studio
– Ancoats Urban Village
168
– Big Science Read 154
– Free & Equal 208
– International Council of
Museums UK 152
– Manchester Literature
Festival 181
– 90 Hairdressing 308
– Rainy City Stories 152
Marnich, Wladimir
(Summa) 24, 44, 66, 314
Martinavarro, Rocío
(Summa) 42
Martinko, John (Landor
Associates) 212
Martynowicz, Michelle
(Design Ranch) 172
Matinsefat, Behrooz 288
Matthews, Daniel (Momin
Branding) 190
Me Studio 64, 74, 114,
156, 242, 278
me&dave 150
Meeks, Alan (Spencer du
Bois) 186
Meier, Sidi (Hotz & Hotz)
278
Meikle, Oliver (Playne
Design) 256, 320
Melnikov, Nikita
(Transformer Studio)
276
Me!Me!Me! 62, 70
Mercier, Arnaud (Area 17)
74, 172, 234
Mesquita, Tom
(300million) 226
MetaDesign China 284
Method, Inc 236, 255
Meulman, Niels 'Shoe'
104
Michaluk, Matt (Mytton
Williams) 176, 192
Miki, Ken see Ken Miki &
Associates
milkxhake 55, 59, 108,
142, 255
Miller, Abbott
(Pentagram) 73, 108,
256
Miller, Jeff (Design
Ranch) 199
Miller, Tom (Bateson/
Studio) 126
Mills, Sarah (Buddy) 140
Minale, Marcello Snr 70,
308
Minale, Marcello M
(Minale Tattersfield)
225, 308
Minale Tattersfield 70,
225, 308
Mind Design
– Circus 55
– Cupcake 48
– John Lyall Architects
230
– Marawa the Amazing
48

– Paramount 268
– Peter Taylor Associates
Limited 128
– Tea 228
– TESS Management 59
– Znips 90
Mir, Josep Maria (Summa)
42, 138, 182, 264
Mission Design 35, 218,
230, 234
Mister Walker
– Bidfreight Port
Operations 42
– Brand Design Council
of South Africa 208
– Constitutional Court of
South Africa 40
– Flow Life Coaching 104
– iwa 74
– Life Assay 273
Mitt, Kadri Maria
(Loovvool) 306
Mixer
– Amazee 56
– The Central 170
– Japlab 66
– Kerik 56
– Wilhelm 138
Mizuno, Manabu (Good
Design Company) 40
Mo, Javin (milkxhake) 55,
59, 108, 142, 255
Mode (UK) 48, 86, 98, 102
Mode (USA)
– College of Arts &
Architecture 206
– Diderot 162
– Kristin Morris Jewelry
160
– Mellow Mushroom 83
– QVC 186
– Valtekz 160
Mody, Nitesh (Moot
Design) 178, 304
Moffat, Samuel see
Studio Paradise
Molinaro, Henrietta
(Atelier Works) 226
Molins, Roderic (Summa)
160
Momayez, Morteza 288
Momin Branding 190, 297
Mondor, Philip (Hambly &
Woolley) 226
Moot Design 178, 304
Morgan, Katie
(300million) 124, 232
Morrow, Sally (Sandstrom
Partners) 56
Morten, Adam (Give Up
Art) 64
>moser
– Christian Constantin
212
– Conservatoire de
Lausanne 240
– HEMU 42
– io 74
– Lara Gut 80
– >moser 248
– Philippe Guignard 196
Moser, Erich (Hotz & Hotz)
118
Mosley, Andy
– (Blast) 92
– (Brownjohn) 202, 262,
278
– (Further) 174
Mould, Sue (Elmwood)
230

Moving Brands 36, 192,
314
Mucca Design
– Casa Lever 142
– The Chelsea 77
– Foodparc 39
– Fornetti 273
– Matta 178
– One Atlantic 280
– Pravda 262
– The Press 88
– Teplitzky's 70
Muller, Viola 126
Murphy, Brendan
(Lippincott) 218, 294
Murphy, Garrett (Creative
Inc) 60
Music 110, 168
Myers, Andy (B&W
Studio) 200
Mytton, Bob see Mytton
Williams
Mytton Williams 176, 192

N

Nanbu, Toshiyasu (Taste
Inc) 214
Nathan Durrant Design
70
Naughtyfish
– Alphabetee 167
– Bluebird 312
– Hans Freymadl 126
– Intersect 278
– Jump Healthfoods 232
– The Malings 178
– Sirca 30
– Sweet Little Things 84
– Tubestation 60
– Workshop Events 248
Neil, Janet (The Partners)
110
Nelson, Anthony
(Cornwell Design) 118
Neon Design 113, 306
Nerinckx, David (Coast)
208, 256
Newark, Glenn (Untitled)
152
Newark, Quentin
– (Atelier Works) 92, 181,
206, 264, 314
– (Pentagram) 195
Ng, Edmond (concrete)
39
Niederer, Andreas
(Bohatsch and Partner)
312
Nielsen, Tom (Me!Me!Me!)
62, 70
Nign 206, 212, 306
Nilson, Greger Ulf (SWE)
84
1977 Design
– Alwyne Estates 208
– Artica 292
– Bespoke Careers 48
– Covert Music 144
– Dutch Uncle 94
– Ice Cream Music 273
– Jelly Products 255
– King's Cross Social
Club 102
NOMON DESIGN 104
North
– AAYA 128
– Arteria 156

– Bettys 88
– Cha Cha Moon 48
– Endpoint 208
– Living Architecture 206
– Opera North 66
– Pleasurealm 226
– The Royal Mint 320
– St Pancras
Renaissance Hotel 228
– 750mph 142
– Urban Splash 30
– Vertigo 140
– Yauatcha Atelier 196
Northern Icon 242

O

O Group, The 174, 206
Obata, Gyo (HOK) 262
O'Dwyer, Philip (Method,
Inc) 236
Oelsner, Joern (Summa)
42
Ohara, Kenichiro (Nign)
206, 212, 306
Okuse, Yhoshiki 126
Oldham, Craig (Music)
168
Olins, Wolff 92, 152, 238,
302, 304, 311
Oller, Marga (Summa) 312
Olsen, Jon (Sandstrom
Partners) 220, 306
Ongarato, Fabio see
Fabio Ongarato Design
Onoma 176, 216, 228,
252, 260, 278
Oosrebeek, Roy
(Burobraak) 311
Opara, Eddie (Pentagram)
62, 94, 128
O+Co 248
Oppenheimer, Brent
(O+Co) 248
OPX 40, 126, 148
Oronez, Cristian
(Concrete) 234
O'Rourke, Mel (Creative
Inc) 60, 132, 159, 236
O'Shaughnessy, Tommy
(The Chase) 225
Owen, Paul (Landor
Associates) 144

P

Palmer Edwards, Paul
(Grade Design) 152
Papazoglou, Dimitris see
Designers United
Paradise, Meg (Mucca
Design) 70, 77
Partners, The 104, 110,
238
Paul, Christian 'Kit'
(Brandient) 172, 222,
226, 248
Pawlik, Wiktor (logotypy.
com) 150, 212, 216
Pedlars 318
Peh, Larry see &Larry
Peloton 252
Pemberton, Sam (Landor
Associates) 302
Pentagram
– ABB Group 60

– Amanda Wakeley 108
– Arup 36
– Asprey 18
– Beacon 142
– Brooklyn Academy of
Music 113
– Capital Partners 124
– City University of New
York 262
– Corridor 170
– The Criterion
Collection 170
– Curious Pictures 214
– Della Valle Bernheimer
62
– Detroit Institute of Arts
256
– The Dorchester
Collection 156
– Eat 232
– Faber & Faber 202
– Fashion Fringe 110
– Gebrüder Heinemann
205
– Heal's 24
– Howcast 218
– Hulton Archive 46
– Institute of Directors
202
– Kubota Corporation
120
– litl 73
– MICA 108
– Mothercare 181
– The Museum of Modern
Art 137
– New York 104
– Saks Fifth Avenue 107
– The Savoy 26
– Sorg Architects 94
– Tiffany & Co. 36
– UCLA Architecture &
Urban Design 128
– Victoria & Albert
Museum 195
– Whitney Museum of
American Art 52
– Wood&Wood 195
Peres, Joao (Landor
Associates) 202
Pernicha, Samuel
(Burobraak) 246
Peter and Paul 78, 84,
189, 190, 200, 238
Peters, Michael 195
Peterson, Daniel (Fabio
Ongarato Design) 52,
88
Phillips, Meg (Fabio
Ongarato Design) 52,
88, 232
Pidgeon, David see
Design By Pidgeon
Pietrafesa, John (Mode
(USA)) 83, 160(2), 162,
186, 206
Piippo, Pekka (Hahmo) 24,
30, 39, 78, 86, 126, 182,
200, 218, 222, 238, 244,
264
Pillai, Chloe (1977 Design)
94, 102, 144, 230, 273
Pineda, Rubén (Emblem)
302
Piyathaisere, Lily
(Dowling Duncan) 190
Playne, Clare see Playne
Design
Playne Design 244, 256,
316, 320

Pobojewski, John (Thirst)
69, 74
Pohancenik, Andreas *see*
Practice + Theory
Pointer, Davon (Uffindell)
259
Poirier, Jordan (Concrete)
26, 314
Pollard, Tom (Studio8)
142
Post, Peter (Teldesign)
117
Powell, Kerrie (Powell
Allen) 186, 308
Powell Allen 186, 308
Powner, John (Atelier
Works) 152, 168, 174,
190, 202, 212, 226
Practice + Theory
– Cally Arts 202
– The Kx 94
– Parfumerie Leni 90
– People Tree 32
– text/gallery 234
– Tossed 140
Preece, Simon (Elmwood)
267
Price, Stewart (The
Chase) 176
Proud Creative 21, 32, 64,
160, 234
PS New York
– Art Matters 238
– Blonde + Co. 110
– NY Arts Program 248
– Wink 248
Punktum Design 208
Purpose
– The Armoury 228
– BullGuard 312
– Consortium for Street
Children 170
– European Farming &
Food Partnerships 314
– Fothergill Wyatt 202
– National Training
Awards 190
– Openfield 21
– UK Skills 225
– Weldon 320
Pylypczak, John *see*
Concrete
Pyper, Martin (Me Studio)
114, 156, 242, 278

R

Raad, Iman *see* Raad
Design Studio
Raad Design Studio
– *Art Tomorrow* 294
– Berardi & Sagharchi
Projects 294
– Magic of Persia
Contemporary Art
Prize 298
– Media Builder 288
Raudaskoski, Antti
(Hahmo) 24, 40, 78, 86,
126, 170, 182, 192, 200,
218, 238, 244, 248, 256,
276
Reardon, Paul *see* Peter
and Paul
Redmayne, Giles
(Purpose) 320
REG Design 44
Reisinger, Dan

– Carmelit 297
– Habimah National
Theatre 292
– The Open Museum 84
– Shenkar College of
Engineering & Design
200
– Tambour 298
– Tel Aviv Museum of
Arts 292
– Teva 297
– Vitamed 192
Renwick, Jack (The
Partners) 110
Rethink
– Crop 302
– Dialog 214
– *Dose* 312
– Fresh Co 44
– Hans Sipma
Photography 52
– Postmedia Network
234
– Qmunity 226
– Slice 268
– Solo Mobile 69
– Tonic 232
Rettenbacher, Martin
(Area 17) 172
Reynolds, Alice (Purpose)
170, 228
Ricci, Franco Maria 318
Richardson, Pete (The
Chase) 214
Ridi, Véronica (Ailoviu)
259
Rigby, Mike (The Chase)
110
Robertson, Dana (Neon
Design) 113, 306
Rodolphi, Giovanni
(Atelier Works) 190
Rogers, Tom 189
– (Brownjohn) 162, 176,
202, 262, 278
– (Felt Branding) 23, 134
Rojas, Cilena (Playne
Design) 256, 316
Rose
– Acacia Avenue 264
– D&AD Congress 214
– Design Ventura 208
– 50 Lessons 216
– Hampstead Theatre
208
– K College 178
– MC Partners 36
– MediaCom 26
– Quintessentially 29
– Westzone Publishing
248
Rose, Jessica 154
Ross, Mark (The Chase)
225
Routhier, Charles (Landor
Associates) 18
Rowles, Ivan (The Chase)
170
Rushworth, John
(Pentagram) 26, 108,
110, 156, 181
Ryan, Vanessa (SML) 84,
86, 176, 192, 236, 304
Rylant, Bart (Studio Hert)
40, 64

S

Sadée, Milena (Method,
Inc) 255
Sadgrove, Brian *see*
Sadgrove Design
Sadgrove Design
– Ashdown Ingram 238
– Bonds 238
– CGA Bryson 264
– Channel 9 TV 51
– Cinema Nova 114
– Dendy Cinemas 114
– Kino Cinema 46
– Leontyna 220
– Libraries Alive 242
– Mayne Health 260
– Passion Foods 268
– Roost 186
– Splitrock 304
Saeedi, Mehdi
– *Art* 287
– Grandmother Co 288
– Mahnab Co 290
– Restaurant Mansour
288
– Sahar Co 290
– Sematak Advertising
290
– Tize Scissors 290
Sætren, Karl Martin
(Mission Design) 35,
218, 230, 234
Salonen, Emmi *see*
Studio Emmi
Salzberger, Claude
(Emblem) 246
Samurai 66, 126, 276, 298
Sanchez, Gonzalo
(Talking) 18, 162
Sandhaus, Shimon 292
Sandstrom Partners 56,
220, 306
Santangelo, Elise
(Naughtyfish) 178
Sato, Kashiwa (Samurai)
66, 126, 276, 298
Schatz, Georg *see* SWSP
Design
Scher, Paula (Pentagram)
36, 52, 113, 137, 142,
170, 214, 218
Schliemann, Udo
(Gottschalk + Ash
International) 46, 274
Schmidt, Wolfgang 26
Schmittel, Wolfgang 24
Scholey, Richard
(Elmwood) 244
Schönhaar, Sabine (Büro
Uebele Visuelle
Kommunikation) 51
Schopf, Patrizia (Summa)
240
SEA
– The Colourhouse 150
– GF Smith 120
– Jamie Oliver 144
– Living Beauty 48
– Matthew Williamson
220
– Mental Health
Foundation 196
– Metropolitan Wharf 134
– OQO 52
– Penoyre & Prasad 132
– Raleigh International
186
– Sansaw 186

Serra, Lluís (Summa) 240
Serra, Quim *see*
Serracatafau
Serracatafau 51, 262, 270
Severinsen, Therese
(SomeOne) 90, 280,
316
Seybold, Herbert (Hotz &
Hotz) 32
Shafei, Kambiz 110, 294
Shalam, David (Further)
242
Shanahan, Aja (Elmwood)
230
Shaw, Steve (Elmwood) 97
Shelley, Shannon (PS
New York) 156
Shortlidge, Tom 21
Sidie, Ingrid (Design
Ranch) 172, 199
Siegel & Gale 24, 156, 192
Sieka, Paul (Cue) 318
Sinnamon, Craig (Mind
Design) 48
Six 24, 59, 168, 228
Skinner, Phil (Purpose)
190, 225
Skype 274
Slink, Nicole (Lockstoff
Design) 102
Sly, Henry (Blast) 195,
280
Smith, Anthony (Music)
110, 168
SML 84, 86, 176, 192, 236,
304
Sobels, Ilka (Jestico +
Whiles) 246
Solé, Tilman (Summa) 30,
40, 42(2), 102, 160,
240(2), 246, 264, 270,
312
SomeOne 90, 104, 176,
216, 267, 280, 316
Sonderegger, Michelle
(Design Ranch) 172,
199
Song, Sunny (CoDesign)
284
Southward, Will (Magpie
Studio) 176
Spencer, John *see*
Spencer du Bois
Spencer du Bois (John
Spencer)
– Active Results 211
– Campaign to Protect
Rural England 252
– Chartered Society of
Physiotherapy 128
– Coram Chambers 214
– The Guinness
Partnership 174
– Intuitive 230
– Merlin 182
– Motor Neurone Disease
Association 120
– Muscular Dystrophy
Campaign 46
– Ramblers 186
– Rethink 132
– Sterling Relocation 189
– Teach First 21
Springer & Jacoby 36
Stafford, Paul
(DesignStudio) 176
Stannieder, Linda
(MetaDesign China)
284
Steinacker, Martin

(MetaDesign China)
284
Stergious, Helen
(300million) 124
Stevens, Richard (1977
Design) 255
Stockholm Design Lab
– Åhléns 167
– Cubus 18
– Digital Illusions
Creative Entertainment
126
– Folksam 32
– Hästens 318
– Hemtex 88
– Magnusson Fine Wine
156
– Moderna Museet 84
– NorrlandsOperan 242
– Peak Performance 186
– Scandinavian Airlines
262
– Stadium 56
– Velux 268
Stone Twins, The (Declan
and Garech Stone)
– Design Academy
Eindhoven 80
– Indie 23
– Kaiser Sound Studios
104
– Moke 222
– Only 62
– SoundCircus Kees
Kroot 42
– Usual Suspects 154
Strohl, Christine Celic
(Mucca Design) 142,
178, 280
Stubley, Jon (Elmwood)
190, 244
Studio Apeloig
– *Afrique Contemporaine*
64
– Claudine Colin
Communication 144
– Direction des Musées
de France 276
– Gallery Litvak 118
– La Maison de Photo 126
– Santarelli and CO 69
– Università IUAV di
Venezia 148
Studio Dempsey
– Beautiful Books 168
– British Academy of
Songwriters,
Composers & Authors
168
– The Faculty of Royal
Designers for Industry
270
– Helen Bamber
Foundation 316
Studio8 52, 88, 142
Studio Emmi 178, 102, 256
Studio Hert 40, 64
Studio/lab 134, 311
Studio Paradise
– Dub Hooligan 308
– Ezst End Arts Club 172
– Fluid Nail Design 174
– Hand me Down 74
– Love Language London
242
– Nine Point Nine 126
– Olmo Reverter
Photography 124
– There Is Sound 320
– Vanity 190

Studio Special 88, 114,
140, 199
Studio Tonne 48, 66, 128,
280
Styles, Ian (Mode (UK)) 48
Sum Leung (CoDesign)
138
Summa
– A la Feina Iguals 240
– Anida 102
– Ars 162
– Barcelona TV 270
– Booket 138
– Certio 160
– Comsa Emte 312
– Derbi 262
– ESADE 44
– espai Maragali 240
– Ferrovial 30
– Grupo Planeta 314
– Inditex 24
– InfoMeteo 246
– Kilvil 40
– Museu d'Arquelogica
de Catalunya 182
– Palau Foundation 66
– Port Vell 264
– Pueblo Chico 42
– RTVE 42
– SOM 42
Sungkar, Jefton (Landor
Associates) 302
Sutherland, Jim *see*
hat-trick
SVIDesign
– Directory 118
– Finish Creative
Services 240
– Finovino 118
– Lusben 73
– Oikos 264
– Ossie Clark 152
– Oyster Marine 314
– Victoria Beckham 122
– Wellicious 78
– Zepter Museum of
Modern Arts 196
Swatridge, Alex (hat-trick)
40, 154, 172
SWE 84
Swindells, Gary (Mission
Design) 35
SWSP Design 64, 114,
190, 248, 314
Sykes, Ruth (REG Design)
44

T

Talking 18, 162
Tam, Jeffrey
(gardens&co) 98, 182,
260, 274
Tamasan, Alin (Brandient)
306
Tan, Adora (&Larry) 94,
228
Tang, Wilson
(gardens&co) 98, 176,
182, 260, 274
Taste Inc 214
Tatarynowicz, Josh
(Design By Pidgeon)
306
Tattersfield, Brian (Minale
Tattersfield) 70
Tau, Ronald
(Joyn:Viscom) 270

Taxi Studio 94, 154, 178, 206, 246, 316
Taylor, Rumsey (Area 17) 62
Taylor, Simon (Tomato) 40
Tegibjærg, Lars (Purpose) 312
Teldesign 30, 117, 120, 248, 252
Templier, Audrey (Area 17) 132, 202, 240
Templin, Joel (Hatch Design) 77, 280
Ter Yeow Yeong (&Larry) 156, 270
Test Pilot Collective 264
Thirst
– The Acting Company 69
– ElAstiC 74
– Infinite Sum 94
– Peter Ellis New Cities 55
– Smith Partners 55
– Thirst 55
Thoelke, Eric (Toky Branding + Design) 262
Thomas, Aurelien (Jestico + Whiles) 246
Thomas, Leanne (ArthurSteenHorne-Adamson) 255, 278
Thomas Manss & Company
– Classé 244
– Depken & Partner 172
– Foster + Partners 246
– Hotel Arts Barcelona 262
– Knabenchor Gütersloh 148
– Lean Alliance 124
– Lill Rechtsanwälte 138
– Oyuna Cashmere 120
– Patrick Heide Contemporary Art 148
– Tim Wood Furniture 159
– TransFormal 206300million
– Crisis 60
– DACS 124
– KidStart 232
– Lea Singers 73
– Moorhouse Consulting 222
– RooX 78
Tinson, Neil (Guild of Sage & Smith) 102, 228, 236, 294
Together Design 104, 190, 316, 320
Toky Branding + Design 262
Toman, Jiri see Toman Graphic Design
Toman Graphic Design 98, 186, 252
Tomato
– Art & Australia 202
– Dab Hand Media 132
– Design for London 270
– Face 122
– FT100 246
– Museion 181
– oki ni 40
Tommy Li Design Workshop
– Asia Pacific Interior Design Awards 97
– Fashion World Talent Awards 78
– Honeymoon Dessert 284

– Radiodada 260
– Slowly 60
– Taste Together 284
– The Vietnam Woods 284
– Ying Kee Tea House 284
Tomohara, Takuya (Good Design Company) 40
Too, Banlee (Grade Design) 152, 156
Törmikoski, Ilona (Stereoscape) 228
Total Design 29, 159
Total Identity 128, 280
Traber, Thorsten (Hotz & Hotz) 147
Transformer Studio 70, 80, 83, 276
Tunnicliffe, Paul (Blast) 92, 195, 280, 312
Turner, Natalie (Atelier Works) 212
Two 142, 162, 268
TwoPoints.Net 234

U

Uebele, Andreas see Büro Uebele Visuelle Kommunikation
Uffindell 92, 208, 222, 259
Umeria, Shammi (KentLyons) 90, 154
Ummocrono 172, 230
Ungar Walker, Emese (Hambly & Woolley) 212, 268
Uniform 62, 199, 259
Unimark International 17, 21
Universal Everything 144
Unt, Hannes see Loovvool
Untitled
– Akerman Daly 208
– Louise Toohey 132
– m/studios 108
– Obsidian 316
– St Mary le Bow Church 150
– Self Publish, Be Happy 152
– Sion College 202
– Synovia 230
– Villalagos 190

V

Vakhovskiy, Maxim (Mode (USA)) 83, 160, 162, 186, 206
Valgode, Filipe (Mode (UK)) 86, 98
Valicenti, Rick see Thirst
Vanhorenbeke, Frederic (Coast) 24, 39, 62, 86(2), 124, 148, 150, 174, 256, 259
Varming, Abelone (Punktum Design) 208
Varming, Søren (Punktum Design) 208
Varrassi, Ian (Mode (USA)) 160, 186

Vázquez, Fabián (Talking) 18, 162
Veniard, Rachel (Uniform) 199
Vermijs, Paul (Teldesign) 252
Vidakovic, Sasha see SVIDesign
Vignelli, Massimo 264 see also Unimark International; Vignelli Associates
Vignelli Associates 18, 192, 255, 314
Vincent, Nick (300million) 60
Vollauschek, Tomi (FL@33) 196, 236, 270, 274
Vongsurawat, Nuttorn (Cornwell Design) 118

W

Wachendorff, Irmi (Gottschalk + Ash International) 192
Walker, Emese Ungar (Hambly & Woolley) 110
Walker, Garth see Mister Walker
Walters, Gemma (Dragon Rouge) 270
Warner, Claire (Browns) 150, 160
Warren, Tim (Landor Associates) 248
Warwicker, John (Tomato) 202
We Recommend
– Douglas Entertainment 18
– Fillet Inc 230
– LazyLazy.com 18
– Leap 256
– Lokalt Företagsklimat 138
– Moving Images 268
– Northsea Capital 36
– Plan 8 222
– Shelta 268
– Slurk 186
– Streetlab 17
– Supermarket 320
– Upplevelseindustrin 60
– Via Snella 36
Webb, Nathan (Purpose) 312
Weber, Kelly (SML) 84, 236
Weicong Lee (&Larry) 148, 284
West, Paul (Form) 80, 108, 185
Westray, Alex (Mode (US)) 83
Wheatcroft, Mark (hat-trick) 268
Whipp, Roger (Taxi Studio) 154
White, Kerry (300million) 60, 78
Wilcock, Andrea (Fabio Ongarato Design) 92
Wilcox, Dominic (The Partners) 110
Willey, Matt (Studio8) 52, 88, 142
Williams, Sarah (Playne

Design) 256, 316, 320
Wills, Karl (Taxi Studio) 206
Wills, Ryan see Taxi Studio
Wills, Steve (B&W Studio) 140, 159, 236, 308
Wilson, Kathryn (Creative Inc) 159
Winter, Romilly (Mind Design) 48
Woliner, Nina (Ummocrono) 172, 230
Wong Kin Chung (gardens&co) 260
Wood, Emily (REG Design) 44
Wood, Lou (Atelier Works) 152, 168, 174
Woodhead, Natalie 244
Woolley, Barb (Hambly & Woolley) 46, 110, 138, 154, 268, 308
Woowat, Stephen (Elmwood) 190, 244
Work, Jody (Studio/lab) 311
Wormell, Christopher (SomeOne) 316
Wright, Ben (DesignStudio) 176
Wyman, Lance
– American Museum of Natural History 276
– The Burgiss Group 138
– Lafayette Centre 200
– La Moderna 306
– Marco 220
– Bob Schalkjwijk 140
– South Street Seaport Museum 318
– Vanity 51
– Nell Cohalan Wyman 196

Y

Yawei Zhai (Hesign International) 192, 298
Youngblood, Margaret (Landor Associates) 216
Youngs, Stuart see Purpose
Yu, Eddy (CoDesign) 138, 156(2), 240, 278(2), 280, 284

Z

Zerene, Marcos (Ailoviu) 259
Zheng Xiaochun 294
Zorraquino 172, 274, 302
Zorraquino, Miguel see Zorraquino
Zulver & Co 244

Sector Index
Page numbers refer
to text

A

advertising
– advertising agencies
23, 35, 62, 69, 77, 118,
124, 128, 218, 290
– advertising
photographer 97
– branding agencies 56,
64, 86, 170, 206, 208,
248(2), 255
– cinema 270
– online 74, 113
see also marketing
agriculture
– agricultural
consultancy 314
– blacksmith 182
– equipment
manufacturer 120
– grain supplier 21
– irrigation provider 205
– mango farms 182
aid organizations 312
see also charities
airlines 17, 262
– luxury jet hangar 199
architecture
– architect's agent 132
– architectural
modelmaking and
visualization 124, 156
– architectural
photographer 144
– books/bookshops 148,
294
– centre 162
– creativity workshop 74
– foundation 238
– landscape architecture
120, 132
– practices 40, 52(2), 56,
59, 62, 64, 86(2), 90, 94,
97(2), 98, 108(2), 110,
126(3), 128, 132(2), 144,
211, 214, 214(2), 230,
232, 234, 236, 240, 244,
246(2), 262, 276(2),
284(2), 298, 318
– schools 128(3), 134,
244
arts (see also film; music;
photography; theatre)
– art historians 44
– art museums 32, 181,
196, 200, 220, 256, 292
– artists 70, 102, 142, 292
– artists' agent 206

– arts district 252
– award 298
– centres 44, 56, 92, 108,
113, 178, 256, 280, 311
– collectives 172, 252
– college 206
– community projects
205
– consultancies 160, 270,
294
– copyright
organizations 39, 124
– education 26, 108, 110,
202, 206
– exhibitions 104, see
also galleries
– festivals 86, 92, 98, 107,
172
– foundations 66, 216,
238
– funding and fundraising
35, 311
– galleries 17(2), 26(2),
29(2), 52(2), 62, 80,
92(2), 118, 120, 148,
152(2), 190(2), 228, 240,
270, 280, 287, 298
– hospital art 246
– institute 290
– internship programme
248
– literary gallery 234
– performing arts 147,
156
– public artworks 202
– venues 23, 60, 94, 234

B

bags see fashion
accessories
banks/banking 192, 252,
262
bars and cafés
– bars 48, 52, 78, 80, 84,
88, 92, 140, 156, 262,
318
– cafés 60, 70, 148, 186,
232, 262, 273, 284, 304,
306, 308
see also restaurants
beauty industry
– bathroom products 278
– beauty products 36,
278
– cosmetic surgery 238,
246
– cosmetics 44, 118
– essential oils 176
– hair care/hair salons
80, 90, 98, 120, 302,
308
– make up and styling
114
– nail products 18, 174
– perfumery 90
– skincare 48, 98
– waxing salon 190
books/bookshops 46,
126, 148, 154, 236, 294
– online literary
anthology 152
– see also libraries;
printing; publishing
broadcasting
– broadcast retailer 186
– cable network 306
– film and TV crafts

agency 117
– online broadcasting
260
– radio 42
– religious 270
– scriptwriting service
316
– TV channels 21, 51,
225, 226, 234, 236, 246,
270, 287, 288
– TV networks 260, 268
– TV presenter 154
– TV production
companies 18, 52, 120,
124, 162, 214, 228
– TV programme
distributor 230
– video conversion
company 230
building industry see
construction industry
business support
– accountancy firms 152,
236
– banking software 192
– business club 297
– business learning
service 216
– courier service 117
– crisis management 316
– data security 312
– directory 122
– electronic payment
system 40
– indoor plants
companies 190, 212
– Institute of Directors
202
– IT 69, 206, 218, 226,
230, 242, 248, 302, 320
– management
consultancies 46, 172,
222, 230
– management training
244
– mediation services 137,
218
– networking club 312
– new business incubator
318
– office development 98,
294
– office equipment 26,
122, 259
– office space providers
77, 78, 92, 98, 278, 294
– product design
consultancy 30
– professional services
252
– recruitment services
36, 124, 138, 159, 160,
176, 185, 189, 246, 256
– research agency 192
– room fragrance
company 240
– signage 124, 170, 195
– social enterprise
promoter 56
– stationery 32, 104, 172,
212
– supply chain
management company
312
– team building
consultancy 244

C

cafés see bars and cafés
campaigns
– against sexual
discrimination 208
– anti car 260
– anti violence 260
– countryside protection
252
– design promotion 256
– enterprise 138, 189
– fundraising 274
– literature 314
– political 206
– talent fostering 199,
206
– children's 40, 256
– community arts
projects 205
– digital technology
provision 238
– disabled motorists 220
– educational 21
– health related 46, 108,
120, 132, 138, 182, 196,
320
– homelessness 60
– international aid 117,
186, 211
– lifeboat institution 320
– poverty campaign 226
– Ramblers 186
– soldiers' 270
– YMCA of the USA 192
– youth development 138
chemicals agency 86
churches/religious
groups 150, 202, 228,
276
cinema see film, cinema
and video
clothing and fashion
– cashmere 120, 212
– children's clothing 140
– clothing retailers 18,
29, 64, 167, 178, 262,
268, 270, 298, 320
– corsetry retailer 36
– Fair Trade fashion 32
– family fashion 18
– fashion art director 104
– fashion award 78
– fashion consulting
agency 92
– fashion contest 110
– fashion designers and
labels 32, 40, 51, 84,
108, 120, 122, 152, 159,
190, 218, 220, 230, 234,
238, 264, 278
– fashion distributor 24
– fashion institute 44
– fashion trade promoter
120
– flame resistant clothing
56
– human rights initiative
78
– maternity fashion 104
– menswear 36, 314
– model agencies 59, 226
– online retailers 18, 39,
40
– sportswear 78, 186,
208
– tailors 36
– textiles 108, 160
– vintage clothing 74

clubs see leisure
conglomerates 39, 314
construction industry
building maintenance
216
– ceramic tile retailer 167
– concrete producer 212
– construction
companies/
consultancies 30, 36,
176, 205, 220, 312, 316
– customized
housebuilding 222
– flooring 168, 189, 320
– heating and air
conditioning 70, 196
– industrial design
company 234
– interior design 26, 48,
62, 97, 102, 126, 176,
232, 240
– interior fit out supplier
206
– metal working tools 214
– paint 264, 298
– safety glass 287
– waterproofing systems
186
– window manufacturers
92, 226, 268
see also architecture
cosmetics see beauty
products
court 40
cultural exchanges 110,
134

D

dance
– ballet company 278
– dance companies 144,
150
– dance events 242
– dance studio 178
design/designers 59,
126, 176
– art and design festival
86
– design awards 200, 262
– design companies 24,
52, 55, 255
– design conference 214
– design consultancies
30, 55, 94, 148, 172,
174(3), 216, 218, 236,
242, 244
– design planning 214
– design promotion 60,
256
– design studios 52, 55
– digital design agency
114
– honorary association
270
– recruitment agencies
48, 77
– website 64, 80, 218
see also graphic design
disabled people 220, 244

E

education and training
– architectural 128(3),
134

– art 26, 108, 110, 202,
206, 248
– business school 44
– charity 21
– colleges 178, 200, 206,
264
– design 80, 206
– drama 88, 90
– examination revision
222
– initiatives for young
people 216, 246
– language project 199
– language schools 83,
242
– management training
124, 244
– music 42, 92, 94, 182,
240, 262
– online videos 218
– presentation skills
training 312
– schools 108, 156, 202,
211
– training awards 190
– universities 46, 78, 110,
138, 148, 154, 195, 196,
199
– women 199
electronics 24, 30, 73,
172, 228, 244
energy 60, 14, 222
– solar 176
– water 92, 117
engineering 84, 212, 220,
246
entertainment
– computer games 126
– DJs 56, 62, 64, 200
– DVDs 60, 170
– hula hoop artist 48
– literary events 181
– lottery 30
– matsuri festival 298
– nightclub 138
– performing arts venue
242
– private event space
274
– social entertainment
group 122
– spa and crèche 48
– theme park 42
see also events; film;
music
environmental issues 83,
97, 211, 222, 248, 302
events 52, 212, 280, 308
– communications
agency 308
– organizers 185, 196,
248
– venues 74, 94, 102, 268

F

Fair Trade 32, 246
fashion see clothing and
fashion
fashion accessories 98,
124
– bags 51, 80, 176, 206,
212, 236
– footwear 35, 36, 154,
190, 222, 226, 292
– jewellery 23, 36, 148,
160, 178, 200, 264, 278,
312

film, cinema and video
  cinema editors 142
– cinemas 46, 114(2)
– film 284
– film and TV crafts
  agency 117
– film awards 56
– film distributor 74
– film event 52
– film festivals 259, 314
– film production 132,
  170, 176, 242, 255, 274,
  284
– film rental 128
– film retailer 128
– moving image
  consultancy 128
– online film tourism 274
– online video sharing
  267
– video conversion
  company 230
– video graphics 138
– video production
  company 60
financial services 30, 108
– accountancy
  consultancy 52
– data providers 30, 66,
  144
– financial advisors 36,
  240, 298
– financial software 218
– hedge fund 262
– investment companies
  24, 42, 118, 138, 170
– investment software
  138
– marketing company
  232
– newsletter 182
– personal services 70
– property services 120,
  190, 192
– retirement services 32
– tax consultancy 128
– trust and fund
  administrator 92
– venture capital fund 36
  see also banks;
  insurance
food and drink
– apple growers'
  collective 308
– bakery chains 60, 152
– bio food supplier 222
– campaign 189
– catering company 297
– coffee 190, 202, 278,
  312
– confectionery 35, 137,
  220, 318
– dairy products 220
– delicatessens 46, 181,
  226
– food companies 181,
  238, 316
– food processing
  companies 73, 273,
  290
– health foods 232, 274,
  288
– industry networking
  group 170
– mineral water 102, 304
– olive oil 220
– online recipe finder 24
– online wine reservation
  service 162
– organic food 268, 306

– pasta maker 306
– power diet brand 51
– pub 228
– retailers 39, 44, 70, 256,
  292
– tea 228, 284
– wine/wineries 48, 70,
  98, 118, 148, 156, 200,
  216, 225, 280
footwear see fashion
  accessories
furniture, fixtures and
  fittings 44, 104
– bathroom fittings 52,
  55
– beanbag furniture 264
– bedding 178, 259, 318
– experimental furniture
  304
– furniture design 126,
  218, 234, 316
– furniture makers 18, 21,
  26, 98(2), 159, 192, 200,
  214, 255, 259
– furniture retailers 44,
  70, 185, 220, 314, 316
– kitchen furniture 60, 66,
  200
– lighting 23, 48, 94, 142,
  172, 228
– online retailers 39, 144,
  228, 242

G

gardens 40, 306
– landscape architecture
  120, 132
  see also parks
graphic design
– consultancies 156, 304
– gallery 32
– professional
  association 208
– studios 54, 124

H

handcrafts 18, 78, 290
healthcare
– acupuncturist 107
– Alzheimer's
  Association 311
– and art 142, 246
– animal vaccine supplier
  222
– condom manufacturer
  267
– diagnostic devices 273
– elderly care home 40
– fatigue management
  320
– health store 24
– healthcare provider
  260
– HIV/AIDS foundation
  318
– home assistance
  helpline 134
– laser eye surgery 234
– massage therapist 174
– medical device
  company 108
– online medical
  information 216
– optometrists 156, 236

– pharmaceuticals 144,
  162, 167, 181, 192, 297,
  304
– physiotherapy
  association 128
– psychotherapists 196,
  273
– rehabilitation services
  252, 267
– speech therapy 242
– strategy company 230
– well being centre 74
homewares 21, 44, 78,
  88, 120, 178, 186, 192,
  196, 230, 306(2), 318
hotels
– Europe 88, 110, 147,
  195, 262
– online booking 60, 232
– UK 26, 98, 167, 176,
  228, 280
– USA 36, 77, 86
human rights
  organizations 170, 316

I

insurance 32, 40, 74, 160,
  186
internationalist policy
  development 226
Internet services 256,
  311
– blogs 56, 83
– community resource
  302
– Google 35
– networking 56, 264
– research service 278
– Skype 274
– website designers 64,
  80, 218

J

jewellery see fashion
  accessories

L

legal practices 138, 160,
  162, 190, 192, 202, 206,
  208, 214, 222, 230, 236,
  246, 252, 259, 267
– barristers' chambers
  214
– litigation budgeting
  software 172
leisure
– clubs 29, 55, 147, 150,
  268
– fitness centres 30
– game manufacturer 24
– gay community centre
  226
– leisure complex 86
– sports club 167
– urban spa 316
– yachts 73, 140, 186,
  314
  see also gardens;
  museums
libraries 132, 134, 242,
  268, 270, 312

M

magazines and journals
  64, 94, 104, 118, 154(2),
  196, 199, 202, 255, 260,
  268, 287, 288, 290(3),
  292, 294, 312
– online 23, 62
manufacturing initiatives
  208, 280
market research 88, 230,
  232, 264, 270
marketing agencies 74,
  154, 170, 178, 195, 200,
  318
married couples 156(2),
  178
media
– agencies and
  companies 24, 26, 104,
  110, 114, 140, 206, 304
– digital media provider
  84
– exhibition design
  company 202
– journalists' centre 24
– media conference 268
– newspapers 234, 284,
  292
– online services 311
– picture library 46
– software service 288
multidisciplinary
  designers 126, 128
museums 42, 52, 83,
  84(2), 137, 150(2), 195,
  276(2), 288(2), 302, 318
– archaeology 182
– art 32, 181, 196, 200,
  220, 256, 292
– book 244
– design 256
– micro museum 59
– professional
  association 152
– science 216
– support agency 144
music
– artist management 144
– bands 18, 32, 66, 80(2),
  90, 102, 159, 208, 222
– choirs 73, 148, 152
– concert promoter 126
– conductor 78
– duo 147
– music awards 168
– music composition
  agency 90
– music events/festivals
  62, 168, 200, 274
– music management
  agency 185
– music production
  companies 94, 114
– music retailer 128
– music venue 174
– musical instruments 77,
  78, 102
– online music platform
  88
– online production
  music library 273
– opera companies 66,
  147, 206, 316
– orchestra 132
– photographic/musical
  project 48
– professional
  association 268

– record labels 17, 90,
  126, 156, 182, 208, 252,
  308, 320
– recording companies/
  studios 42, 66, 69, 102,
  104, 122, 142, 276
– singers 102, 108, 182

N

9/11 Memorial 211

O

observatory 297
oil and gas industry 192,
  208, 216, 222

P

paper and packaging 120,
  240
parks 51, 308
personal services 174
– garden design 306
– life coaching services
  104, 248
– lifestyle management
  56, 62, 298
– skills and leadership
  developer 84
photography
– editorial photography
  agency 126
– photobook printer 113
– photographers 32(2),
  52, 84, 86, 94, 102, 110,
  114, 124, 140, 144, 156,
  160, 212, 280
– photographic
  exhibitions 150, 186
– photographic/musical
  project 48
– photographic prints
  retailer 126
– picture library 46
portside logistics 42
post production
  companies 226, 232
printing 88, 134, 150, 268
– foreign language
  service 232
– type design/
  typography 48, 292
  see also publishing
property 137
– affordable homes 174
– estate agents 102, 172,
  202, 208, 232, 248
– historic properties 44,
  94
– leasing brokerage 168
– mixed use development
  142, 168, 176, 182(2),
  185, 186, 200, 278, 294
– online property search
  278
– property developers
  30(2), 55, 56, 70, 118(2),
  124, 134, 150(2), 162,
  170, 190, 264, 276, 316
– property services/
  investment 190(2)
– rental services 73, 108,
  206

  see also construction
public engagement
  consultancy 26
public relations
  companies 48, 144,
  170, 176, 228, 244, 280
publishers/publishing 64,
  110, 148, 168, 174, 178,
  196, 202, 208, 212, 315
– art 182, 248, 287, 311
– author 110
– copyright organization
  39
– copywriter 308
– directory 122
– illustrators 94
– literary agent 214
– paperbacks 138
– self publishing 152
– technical information
  publisher 126

R

radio broadcasting 42
recycling 64, 140
religious organizations
  see churches
removal firms 80, 189
research 113, 186, 278
  see also market
  research
restaurants
– Australian 84, 122, 260
– Belgium 64
– Canada 46, 107
– China 284
– France 240
– Germany 190
– Greece 260
– Hong Kong 88, 128,
  276, 284(2)
– Iran 288
– Ireland 159
– Italy 39
– The Netherlands 280
– Spain 110, 118, 148, 189
– Switzerland 29, 118,
  170, 196
– UK 52, 55, 102, 150,
  152, 168, 200, 226, 238,
  267
– USA 70, 83, 98, 104,
  142(2), 174
  see also bars and cafés
retail centres 148, 170
retail trade event 154
retailers 90, 181, 205,
  262, 206
– department stores 24,
  70, 74, 107, 142, 167,
  192, 218
– florist 104
– loyalty scheme 232
  see also clothing and
  fashion
Royal Mint, The 320

S

security products 137,
  244, 287
shoes see fashion
  accessories
society/societies 126,
  128, 174

– arts projects 205
– equal rights agency 240
– social issues 42, 122
– social networking 56,
   192, 264
spaceflights 40
sport 225
– angling/fishing 66, 220
– boxing 225
– climbing 86, 178
– cycling 66, 122
– equipment 40, 56, 86,
   276
– exploration 142
– film editing 88
– Olympics/Paralympics
   302
– skateboarding 17, 40,
   172
– skiing 80
– Tae kwon do 59
– tennis 306

T

telecommunications 42,
   78
– mobile phones 69, 196,
   216, 218, 228(2), 288,
   294
television *see*
   broadcasting
theatre
– theatre companies 69,
   274, 280
– theatre festival 292
– theatres 117, 208, 292
think tanks 46, 124, 294
timber companies 178,
   270
trading companies 24,
   168, 290
transport
– bus services 176
– public transport group
   252
– subway system 297
travel and tourism
– city wayfinding system
   212
– highway service
   stations 162
– sightseeing
   information service
   220
– taxi service 220
– tour operators 90, 304
– tourist boards 222, 302
– travel agency 216
– travel software 230

U

urban planning and
   initiatives
– commercial zone 202
– design advisory group
   270
– districts 205, 240, 302
– environmental
   department 168
– local councils 140, 200
– market 314
– planning 110, 304
– regeneration 168, 178,
   264, 274(2), 306

V

vehicles
– campaign against 260
– car dealership 168
– car rental companies
   18
– components
   distributor 238
– fuel and lubricant
   company 220
– highway service
   stations 162
– motorcycles 107, 264
– off road vehicles 18
– roadside assistance
   service 314
– used car dealership
   252
– vehicle certification
   centres 160
– vehicle charging
   stations 212
video *see* film, cinema
   and video

W

watch brand 248

Y

young people
– centre 308
– development charity
   138
– student organization
   148

Dedication and acknowledgements

This book is dedicated to John Taffinder, my much-missed father-in-law, who died suddenly during its making, and to his daughter Samantha, without whose care, commitment and patience, both as a research assistant and a wife, this book would not have been possible. To Samantha, let me say in print: I love you. And, to our two mini-logophiles, Lucas and Thomas: you make everything fun x.

I would like to thank every one of the 230+ design companies across the world whose work was selected for the book, and the organizations that agreed to the inclusion of their logos. I am especially grateful to the following individuals for their time, help and contributions: Jason Smith of Fontsmith; Holger Jacobs of Mind Design; Tiffany Foster and Hope Morris of Pentagram; Rick Valicenti; Mike Dempsey; Quentin Newark; Ian Chilvers; Tom Rogers; Rietje Gieskes of Landor Associates; Beatriz Cifuentes of Vignelli Associates; Javin Mo of Milkxhake; Olga Llopis of Summa; Majid Abbasi; Tom Shortlidge; and Hannah Davey of Greenpeace. Finally, I would like to thank Jo Lightfoot and Susie May at Laurence King, Catherine Hooper, and Chrysostomos Naselos of Company, for their talent, toil and tolerance.